AND STILL
PEACE
DID NOT
COME

AND STILL PEACE DID NOT COME

A MEMOIR *of* RECONCILIATION

Agnes Fallah Kamara-Umunna
and Emily Holland

HYPERION
•••••
NEW YORK

SUSTAINABLE FORESTRY INITIATIVE

Certified Fiber Sourcing

www.sfiprogram.org

THIS LABEL APPLIES TO TEXT STOCK

We try to produce the most beautiful books possible, and
we are also extremely concerned about the impact of our
manufacturing process on the forests of the world and the
environment as a whole. Accordingly, we've made sure that
all of the paper we use has been certified as coming from
forests that are managed, to ensure the protection
of the people and wildlife dependent upon them.

To my mentor Patrick Coker, for believing in me and being loyal to our relationship; my boss Joseph Kojo Robert-Mensah, for a thousand reasons; my father, Dr. Joseph I. Kamara, for loving me and letting me know he is my real father; my son Alusine Reginald Turay, who always believed in me and knew I could do and be anything I wanted in this world; to my Kalf' Allah, who is deep in my heart, and to Master, who is my brother, friend, love, hope, and strength and for reasons best known to both of us.

—Agnes Fallah Kamara-Umunna

To the children of Liberia, especially the brave young people who endured the unthinkable and are building brighter futures. You have my deepest gratitude and admiration. And to my family, Nicole, Lindsay, and Peter Holland, who have supported every dream and step of this journey. And who have never, no matter how dark or steep the climb, stopped believing in me. I love you.

—Emily Holland

Acknowledgments

I wish first to thank the many people that I have worked with, for their courage and for the privilege of having me walk with them on their journeys. In particular I am indebted to those men and women who were ex–child soldiers, female victims, female victims who became female fighters, who allowed me to listen and permitted me to air their stories publicly. My appreciation goes to Mary, Rita, Gladys, Butt Naked, Edward, and Fofee.

I want to thank my parents, Joseph and Lucy, for a thousand reasons.

Thanks to my three wonderful daughters.

To my daughter Neima N. Amara-Candy, I don't know where I would be without you, but it wouldn't be here.

Thanks to my friend Mabel George, who is always there to share laughs and tears.

I thank my amazingly talented former workmates: Patience Goanue—you first taught me all I know about radio; Facia B. Harris; and Macdonald M. Metzger for their support and the courage they gave me in my work and being there for me in bad and good times. Special thanks to Sharon Andrena Vincent, my formal workmate, who allowed me to look at places for stories not just in displaced camps and ghettos.

I thank, especially, my dear friend and my best guest on *Straight from the Heart* radio program, Ezekiel Pajibo, who opened my eyes to the Liberia Truth and Reconciliation process and wanted me to be part of the Liberia Truth and Reconciliation Commission.

My appreciation goes to Councillor Jerome Verdier, Jr., who gave my boys and girls the platform to be recognized at the Truth and Reconciliation Commission.

My best gratitude and appreciation to Abigail Disney, who I am grateful to in many ways: the many ways I cannot talk about, but she knows what I mean.

My gratitude to my new friend Gloria Marie Steinem, for her support and encouragement to make me own an all-victims female radio station in Liberia. I give thanks for the gift of friendship.

Paul Martin, my mentor, who saw something in me and my work as a Human Rights Activist. To Elizabeth Boyyeneh Nelson, Nathaniel Milton Barnes, Abla G. Williams, and President Jimmy Carter.

I thank, especially, my dear friends Kevin and Venus Wilson, who gave me their daughter's room to stay in while I was looking for a place to stay in the U.S.

To all of you and to others too numerous to list here, thanks for touching my life and offering me new ways to understand the world!

—AGNES FALLAH KAMARA-UMUNNA

First, to the many individuals who selflessly and courageously contributed their stories, time, and heart to this project, especially the young men and women from Straight from the Heart Center, the Liberia Truth and Reconciliation Commission, and UNMIL Radio.

Second, to our agents Peter McGuigan, Stephanie Abou, and Hannah Gordon and to our gifted and visionary editors Gretchen Young and Elizabeth Sabo, without whom none of this would be possible. For your belief, encouragement, and your extraordinary person-alities, thank you.

Next, to the International Rescue Committee, whose heroic em-ployees work on behalf of refugees and displaced people every day, and to the exceptional mentors I was lucky to find there, especially George Rupp, George Biddle, John Keys, Anne Richard, Carrie Welch, Ed Bligh, David Gatare, Nicky Smith, Heidi Wagner, and Michael Amanya.

With huge appreciation to my long-term champions and friends, George and Mary-Beth Hritz, and to the Princeton in Africa pro-gram, which first opened my "Africa eyes."

To Tressa and Brian, my godparents and so much more, and to Patrick, who loved Africa while he was with us, and to Suzanne, who helped so many young people during her short time.

To Rebecca, for transforming friendship and true generosity. To Kirsten, a real sister and sage. To Ben Heller, a life changer. And to Dr. Matthew Stremlau, whose selfless spirit and dedication to the African continent will always inspire me.

To outstanding teachers from various life chapters: Jim Upde-graff, Otto Mower, Courtney Flanagan, Robert Fagles, Emmanuel Kreiks, Michael Doyle, David Caron, Jamie O'Connell, Kate Jas-tram, Dean Tom, Ted Braun, Missie Rennie, and Justice Carlos Moreno.

To my best friends, as true blue as they come, and to a few who played pivotal roles in this endeavor: Abigail, Anne, Ashton and Chris-tina, Carolyn, Christian, Frank, Greg, Heather, Hilary and Bobby, Kim, Lauren, Pepper, and Sarah.

With enormous love to my grandparents, Dr. Peter and Barbara Murphy and Howard and Priscilla Johnston, and my practically-grandparents and life compasses, Jane and John Graves. Again to my family, remarkable and extraordinarily loving people, and so much more than I deserve. This is for you!

Finally, to the Liberian people—strong, brave, bold survivors working to rebuild their country—and to all those who strive hard so others can live in peace.

—EMILY HOLLAND

PROLOGUE

W ELCOME to another edition of *Straight from the Heart* on UNMIL Radio, 91.5 Monrovia, Harper, and Zwedru; 90.5 Gbanga; 97.1 Voinjama and Greenville; and 95.1 Sanniquellie. *Straight from the Heart* is a live, phone-in program designed to air your true-life stories and look at how we can become reconciled to what happened to us . . . and, in some cases, the shameful things we did to others . . . with the hope that we Liberians can reunite with one another.

Getting over the past is never easy. It does not mean forgetting. But rather, acknowledging what came before in order to live together once again. What does reconciliation really mean? What are the fundamental issues? Is reunification a desirable goal for us in Liberia? After years of civil war, how can Liberian society achieve peace?

My name is Agnes Umunna. Today we will hear the story of a former child soldier, Jefferson, who was just two years old when he was captured by the rebels. Now he finds it difficult to live in his community and seeks forgiveness. How do we talk to Jefferson about asking for forgiveness, being forgiven, and becoming reconciled with the people he hurt as a child soldier during the war?

First, let us listen to his story.

AND STILL
PEACE
DID NOT
COME

1

—◆—

MY FAMILY IS GIO. We lived in Monrovia when the soldiers started hunting people from our tribe. I was two years old and lived with my auntie. When the soldiers came, my parents ran to the church and we were going to run with them, but my auntie said we should wait. While we were waiting, we heard on the news that they were carrying on a massacre at the church. Everyone was being slaughtered. My mother, my father, my little sister! When this happened, my auntie screamed, "I am a Gio woman! See what they did to your mother, your father, and your little sister? If the people come and find out we are Gio, they will kill us, too!"

We could not stay there any longer. We ran to Nimba, which is where the revolution started and where my family comes from. My auntie thought we would be safe there. But she was an old woman, and when we got to Nimba she could not take the gunshots anymore. As soon as we got to our village, she died.

I remember crying, crying, my auntie dead and wondering who would take care of a little boy like me? People were running into the forest, so I followed them. I didn't know nobody, nobody know me. Suddenly, one of Charles Taylor's leaders jerked his thumb in my direction. He said I should follow him. He said he loved me because I was a bright child and had high-headed ways. He would promote me to the Small Boys Unit, which is what they called "The Marines" back then. And you know, as a child, you don't have any sense, so I ran with that group until I was four or five years old.

At seven years, he gave me gun. I didn't even know about guns, but he taught me to shoot and I did some things I still regret. Once, I was standing there and my commander and one of his deputies starting arguing. They made a bet about a pregnant woman—and if anybody is related to that woman, please forgive me. The rebel leader said the woman had a boy child in her stomach. His deputy said she had a girl child. They bet two hundred U.S. dollars.

Then my commander called me over. He said, "Jefferson!" I said, "Sir chief?" He say, "Open that woman! I want to see which child is in her stomach!" She was screaming. Crying "Lord, Lord, Lord." But because we were all on drugs, we didn't do things normally. I opened that woman raw to see what sex she was having. And the child was a male child, so my commander was happy. He got two hundred dollars U.S. for his trouble. And the woman died. And her baby died. And after I cleaned up the operation my commander said, "You are good to go."

—Jefferson

PEOPLE THOUGHT it was Judgment Day. The end of the world. Suddenly everything we heard would happen if we didn't live more righteously—*Turn to God! Before it's too late!*—was raining down on our tiny African nation. Brother killed brother. Sons were forced to rape their mothers. Fathers were forced to sleep with their daughters just to save their lives. Children were sacrificed. Those who weren't sacrificed or kidnapped stayed close to their parents. It was too dangerous for them to play outdoors. The beaches, the jungle, even the schoolyards, were full of bullets. For fourteen years, it was like the last day on earth.

Why God had chosen to start with Liberia was a mystery. So far as we knew we had done little and mattered less in the world's eyes. We had waged no wars, built no nuclear weapons. The average Liberian's salary would make you shake your heads in piteous disbelief. Still, we looked for answers: *Would this be happening if I had worked harder? Been kinder to my loved ones?* It took a long time for us to understand that the darkness swallowing our country had been building for a long time. We were demanding answers for actions that went back decades and, in some cases, centuries.

If you do not know Liberia, you are not alone. Most people can't point to it on a map or know about the nightmare that for fourteen years tore our country apart. The few who do often lump it together with Africa's other fifty-two countries and island nations and dismiss us. In telling you this story, I hope to change that perception, but not for the reasons you might think. What's done can never be undone. We are responsible for our sorrow, and it is up to us, the Liberian people, to look back, look past, and move on. No one can do that for us. Still, everyone knows history's talent for repeating itself. I am an optimist, but we live in a world where terrible things can and do recur. While I hope with all my heart that what happened to *us* never happens to you, we can learn from Liberia's tragedy. If we don't, someday our grief could be yours.

Of course, to understand the story of the Liberian child soldiers you first have to understand the story of our land. The Liberian people have a unique past. No matter what side of the war we were on, we possess a shared story. I am no historian. Or, rather, we are all historians in Liberia, and this gets us into trouble. Nevertheless, to help you grasp Liberia's child soldiers, and also myself, a little better, I will do my best to lay down briefly the events and individuals that led to Liberia's civil war. That war being two wars that left as many as three-fourths of our women raped, more than 250,000 people killed out of a population of 2.5 million, thousands more killers, and everyone knowing somebody buried under the earth.

Most people trace our nation's beginning back to the early 1820s. It was then that a group of Americans decided the best way to manage freed black slaves and slaves coming into their freedom was to ship them roughly six thousand miles away to Africa. The American Colonization Society sent former slaves from the sweltering plantations of the southern United States to the sultry shores of modern-day Monrovia. Slaves freed from slave ships were also directed there. The settlers who didn't die from malaria, yellow fever, hunger, or poisonous arrows courtesy of the native peoples went on to Christianize and subdue the natives and purchase or seize their land. In 1847, the colony of Liberia (meaning "liberty") was founded. Its constitution was drafted in the United States. The freed slaves, now called "Americo-Liberians," formed the True Whig Party and would dominate Liberian politics for the next 133 years.

As their dreams of independence took hold in a jewel-green land of jungles, snaking rivers, and a turquoise sea, the political and socioeconomic differences between the Americo-Liberian settlers and the natives grew. Draconian rule was punctuated by periods of diplomacy. The inequality increased and tensions built and built, and finally sparked the bloody war that devastated families, decimated communities, obliterated Liberia's economy, and left profound physical and psychological scars. We called the first war, the one fought from 1989–1996, "World War I." We called the second war, the one fought from 1999–2003, "World War II." Which goes to show you just how horrific they were.

War doesn't happen overnight, of course, and there were many good years before it came. At least that's how it seemed to me, a small child whose world was shaped by the usual things: food, sleep, and smiling faces. In those early days, we had electricity in our house. Light shone from the streetlamps. Even the poor Liberians living in the zinc houses had freezers, rugs, and television sets. I remember a market near Randall Street where huge trucks would rumble in from Guinea, the Ivory Coast, and Sierra Leone. Townsfolk bustled about to buy and barter goods imported from America. For a time, among African nations, Liberia was seemingly a model of wealth and peace.

Only later did I learn the truth: that many Liberians who sold things at Randall Street or smiled and asked me my name in their native languages weren't happy at all. They had few rights. They were treated like second-class citizens. Their futures weren't futures, but shut doors. By the time these Liberians started advocating for their rights, however, we had moved to Sierra Leone. Although we made trips over the years, my memories of Liberia's downward spiral are fleeting at best.

This prompts an obvious question: Who am I? Where do I fit into this picture? I am not a former child soldier. Nor an Americo-Liberian descended from slaves. Nor do I come from the bush. I am a forty-three-year-old woman and the daughter of two hardworking parents, a Sierra Leonean doctor and a Liberian nurse. If it weren't for them, their good jobs and the modicum of privilege it brought me, I might be telling these child soldiers' stories as my own. Heaven's coin toss is mysterious, and why I was born at one time and children like Jefferson at another, no one knows. I share the details of my upbringing to give you some context, contrast my life with theirs, and tell you that, however complicated, my childhood was a paradise compared to his. It is the garden we Liberians are trying to get back to.

I entered the world on October 2, 1967, at Monrovia Catholic Hospital. When I turned two, my mother, Lucy, married a shy accountant named Reginald, who was not my father, and we moved to Sierra Leone. I grew up in a town called Kenema, which is located in the southeastern part of the country. It is a wet, tropical place with umbrella-like trees, impish monkeys, and cinnamon-colored roads. Hiding places abounded, which was perfect for me, a mischief-maker and frequent fugitive from dinner and bath-time.

Sierra Leone's literacy rate isn't anything to brag about now, nor was it then. A group of Peace Corps volunteers rented a house across from ours, and as a little girl, I was mesmerized by the smiling college graduates who taught in village schools. Motorcycles were the only way they could reach the remote places where they worked. Every day I would run to the big window in our living room and wait expectantly for them to return. I heard them shout, "Hello!" and "Good-bye! Safe journey!" It was like waiting for the ice-cream man.

Finally, one day I summoned my courage and made my move. Swishing my dress from side to side, I walked right over and recited the alphabet for the Americans. From that day forward, I was a welcome guest in the house across the street. I'd sing songs for them, flirt. They'd clap their hands encouragingly, let me touch their blond hair and try on their funny sandals. At one point, a woman who lived there came and asked my mother if she could take me back to America, where she lived. Sierra Leone was a peaceful place then, but perhaps this woman had a premonition of things to come. My mother considered her proposition, but in the end could not bear to part with me. What "international adoption" meant, and whether it would be a good thing for her daughter, were unclear.

As I grew older, I often thought about this missed opportunity. When I became a teenager, and later, when things got bad and people were desperate to leave Sierra Leone but couldn't, I wished my mother had let me go. Now that I am in America, I realize that while it was my destiny to come here, that was not the time and way.

The trouble began when I was eleven. Sierra Leone's president amended the constitution and banned all political parties aside from his. When this happened, my mother and stepfather exchanged concerned glances across the dinner table and clutched their newspapers with a tighter grip. One day, my stepfather had to come and rescue me from school when the president's party started bombing the houses of people who supported his rivals and lived in our village. My stepsister and I were not allowed to play outside that day. The next morning, my worried mother stroked our hair and tried to do what adults everywhere, across the world, confronted with human cruelty, cannot: explain evil and assure us that everything would be all right. Later at school, I held my breath as I counted my classmates and breathed a sigh of relief to find all were present and accounted for.

When I turned twelve, like many African children, I nearly died from the measles. My grandmother ministered to me using native herbs, grinding up large-lobed leaves from the bush and mixing them with cane juice, rum, and sticky white clay, then smearing the paste all over my body. I looked like contemporary art. When my mother saw me, she scolded my grandmother for being "so backwards." As a nurse, I think my grandmother's techniques threatened her pride and sense of modernity.

Not that we were modern by your standards. Out behind the house, we had a big water tank where everyone took baths: children in the morning and adults in the evening when it was a bit more private. My little stepsister, Regina, was modest and didn't want anyone to see her without clothes on. She took her baths at night by candlelight and arranged her hair for hours in front of the mirror my mother had hung from a rope above the sink. One night, while Regina was bathing, I took a white sheet and draped it over my body. Silent, lantern-like, I snuck behind the water tank and floated past her making chilling noises: "WhooOOOOoooo! WhoooOOOOOOoooo!"

Regina screamed. She dropped the bar of soap and sprinted into our living room at breakneck speed. My mother and stepfather glanced up from their newspapers to find a very wet, terrified, and naked Regina struggling to cover herself and bawling. Sisters.

I would always make it up to Regina. At night, curled up on the mattress we shared, I defended her from mosquitoes and told her stories about noble princesses and wily hyenas. I walked her to school. Every morning, my mother gave us five cents each to buy our lunch, but I would give Regina mine, and she would buy the cassava cakes that she loved. We made a funny pair: me tall and thin, and Regina small and chubby.

When I was thirteen, I transferred to Queen of the Rosary Secondary School, a preparatory institution full of girls in starched dresses with their hair combed in cornrows. An obedience chart hung upon the wall of our classroom. If you did something naughty, such as talk in class or fail to finish your homework, the teacher scrawled a big, red X next to your name. More than 20 X's a month resulted in a conduct card. If you received one of those, the principal called you up in front of the entire school at morning assembly to apologize. As if that weren't enough, he called your parents in for a conference.

My mother had attended Queen of the Rosary Secondary School and still knew the principal and most of the teachers there. For that reason, I had to be extremely careful. When my friends got into trouble, they just went outside on the street and hired a total stranger to impersonate a relative: "When you come to school, make as if you are my uncle! Make as if you are my auntie! P.S. My name is Blessing!" But I had no such alternative. If I got ten X's next to my name, I held my breath until the end of the month when, *ahhh*, our teacher took an eraser and wiped the slate clean.

One day, I don't even remember what I did, but the principal called my mother in for a conference. When she arrived, without even hearing what I had done, my mother said the principal should flog me.

"Agnes is a good girl!" my teacher protested. "Don't flog her! Her *friends* are to blame!"

My mother shook her head. "It's not her friends, it's *Agnes*," she said, and pointed right at me. Her fists curled. Her eyes glowed like cooking coal. Collecting her handbag, she rose stiffly, exited the principal's office, and proceeded to scan the schoolyard looking for someone man enough to do the deed. None of my teachers wanted to flog me, though. I grinned, believing I was in the clear. Only then, my mother found a teacher who had married one of her friends. He knew the consequences of crossing my mother, a woman whom no one in the community dared disobey. He flogged me twenty-four times with a switch. My classmates jeered. My backside was on fire!

It was moments like these when I wondered who my father was, and when he would come to rescue me. All these years, my mother had kept his identity a secret, and though I often asked about him, she refused to discuss the matter. I interviewed relatives, ransacked my mother's closet, and even tried to bribe my stepfather, Reginald. All my sleuthing resulted in dead ends.

"Go ask Uncle Joe!" my mother would say, when I really started testing her patience. This seemed strange to me. Why would my mother send me to ask someone else? But of course, Uncle Joe was a wise doctor who taught anatomy at a medical school in Liberia and knew many things. It was highly possible he held the clue to my origins.

Joe had relatives in Sierra Leone and visited on a regular basis. There weren't many African doctors in West Africa—there are few now—and his visits were always cause for celebration. Men admired his calm, amiable nature. Women, his movie star looks. To me, Joe was an easy hero who had been a part of my life for as long as I could remember. I adored his stories, his kind smile, and the chivalrous way he treated my mother. No one in our village made me feel as special or important as Joe did, and for no apparent reason, either!

On summer breaks and holidays, I would return home from school, and there Joe would be: in our living room, or standing at the gate with outstretched arms, waiting for me to run, zigzagging, into them. Every time he came to visit, my mother cooked a big meal. She brought out plates heaped with food—hills of check rice, pyramids of fried fish and plantains—and I would carry them to him. My mother and Joe talked quietly as I shoveled mouthfuls of rice with my fingers. I loved how she let her hair down, literally and figuratively, in Joe's presence. What an effect he had on people! When I finished my plate, Joe would take me for a ride in his small car all over town. I would tell him what I was learning in school: poems, jokes, and multiplication tables. Joe would share funny stories about his village and the medical students he taught. His shining eyes would crinkle into a smile as I doubled over in laughter. At the end of the ride, Joe handed me money for a treat.

"Thank you plenty, Uncle Joe!" I would call after his car, clutching my coconut candy. I adored him.

Uncle Joe's relatives lived nearby. Whenever I would pass by their houses, they would stop whatever they were doing and come outside and point at me. "That's Joe's child!" they would shout.

"Hello!" I would smile at them and wave.

"She smiles just like her father!" Uncle Joe's relatives would slap their knees gleefully. "She is a *replica* of him!" And I would scamper off, never putting two and two together.

Until one day, when I was passing by one of these houses and saw Uncle Joe in the window.

"Hello, Uncle Joe!" I singsong shouted.

He waved. But then another man, I think it was his brother, walked out of the house and started shouting. "Why are you calling this man Uncle Joe? This is your Daddy!"

I stopped dead in my tracks. Images of Joe's visits flashed through my mind like the movies broadcast at the village cinema. Suddenly, I realized I'd known all along.

"Is it true?" I asked Uncle Joe.

I didn't need to. He was walking toward me with tears in his eyes, mirror images of my own.

I don't know why he didn't tell me before. We've never really talked about it. I think Joe wanted to, but was struggling to find a way. Now he saw that I was growing up and needed to know these things. It was strange, you know? I was thrilled to have a father . . . and not just any father: Uncle Joe! Still, I wondered why he had kept this secret from me, and what he had been worried about. Had Joe been testing me? Was he ever going to tell me? Had I not measured up to the daughter of his dreams? Our easy relationship was suddenly freighted with questions and alien emotions. Now that I came from Joe, I didn't know how to act around him.

Then there was being Dr. Joseph Kamara's daughter. When I did right, people clicked their tongues and pinched my cheeks and said I was destined for greatness, just like him! When I did wrong, which was more often, these same people reminded me how unlike Joe I was. It was like running a never-ending race. In those early days, I often grew exhausted and frustrated trying to live up to my new name: Agnes Fallah-KAMARA.

Still, there were perks. My school friends were dazzled. The principal was impressed. I quickly adapted to my newfound celebrity. As for Uncle Joe, from that day forward he introduced me proudly, using my first and middle name:

"This is Agnes Mam, my daughter. My *first* daughter."

In Africa, it's special to be the first child. We get the most privileges but feel the most pressure (you can think of it as favoritism with a hitch). Around his friends and relatives, Joe would brag about my achievements, however small, and not even mention his children by a different marriage. Everywhere we went, he introduced me like that.

Happiness doesn't last forever, and new relationships are soon challenged. When I turned sixteen, my stepfather, Reginald, died from a heart attack. He had never treated me as a stepdaughter, but a daughter with full rights and privileges, and I was very sad to see him go. My mother held a funeral. My father, wearing a distinguished suit and tie, came to pay his respects. He returned a few days later with a proposal:

"I'm sorry your husband has died, Lucy," he consoled my weeping mother. "Why don't you let me take Agnes Mam to relieve some of the burden?"

My mother is the sort of woman who always seems to be wearing shoulder pads, even on holidays, even in the summertime—and certainly in crises. She put her foot down. In desperation, I reminded her she had nearly given me up for adoption when I was small, but she wouldn't budge. At the time, I accused her of engaging in a "power struggle." It wasn't my fault my parents had broken up. I said it wasn't fair for her to sacrifice my happiness and relationship with Joe, just because she hadn't been able to make her own work. Now, knowing what I do about what was happening in Liberia, I wish I hadn't said those things.

The country of my birth was no more. Just three years earlier, a Liberian soldier with a sixth-grade education named Samuel Kanyon Doe, had seized power from Liberia's president, William Tolbert. Doe and his fellow coup-makers assassinated Tolbert in cold blood inside his presidential mansion, incarcerated dozens of Tolbert's officials, and executed thirteen of his cabinet members on a public beach. In that instant, the 133-year rule of the Americo-Liberians came to a close. So did life as Liberians knew it. Doe established a military government. The ethnic groups that had lived side by side in peace for generations drew lines around their homes, properties, and hearts. Over time, as resistance to Doe's government intensified, human rights abuses escalated. Torture, disappearances, extrajudicial killings, and other forms of impunity became routine. Doe manipulated ethnic differences, laying the groundwork for the ethnic cleansing that would take place during the war. Although my father was in no immediate danger—he did not come from a tribe Doe targeted—people can make mistakes in wartime. I don't know for certain, but I think these events might have played a role in my mother's refusal to let me go and live with him. In typical teenage fashion, I couldn't see past my own nose, however, and accused her of making me "suffer for her mistakes."

My father was disappointed. Over the years, he would try to explain what had happened between him and my mother and get stuck. "It was true love in youthful thinking . . ." he used to say, dabbing his eyes with the hem of his white coat.

My mother kept a large wooden chest stashed in her closet, which I was forbidden to touch. One day, when she was out, I dug through her chest and found love letters they had written when they were teenagers. *Lucy my love* and *Joe my darling . . .* Triumphant and annoyed, I brought them to my mother.

"You see! He was my father all these years and you never told me!" I said. "What is going on between you two?"

My mother shrugged.

So, I don't know what happened, but here is what I believe: My parents are *still* in love. And here is how I know: Anytime my mother sees a picture of my father, she grabs it from my hand, takes her stick of glue, and pastes it in her scrapbook. "Why are you stealing all my pictures?" I say. "You say you don't love this man, but you do! It's written in your face! It is *there*!" Closing her scrapbook, my mother shutters her face and smiles mysteriously, or she complains that my father spoils me and doesn't spoil her. And when I tell my father this, he says, "I called your mother!" And when I tell my mother this, she just laughs.

I suppose I'll never get an answer. Still, after all these years and all the things I've seen Liberian people confront and overcome, I want them to reconcile. I want to say, Mom, I love Dad. Dad, I love Mom. I just want peace between you two. There is too much war in the world as it is.

2

THE REBELS CAME in the night to the village where I lived with my grandmother. They took me from my bed, just as they had done with so many other children. For the first two days, I had my hands tightly bound. But as we approached the Sierra Leone border, they loosened my hands and gave me bags to carry. All this time, I kept my eyes down. I was terrified. I knew that I would soon be given my first assignment. I didn't have to wait long.

When ULIMO rebels saw anyone riding a bicycle, they had a policy of killing them. People on bicycles pose a threat, as they can ride to the next village and raise an alarm. We came across a man on a bike, and I was told to beat him to death with a piece of wood. I didn't hesitate because doing so would have meant sacrificing my own life. Boys who were unable to kill—and there were many—were subsequently killed themselves.

After several months, I was given a gun. They told me to smear shea butter over my hands, feet, and forehead. This, the rebels said, would give me the courage to kill, but it would make me fall to the ground should I try and escape. Unfortunately, I believed them.

I don't know how many people I killed while I was in the bush. I would use my gun and fire indiscriminately into the crowd as we raided villages for food and children. Many people died because of my actions. Finally, after two years I began to doubt the rebels. Me and another boy decided to escape. During the next attack on a village, we took our chance. We ran and ran and ran.

—Gabriel

[decorative divider]

DOES GABRIEL'S early experience losing his family help explain why he went on to do terrible things to other people? Should he go and try to find that man's relatives? What could he possibly say to them? Could they ever forgive him? These are questions I have and try to help other people answer. Questions you probably have: How could Gabriel *do* that? Isn't there some switch, some point when a person says *stop*, this is evil? Maybe you are wondering how a "normal" life like mine could intersect with such extremes, let alone help to alleviate them? We are coming to that. But you know, I still don't have answers. Only this: Perhaps we can never foresee the way violence starts to approach the safe circles of our worlds . . . and sometimes, overtake them.

In my own way, I wish I could turn back time. I wish I had realized what was happening in Liberia and made use of the opportunities I was given: schooling, financial support, and African medical worker-parents in a country that needed more of them. "Remember, if you're headed in the wrong direction, God allows U-turns," I tell my child soldiers in Liberia. Still, I wish I had been a true first child who took the straight path from the beginning, instead of a child who squandered her privileges and chances. Although I spend my life encouraging people to open up about their pasts, this next chapter of my life is one I would rather keep the lid on.

I failed and had to repeat the tenth grade. My father was giving me money all the time now. To make up for lost time? Probably, but I was not interested in the psychology behind his handouts. I was rebellious, careless. I took and spent his money at nightclubs and at the movies with my friends. Wearing perfume and expensive blue jeans, I traipsed around town like I knew what was *up*. I was trying to fill a hole inside myself, or increasingly, get out of one.

When my father denied me an allowance increase, I became furious. I wrenched up the dial on my stereo. I would scream and crank the song volume to MAX and dance wildly in front of him. My father would hold his hands over his ears like a terrified child. "You were always talking to me through your radio," he chuckles now. It drove him crazy back then.

I started dating a boy in our neighborhood. There was no sexual education in Sierra Leone in those days. I didn't know what I was doing, and when I turned seventeen, I found out I was pregnant. I dropped out of high school. Delivering the news to my mother is an experience I wouldn't wish on my worst enemy. When I told her, the way she looked at me? I felt I hadn't just let down my mother, my unborn baby, and my family, but all women everywhere. For nine months, the door to our small house didn't close. It *slammed*. The echoes reverberated off the walls, punctuated by her rants and my regretful tears.

As one of my girls, Finda, says, "I believe there is nothing sweeter than a mother's love, nothing more precious than the attachment which begins in the womb and grows for nine months until a human being is born." But I had broken this bond. I had been my mother's pride, and now I had disgraced her. During the months I carried my son, my relationship with my own mother crumbled.

My mother delivered my baby, Reginald. More tears . . . of pain, of shame (which were of course more painful). After that, she threw me out of the house. I didn't know what to do. For a while, I sold wood on the street to make a little money. I would take the small change to the store that sold old clothes and buy my son musty pants and jumpers from America. When I became anemic, my mother took me back but treated me like a servant.

For a long time, I felt like my life had ended. I felt helpless and confused. I believe we make things work out for us if we want them to, and once we are determined. Still, everybody has their moments. This was mine.

People show their love in different ways. When my mother decided to raise my son, I cried tears of gratitude. She saw what I was, a scared child who needed time to climb life's ropes, and sent me to live with my father and stepmother in Monrovia. While it may seem very irresponsible to you, my leaving like that, I knew she would take better care of my son than I could. In Africa, we help each other out in ways you might not in your country. Even these days, in countries like Sierra Leone and Liberia, where there is so little education about sex, pregnancy, and disease, mothers like mine do the lion's share of the child-raising, helping their daughters cope until our countries get with the program.

Unfortunately, living with my father and his wife did not work out. To this day, my mother believes my stepmother was jealous and secretly practicing juju—African witchcraft (which of course she wasn't)—against me. "She envies you, Agnes!" my mother would hiss over the telephone. I said I couldn't imagine why. While not exactly juju, my mother took to wandering around the house muttering incantations of her own against the green-eyed woman who derailed my dreams. You know, typical things about wicked stepmothers poisoning their husbands' minds toward their children.

Licking my wounds, I went to live with my friend Mariam and her family in their house near the airfield. Mariam's father was known as "J.P." and worked at the Coca-Cola bottling plant. Several hundred Liberians bottled fizzy drinks for a respectable paycheck at this sprawling red and white compound on the outskirts of town. J.P. was a foreman there, I think. Unlike most employees, he had a desk and even a telephone. At home, J.P. was certainly king, with two wives and several children who all lived together under one roof in a tense, constantly renegotiated truce.

He was a strict man, J.P.: the type of man, who, if he was outside, everybody stayed inside, and vice versa. He used to send his two wives, Mariam's mother and the younger one, to the market to buy rice. When they returned, J.P. would count their change and lock the bags of rice in his room. When he returned from work, the house had to be spotless, dinner on the table, everyone's sandals off the floor and aligned in tidy rows. "J.P. is coming! J.P. is coming!" his wives would whisper as he approached the house, frantically scrambling to arrange the children. Having grown up in a different kind of household with a mother who wore the pants, I couldn't understand why a wife, let alone two, would be so terrified of her husband.

J.P. rarely spoke to anyone. When he did, it was to waggle a reproving finger in our faces. "Stop going to clubs!" he barked at Mariam and me. "The war is coming!"

He was right, of course. The drumbeats of war had been growing louder and drawing closer for some time. Ethnic tensions were at a fever pitch; Liberia's standard of living had plummeted. Following a five-year ban on political parties and elections, President Doe had held (and won) a presidential election. Some people accused him of ballot-rigging and human rights violations. When a general named Thomas Quiwonkpa tried to overthrow Doe, Doe put him to death and launched a killing spree in the county the general came from. Now this same county, Nimba, was on everyone's lips. It was said that a fierce, young warlord—"American-educated"—named Charles Taylor was amassing a rebel army there. Liberians didn't know whether this was a good thing or a bad thing, but they had seen what Doe was capable of and encouraged each other to stay indoors.

Mariam listened to her father, but I didn't. I suspected J.P. was over-reacting and using war as an excuse to get us home at a respectable hour. Can you believe my naïveté? The fate of our nation was farthest from my mind. Late at night in the bedroom Mariam and I shared, we would lie awake talking: me about boys, and Mariam the disturbing rumors she had heard . . .

"The Congo people are packing up their houses to go to America!" Mariam wept.

Congo is a colloquial term people use to describe the Americo-Liberians. When Doe became president, he had allowed the Congos to stay in Liberia and a group of them lived in decadent homes like fancy cakes up the road from Mariam's family.

"Don't be a worrywart, Mariam," I teased. There was nothing to fear. President Doe was on top of things. He had survived several coup attempts already. Living in my teenage dream world, I reminded Mariam the Congo people were rich and traveled all the time. They were probably just going on vacation!

Mariam looked unsure. She wasn't the only one hassling me. For the last year and a half, my father had been pressuring me to go back to school. He had abandoned his private dream that I would follow in his footsteps and become a doctor, but publicly hoped I'd start taking some steps in the right direction. Soon, though, like Mariam, he had different concerns.

"Mariam is right." My father nodded. "If the war comes, and you are not in the house, how will I find you?" He implored me to heed Mariam's warnings and stay put.

I didn't stay put, but I did start to wonder . . . Like a ground tremor, more and more people swore a war was coming. On the bus, in the marketplace, and even at the nightclubs, Liberians said Charles Taylor had invaded Liberia from the Ivory Coast and was headed our way with a rebel army. *He means business!* people said. *His guns are massive and powerful! He is prepared to make tough decisions for political freedom!* He was a complicated showman, too. According to the news reports, when Taylor invaded Liberia, he phoned the BBC to announce his plans to overthrow the president. Taylor said he had no desire to *become* president. He was merely interested in returning power to the people.

"Charles Taylor," Doe retorted in the press, reported the *New York Times*, "wouldn't last an hour if he entered Monrovia."

Doe told people not to worry, but Liberians weren't so sure . . . Many were tired of Doe's repressive regime and supported Taylor, initially. This deadly mistake would cost them their families, their freedom, and in many cases their lives, by allowing Taylor to gain territory quickly. They did not resist when they had the chance. Soon the stories and images in the newspapers in the market began to change. The front page chronicled Charles Taylor's grisly advances rather than President Doe's corrupt practices. Taylor conquered villages overnight. He was dragging a knife through the belly of our country. He left behind a blanket of blood! People with relatives in the invaded towns communicated stories of rape and murder so elaborate they had to be fake. They said that Taylor kidnapped children—that he was turning them into drugged agents of murder! Killing machines! People said Taylor took small girls and gave them guns to fight, *when they weren't pleasuring his troops.* "Can you believe these tall tales?" I shook my head in disbelief. Who in their right mind *would* believe such things? Young and caught up in my own world, I refused to entertain the increasingly unavoidable truth: that war, tragic and terrible, was coming.

"We will be fine," I tried to console Mariam. "These are just stories." I thought they were just stories. Until one night, when Mariam's father didn't come home from the factory.

You could almost set a clock by the twilight hour when J.P.'s heavy footsteps trudged up the path, his whispering wives and children frightened into submission. But tonight six thirty passed. Seven o'clock. Seven thirty, eight, eight thirty, nine o'clock . . . nine thirty p.m. Everybody's eyes were glued to the clock in the living room. "J.P.'s not here! Where's J.P., oh?!" his jittery wives exclaimed each time the minute hand lapped twelve. Mariam's brothers and sisters kept quiet. Finally, around midnight, we heard a key turn in the lock. Clinging tightly to the children, we waited with bated breath as the door creaked open to reveal a rectangle of blackness.

"J.P.!!!" his family cried, relieved. But it wasn't him—not the J.P. I knew. He stood there in the doorway while his wives and children rushed around him. How did they not see? Not sense the difference? I hung back, not because I wasn't happy to see J.P. home. I had seen an expression on his face that frightened me.

"What happened? Why are you so late?" his wives and children clamored. They asked him whether he had eaten and smoothed his uncharacteristically sweat-stained shirt. "We were worried about you!" they scolded.

J.P. was silent. He sank into a chair and didn't speak for some time. "There is trouble . . ." he finally said. His voice was gravelly and strained.

"What kind of trouble?" they pressed.

But J.P. refused to say anything more. He just sat there, staring. Staring at his wives and children. He looked at them as if they were not his family at all, but deluded visions sent to play with his mind.

Mariam was terrified. Is there anything more frightening for a child than an adult without answers? It wasn't until later, after she and I had gone to bed, that we learned what had happened. J.P.'s younger wife came and knocked on Mariam's bedroom door. Wall-eyed, she told us J.P.'s news: Charles Taylor's rebels had reached the Coca-Cola factory. J.P. and the other employees had spotted them on

the horizon that morning. By evening, the rebels had reached the perimeter of the plant and pitched camp. Though some distance away,
there was no mistaking their large numbers, or formidable weapons.
"But the strangest thing of all?" J.P.'s wife placed a hand over her heart
and her eyes fluttered, eyes not much older than our own. It appeared
to be an army of *children*. Boys three and four feet high, she showed us
with a trembling hand. It was clear that J.P. had no idea what to say or
do, only what the incursion meant:

"The war is here," J.P.'s wife echoed with trembling lips.

The same message reached my father, who came for me the next
morning. "Bullets hit our house, Agnes," he said. "We have to run."

Run? Had I heard him correctly? What did he mean "bullets"? I
didn't believe him. He insisted this was not a joke and told me to get
going. Then I noticed his drawn face, the dark circles under his eyes.
Sensing my growing alarm, my father put a hand on my shoulder and
said he would explain everything once we got to Freetown.

"Freetown?" I stammered. The capital of Sierra Leone was 228
miles away from Mariam, and the last place I wanted to be.

J.P. appeared and the two men went into the next room. Mariam's
mother was crying. I don't know where the younger wife was. Mariam
grabbed my arm and hurried me back into her bedroom. With panicked eyes, she helped me stuff my clothes into a sack. "My father is
crazy," I cried. "The war will finish in seconds. There is no need to
run!"

Mariam didn't respond and kept packing up my life for me, and I
didn't know what to say after that. Things were happening too quickly.
I needed more time. I had to say good-bye to Mariam and my other
friends, and to deal with the shock and confusion I was feeling. When
we emerged from her room, my father was hugging J.P. I embraced
Mariam fiercely, wondering when we would see each other again. J.P.
didn't have connections like my father, so her family would stay in

Monrovia and hope for the best. My father nodded when J.P. told him this, and I could tell he felt guilty he couldn't do more for my friends. Leaving them felt like desertion.

"I will write!" I called to Mariam. I could barely meet her eyes, which were glistening with tears. Mariam had been right about the war, but I was the one who got to escape. Somehow I knew things would never be the same.

With that, my father shoved me into his pickup truck and we were off.

With the little money my father had packed, we bought petrol and drove to the Sierra Leone border. In the past, this trip would have taken no time, but now soldiers guarded every county—Tubmanburg Junction and Klay. We had to show our identification cards at each stop. My father drummed his fingers nervously and turned his watch around and around on his wrist. *Who shot our house? Where is your wife? How long are we going to be away?* I had so many questions but kept silent. I feared the answers to them, and I could tell my father was concentrating deeply.

When we reached the border, my father groaned. A long line of cars stretched for miles in either direction. He got out to assess the situation, jogging down the spindly dirt road bordered by glossy trees, inhaling the fumes from dozens of exhaust pipes. Inside the cars, anxious people stared straight ahead. None of them were moving. Towers of suitcases and animal cages wobbled on car tops and trunks. I waved feebly at the people in the car behind us: It was full of men, women, and children sinking beneath baskets and looking very uncomfortable, their limbs jutting out of the vehicle in every direction. Tense, tired, nervous.

When my father returned, he explained why he was so desperate to leave. Apparently, Charles Taylor had vowed that citizens from ECOWAS countries, those West African states that contributed soldiers to the Economic Community of West African States Monitoring Group, or ECOMOG (the peacekeeping force sent to fight him), would be targeted for elimination when he took Monrovia. ECOMOG would initially prevent Taylor's takeover of Monrovia, but not for long. Sierra Leone, my father's birthplace, was an ECOWAS country. Not only that, but Taylor was hunting people from the Mandingo tribe. While my father is not a Mandingo, his father is, and he looks like one. It could be very dangerous for him. And for me.

When my father told me this, I started shaking. Suddenly I understood. The bullets weren't meant for my father's house. They were meant for my *father*. I envisioned a list of execution dates and names: my father's, mine, the names of people we knew from the other ECOWAS countries—Gambia, Ghana, and Nigeria. My mind reeled. We hadn't done anything. Why was Taylor hunting Mandingos? Where did he get the idea that killing innocent people was the way to change a country? Me, a young woman, and my father, a humanitarian doctor? I thought back to J.P.'s story, as relayed by his wife. An army of children was coming.

On that day, I experienced a feeling that would haunt me for the next fourteen years. It was a feeling of perpetual insecurity. Of being hunted. Your eyes change, your ears change. They become attuned to the slightest abnormal sights and sounds. You're jumpy and on edge. You breathe as though you're suffocating. Worst of all: Your skin crawls with the tactile knowledge someone may be behind you, stalking you, ready to pounce. You grow invisible bonds with total strangers who are being hunted too.

That afternoon, I pressed my nose to the glass and looked at the cars in front of us and behind us, wondering if they came from ECOWAS countries. Wondering if license plates were now death certificates. What were they telling their children, these adults who no longer had any answers, no power over the worlds they had built? I said a prayer for each car I could count. Finally, as night fell, we crossed the border into Sierra Leone.

We felt the invisible line of a border pass through our bodies. Safety. I hadn't eaten anything the whole day, but fear had taken up all the room in my belly. My father looked relieved for the first time that day. He put a hand on my head and patted it as he had when I was little.

In Freetown, my father's colleagues helped us to rent a house. It was a cement block situated on a road right next to the Sierra Leonean military cemetery. This eerie, morbid place would be my home for the next several years.

Then finally, my father and I went to see my mother, who was living in the South and raising my son, Reginald. When my son called me "sister," my heart tightened with guilt. Still, I managed to smile because I knew he was in better hands. My mother said not to mind, and that she was saddened by the changes in me, but happy that I was okay. I think it is hard for any parent whose child starts to see the world as it is, and the darkness it's capable of.

We stayed with my mother for a week and then returned to Freetown. At last, aside from that brief period in Monrovia, and under different conditions than I had envisioned, I was living with my father. Most days, we sat glued to the radio and TV set. Liberia was all over the international news. Every day, I would turn on the radio and listen to foreign journalists with dramatic accents describe the deteriorating situation in my country. They said it had taken Taylor's forces just six months to reach Monrovia. Fighting between Taylor's NPFL (National Patriotic Front of Liberia) soldiers and Doe's AFL (Armed Forces of Liberia) forces was devastating towns and sending thousands of Liberians fleeing across the border.

Doe enacted dusk-to-dawn curfews. From his heavily barricaded mansion, newspapers like the *New York Times* reported Doe had criticized the United States for not selling Liberia arms, or assisting the Liberian government, "its oldest ally on the African continent," in its time of need. Taylor's forces targeted ethnic groups. Doe launched counterattacks against Taylor's forces. He accused Taylor of giving little boys guns bigger than they were, and opium and cocaine so they became psychopaths and murderers. Every day, according to the papers, Taylor's juiced army of senseless boys closed in on the capital.

More news bulletins: The expatriates were evacuating, even the humanitarian organizations were pulling out! In the papers and on the radio, I read and listened to frightened ambassadors and aid workers, pressed for apocalyptic numbers and speculating about their departure plans: "Monitoring the situation" . . . "Day to day assessment" . . . "Last man on the ground" . . . We had a television in the house, and I used to scan the alarming footage of familiar places. Sobbing people giving their stories to cameramen. Begging for someone out there in the world to intervene. I watched for people I knew and worried what it meant when I actually saw them.

People who had stayed in Liberia during those early days of the conflict started arriving in droves. They came by car, by boat, and on foot. Every day, my father and I would journey down to the port in Freetown and scan the new arrivals to see if there was anyone we knew. What should have been a two-hour journey by boat for these destitute people had taken days. Many families were at sea without food or water. When the boats docked, wretched-looking women and children, green with seasickness and hunger, stumbled off boats and collapsed on the land, vomiting bile and blood.

We listened to endless stories of death and destruction. Whole families killed . . . by children! Children who had lost their parents at the hands of boys and girls *their own age* combing the junkyards for scraps. Most of the rich people in the cake houses near Mariam's had left. Now drunken, demoralized government soldiers were looting the wealthy suburbs, terrorizing and killing the people who had remained. "Where is Mariam?" I asked the new arrivals. "Do you know J.P.?" They did not. They stared into space like zombies, already dead. "We tried to get to America . . ." some would say, their voices trailing off into a whisper as if some unseen hand was turning down the volume . . . a glove closing in on the throat.

According to the *New York Times*, the embassies were choked with requests from Liberians seeking shelter and asylum. Most were denied. Refugees flooded the already overcrowded humanitarian centers, only to be turned away. Frantic and losing hope, these poor people took up residence anywhere they could—in the entrances of eviscerated office buildings, abandoned schools, and looted stores. There was no food. No electricity. Patients fled the hospitals. Doctors and nurses, including some of my father's colleagues, followed them. We read that bodies were dumped outside the doors of the morgue at night. In the morning, small groups of people gathered to identify the dead. It looked to be the busiest doorway in the world.

I met people who had owned large properties and businesses in Liberia and lost them overnight. Whatever they had was jammed into bandaged-together suitcases or piled in bundles on their backs and heads. They looked like broken farm animals. Was this all they brought? What about their savings? "Gone," my father said with a faraway look. I saw a government minister shuffle off a boat wearing a pair of pink ladies' bathroom slippers. I tried not to stare, but I *knew* this man. He was a powerful man who used to give people money. Now he was begging for it on the street! We found my uncle among the refugees. He was so lean and weak it broke my heart. More of my uncles and aunts arrived with their children. All of them were hungry and crying for those left behind. Nobody had time to say good-bye.

My father was determined to help as many people as we could. If we didn't find anyone we recognized at the port, we would check the Mobil petrol station. This was the place where newly arrived refugees would congregate and, if they had a little money, eat and drink. These were the luckier ones, my father said: still one step away from the refugee camps.

There were no cell phones back then, but the owner of this petrol station owned a landline, which he let the refugees use for free. People waited in line all day to use that telephone. When a refugee reached the front of the line, he would dial his family and friends. "Come for me between ten and twelve!" he would say. If no one picked up, he would have to walk all the way back to the end of the line and wait for hours, hoping someone would be there when he reached the front of the line again.

"Do you recognize anyone?" my father would ask. If I shook my head, he would frown and say, "Look harder." Any glimmer of recognition and my father would rush over, shake the person's hand, and help him find shelter or something to eat. The few familiar faces among the countless unknowns.

One day, I saw three little Liberian girls in soiled dresses crying in a ditch by the petrol station. The littlest girl was shivering uncontrollably. The middle girl, looking as if she could not cry anymore, was trying to soothe her. I went up to them and said my name was Agnes, asked them theirs. They were just seven, nine, and twelve years old. The oldest told me they had fled from Liberia with their parents. At the border crossing, government soldiers had arrested their families and accused them of being rebels. The soldiers shot their parents at point blank range. I gasped. How had these girls escaped? The oldest girl spoke in a strange monotone. I don't think she comprehended what she was saying. The youngest kept asking when her mother would be coming back and when they would go home.

They are me, I thought.

"Wait here," I told the oldest girl and went to find my father. I pointed at the ditch and their sad, shell-shocked faces. "We have to help these girls," I said.

My father agreed. He went over and knelt beside them. The girls agreed to let us take them in. My father bought them clothes and food. He paid for them to take classes in Freetown. The girls slept in my room, which was nice, but difficult for me, too. As they told me stories of what was happening in Liberia, all I could think was *This could be happening to Mariam.*

Those girls stayed with us until they got hold of their relatives in America. I told them to write when they arrived, so I would know they were okay. Eventually my father left, too. The WHO (World Health Organization) needed him to help the sick and wounded in Liberia. It would be the first of many times my father would risk his own life to save other people's. He promised to visit when he could, and when it was safe to do so.

My uncle didn't want him to leave. "Do you see what is happening in Liberia? They will kill you, Joe!"

His words shook me to the core. Do you know what it's like hugging your father for the last time? Because you never know. It might be! All the things you never thanked him for, all the pain you caused him—it starts bubbling up inside you. You hug him long and tight, tight enough to last the many days and months that lie ahead. One hug to say *Thank you, Daddy, for my life . . . for loving me . . . for being my father, in case . . .* One clasp to sum up all your love.

When I promised my father I would be careful, he saw that I meant it. War wasn't something I had understood right away. Now its consequences were becoming clearer. War separated people from their countries and each other. It wiped out families and people's hope.

War was the nightmare happening to Liberia in the brightest African sun. To what reality would Liberians awaken when the sun rose?

Yet, on balance, how lucky I had been: twenty-three years old, alive, and unharmed. I had made it out of Liberia intact. Many Liberian young people were robbed of even that . . . For the next fourteen years, children would grow up in a land that was no longer any place for children. For them, the nightmare was only beginning.

3

A TRUE LIFE STORY that happened to me: My name is Finda. Since I was a kid, I was always in tears. I do not know how to call that war, because it a senseless war. The war they fight had no meaning. I saw so many things I don't know how to get them out of my mind. I think these people were thirsty for blood. I think that they were vampires.

It was December 1989. We hear over the radio that rebels are in Liberia, so if anyone see them they should tell a government office. My father called a family meeting. He said, "The thing that is coming will be very bad, so let us take our children out of this country before it's too late." My mom told my dad that nothing would happen, he just afraid that's all.

One day I was at school when everybody started going for their children. So I ask my teacher, "What's happening?" He said, "The war is coming. So please ask the pastor to call your parents, because it will destroy many things."

I was twelve years old when I see this man enter our yard with a gun. He was a warlord dressed with all kinds of things on him—so fearful! He killed my grandfather. When my auntie's baby started crying, that warlord got angry and knocked the baby's head against the wall until it died.

My mother cried, "Kill me and let my children go!" That warlord refused bitterly. She begged for our lives as if he was the giver of life. At last he accepted. He told his bodyguard to keep us in jail until my mother got fat. He said my mother was dry and he wanted a fresh human body.

I myself stop eating. But when we got out of jail, my mom told me to eat because my brothers and sisters would need me to be strong. That warlord slaughtered my mother like meat. He started from her feet. He made us stand there until he was through. My mother kept on telling me that no matter what he did, we should not cry. If we cried, he would kill us. Instead of crying, she was blessing me and making me promise never to let her children go. She promised me that come rain, come shine, I would take good care of her little ones. After that, the rebels took my brothers away and the warlord took me for himself.

I REMEMBER THE DAY I saw child soldiers for the first time. It was August 24, 1992, the day after my father's birthday. I was twenty-five years old and had traveled to Monrovia during a lull in the fighting to be with him. Sierra Leone had descended into its own war at that point, so nowhere was really safe.

All that year, Sierra Leonean rebels from the Revolutionary United Front (RUF) had been attacking villages. They raped and mutilated people in a grisly form of "scorched earth policy." In April, the RUF took Freetown and ousted the Sierra Leonean president. Because most of the fighting was confined to the rural areas, I never saw any violence. My mother did, though. She was in Pujehun in the South when the rebels came. They ransacked her house and took all her things. Fortunately, she wasn't at home or it could have been much worse. Instinct told her to run, so my mother took my son, Reginald, and fled to a place near Bo Town. She worked as nurse in a camp for traumatized Liberian refugees and Sierra Leoneans.

I was so scared when she called to tell me this. "Reginald is fine," she confirmed, and I heard him playing in the background. I looked at the snapshot my mother had sent and wondered if I should go and see them. Back then, traveling through Sierra Leone was dangerous and my relationship with my mother was still quite brittle. It was hard to know what to do. I'm not blaming the war for my reluctance, but I wonder if we might have been closer if violence wasn't always at our heels, threatening to tear everything apart.

It was different with my father. Perhaps it was that he and I shared the same experiences. We had escaped from Liberia, helped people at the port, and listened to story after story from Liberian refugees reminding us we might be gone tomorrow. If there is one silver lining to terrible experiences like war, perhaps it's the fact they *can* bring some people closer together. War brought my father and me closer together. And now, front and center in my mind was the understanding that nothing was certain. Monrovia was a place where there was fighting one day, and people went about their business the next. Given a chance to celebrate my hardworking father's birthday, I didn't think twice. I booked a ticket.

Back to that day: I am no cook but had risen early to make cassava soup, my father's favorite. I was stirring the pot vigorously and listening to the radio when my father's walkie-talkie started crackling in its cradle. It was unusually early in the morning for the walkie-talkie to come to life.

"Kilo kilo . . . kilo kilo, are you there? Pick up!" a familiar voice using my father's code name ordered (it was too dangerous for UN agencies and humanitarian organizations to use real names over the radio). It was Dr. Tshabalala, the South African lady who ran the

WHO office where my father worked. I rolled my eyes. I had met Dr. Tshabalala before. Like many expatriates, she didn't have a life outside of her job and acted like nobody else did, either. My father bounded into the kitchen, still in his bathrobe. He took the walkie-talkie into the next room, and he and Dr. Tshabalala talked for a moment. "Agnes, I must go," he said when he returned, putting the walkie-talkie back in its charger. "There's been an attack at Tubman-burg Junction."

Tubmanburg Junction is the capital of Bomi County, located about thirty-five miles north of Monrovia. I had been there a few times and knew that it was an area controlled by Charles Taylor, rich in diamonds. I asked what had happened. My father told me what he knew. Thousands of war-displaced civilians had gathered at the junction to wait for humanitarian assistance. Among them were many starving and seriously wounded people. Child soldiers from all sides of the fighting. "Child soldiers?" I asked. My father said it was so. They had left the war or escaped and were trying to blend in with the other people. Charles Taylor's plan was to take over the country, my father explained. In that moment, he had decided to overrun Tubmanburg Junction. The relief organizations were being summoned to register the sick, elderly, and the children and transport them to displaced persons centers near Monrovia. Dr. Tshabalala needed my father to accompany her to Po River in the buffer zone and assist her. I asked if anyone had been killed.

"Yes," he said.

"I want to come with you."

He just looked at me. "Fine," he answered, probably to save time and stop me from arguing. "You can come as long as you stay in the car."

I nodded, not knowing why I had asked. I suppose I wanted to see my father at work. Maybe I thought I could help him, or make him proud. Probably it was a mixture of all these things.

Moments later, Dr. Tshabalala's Jeep growled into our driveway. She honked the horn loudly several times. My father grabbed my arm, and we hurried outside, me wearing a skirt and impractical shoes. Luckily, I had remembered to turn off the stove.

"Good morning, Doctor." My father nodded, deferential and serious. He took the passenger seat as I clambered into the back with the medical kits. Dr. Tshabalala didn't acknowledge me, and I could tell that she wasn't pleased I had come along. What could the daughter of Dr. Joseph Kamara possibly do in a disaster area, besides be a pain in the neck? Reports filtered through the static on the radio, confirming the situation in Bomi County. Voices describing the horror in staticky fragments:

"... Thousands ..."

"... small children ..."

"... crisis ..."

"Come quickly!" a voice gurgled on Dr. Tshabalala's walkie-talkie. We drove for a long time, traveling over dirt roads that rolled like waves. Dr. Tshabalala did her best to approach the tire ruts from the side to prevent shock and bruises. Heavy clouds rumbled overhead. The stone-gray sky seemed to cave. It was the rainy season, and the air rushing through the windows smelled like wet cement. Looking out, I remembered that the last time I'd ridden this direction in a car with my father, we were fleeing Liberia.

Civil war had been raging for two and a half years at that point, and much had changed during that time. Returning to Monrovia, I had been appalled to see what my country had become. Food was scarce. Empty bellies plentiful. Rebel forces used the braided straw roof huts that dotted the countryside as if they were free hotels. You could feel war's presence everywhere you went: in the shadowy gazes of abandoned streets, or on the store fronts smeared with graffiti of sex and guns. Violence didn't need to actually be happening to imagine, in graphic detail, how it might.

"Wake up, Agnes," I heard my father say. "We are here."

When we arrived at Tubmanburg Junction, I couldn't believe we were still in Liberia. Men and women were streaming out of the bush and running in all directions. Tiny children, half-dressed and crying. Older children pushing their grandmothers in wheelbarrows, or running with them on their backs. Old women riding piggyback—reduced to children! People ran as if they were being chased by a predator or a flash flood.

"Where are my babies?" a woman wailed. Other women waddled like babies themselves; I wondered what had happened to them. International aid workers raced around madly, trying to organize and register people so they would have a place to go, food to eat, and medical treatment. Everyone was terrified. Everyone looked malnourished. In Freetown, I had seen news reports of displaced people running for their lives and shaken my head in disbelief. But now they were *here*, running before my own eyes, just footsteps away. I pressed my nose against the glass of Dr. Tshabalala's truck and stared at them like a movie. I put my auntie's face on their aunties' faces, my father's face on their fathers' faces, Mariam's face on the women's faces . . .

"Agnes!" my father yelled. "Stay in the car!" He started to say something else, but Dr. Tshabalala shoved a clipboard into his hands and screamed, "Get going!" Petrified, I sat in the Jeep with the engine turned off and watched my father run straight for the chaos. He hoisted old women off the muddy ground. He carried small children to tents so they wouldn't be trampled.

I sat on my hands, watching. I wanted to help, but I didn't know how. If asked, I doubt that I would have remembered how to open the

Jeep door. All of a sudden, the crowd parted. A woman sprinted out of the bush and into the clearing. She had a wild look in her eyes and an enormous belly covered by a thin piece of torn fabric. Her face was contorted in fear and pain; both were struggling inside her. Her pregnant belly jiggled up and down. I didn't see anyone behind her, but I could tell she was running for her life.

"Eleuleuleuleuleuleuleu!" she screamed. Her belly was so big. It was raining hard now, and the water poured down upon her. Suddenly, she sank to her knees. She lifted up her arms. With a last shout, her knees buckled and she fell facedown into the mud. She lay motionless on the ground. I shrieked inside the Jeep. This is when I saw the baby coming out of her.

Two NGO workers rushed over to try and save the woman. She was dead by the time they checked her pulse. I don't know if the baby survived. The NGO workers were covering the mother's face with a cloth as they lifted the tiny body from her womb. The hard rain drove down on them like a curtain.

I turned away. I felt sick. My hands were shivering uncontrollably. "Daddy!" I shrieked. A twenty-five-year-old woman. *Daddy.* I looked out the opposite window to the tents to try and find him. He was nowhere. I looked for Dr. Tshabalala and didn't see her either. I trembled, realizing the only thing separating me from the madness outside was a thin pane of glass.

My stomach lurched. A chemical taste filled my mouth. Thinking I might vomit, I rolled down the window a crack, but the rain came pouring in. I rolled it up quickly. Raindrops drummed on the window like the sound of so many spirits trying to get inside. Shivering, I told myself to stay calm, but my breath came in short spurts. I wanted to cover my eyes, go to sleep, rewind back to that morning and make another choice: be anywhere but Tubmanburg Junction. I didn't know how to drive, but in a moment of desperation, I crawled into the front seat. Had Dr. Tshabalala left the keys in the ignition? She hadn't. Scrambling back into the backseat, I checked the trunk. Was there a blanket? A tarp? Anything to cover myself and shut out the madness? Nothing. Desperate, I glanced out the back window and saw the people running and wondered if I, too, could escape.

It was then that I saw them. Boys. Teenagers and little ones. Boys cruising the perimeter of the clearing and looming in the shadows of trees. More approaching the registration tents and turning back, changing their minds, at the very last second. I blinked to make sure I wasn't imagining them, but they were real. Small boys dissolving in and out of the crowds of people. Unlike the displaced Liberians who toted heavy bundles on their heads or babies on their backs, these boys had nothing . . . nothing that I could see, at any rate. And yet, as they sloshed through the cavernous ruts of water, navigating the slick mud and rain, there seemed to be awful and inexplicable burdens weighing them down. Invisible but unimaginable loads.

My pulse quickened. Could these be the boys I had heard stories about? It was hard to tell, because there were so many people around, but these boys were wearing costumes—long, dark coats smeared with streaks of mud and ugly stains. They wore ladies' dresses and head-scarves. Some of them wore dresses like bandanas around their heads. Women's clothes they shouldn't be wearing, men's and boys' clothing that wasn't their size . . . They had chains and crazy totems looped around their necks. Sunglasses that didn't sit right on their faces or seem to match their frightened, paranoid movements. They looked like clowns. Clowns that didn't smile. It was like a crazy, cross-dressing costume party. Mesmerized, I processed the disturbing outfits and their skin: slashed, putrid with scabies. They were trying to blend in and disappear, but couldn't.

Suddenly all the stories I had heard—radio stories, newspaper stories, the first-hand accounts from refugees at the port—rushed through my mind. *Child soldiers.* These boys were child soldiers! Real, live boys who killed and tortured!

I unlocked the passenger side door. Hypnotized, I got out of the Jeep to take a closer look. Why? I don't know. I was *drawn* to them. Drawn to know what they were, how they talked, why they looked the way they did. Were they really boys? Or ghosts? Would they speak to me if I tried talking to them? *What are you doing, Agnes?* my rational self scolded as my body pressed on. In a trance-like state, I started moving toward them.

I had never seen child soldiers before, you see. People who had suffered at their hands said it didn't matter if you were old, or a woman, or even a child. "These boys will still kill you!" people said. "They will invent 'charges' against innocent people! They kill their village friends! The older ones kill their own wives!"

Then there were the pictures of child soldiers: disturbing photos in black and white. You would see dozens perched on the backs of white pickup trucks, their matchstick legs dangling over the sides, their bodies packed in like sheep. They flashed victory signs like a sports team or any young gang on a joyride. Only this gang didn't kick footballs. They sprayed bullets as if it were a game, brandishing their AK-47s in the air and shouting. Some slung them over their backs. Others hauled bushels of AK-47s as if they were bundles of wood. I saw a picture of a tiny boy with a bald head and no shirt, just a bullet belt strapped to his chest and wearing bright flip-flops. Had it not been for that bullet belt, he would have looked like any young boy carting a bucket of water for his mother or helping his father on the farm. He struggled under the weight of the bullet belt as if it were crushing him down.

Some wore wigs in the photos: thick sausage curls in wild colors. They wore wedding dresses, choir gowns, graduation outfits . . . they carried ladies' purses . . . baseball caps, shower caps, headphones. Some wore thick, white smears on their faces: dabs above their eyebrows and lines like prison bars running up and down their lips.

And yet . . . even with all this documentation? I had still found them hard to believe. After all, these were children—children much younger than me. The boys at Tubmanburg Junction couldn't have been older than twenty, the youngest was probably seven. *Maybe the older boys are capable of those bad things*, I thought. But the younger ones? Impossible! No little boy I knew was capable of murder or rape. How would a boy even know how to do those things?

Still, gazing at these boys, I began to shiver. Their eyes seemed funny and detached. The glance felt somehow wrong, disembodied. Then there was the way they moved, imperious and as if in a dream, as if motion was disconnected from purpose. Later, I would learn about the drugs. I would learn that child soldiers often wore outfits to disguise themselves as they committed atrocities. Costumes prevented people from seeing their faces. The dresses were torn from women and children they'd killed.

I didn't know this at the time. Nor did I consider the consequences of my actions. Even when some of them started fighting, roughing each other up and pantomiming a gunfire, I didn't stop walking. It was as if I, too, was in some sort of a dream. I was too shocked by how strange they were, how young they were. I was far enough away that I didn't think they saw me. I wanted to see their faces. I wanted to know if they were boys, animals, devils, or truly human beings. I looked at them because I didn't want to think about the pregnant woman who had died.

"Agnes!"

My father.

"Don't look at them!" he ordered. "Those boys are bad. You don't talk to those boys!"

Suddenly, my mind snapped back to the pregnant woman giving

birth in the mud, and it was as if I'd woken up and made the connection. Those stains on their coats were blood. She had probably died because a boy had done something terrible to her! I pleaded with my father not to leave. The child soldiers had made me forget about the woman, but now she was back, and I didn't want to be alone.

At last, my father assented. He called me over and told me to lend a hand. I remember helping Dr. Tshabalala board elderly people and pregnant women onto vehicles. Cars were coming and going from the junction, and I would line people up and wait with them while they hugged each other and cried. I remember holding a baby and trying to calm him down. I don't know who was crying harder, that baby or me. Looking into his eyes, I wondered if he would grow up in Liberia— this Liberia. Briefly, I wondered if this baby would become a child soldier, and I didn't want to hold him anymore. The rain grew colder. The baby started to shiver. I ducked under the tent, trying to keep his tiny head dry. I felt that if I could just keep him dry, that maybe that was something.

Inside the tent, I sat beside my father at the registration desk. I watched him and Dr. Tshabalala take down people's names, ages, counties, and the number of missing persons in their families. Occasionally, a child soldier would make his way to the table. My body would tense, but my father would pat my hand and say, "Stay calm." My father would ask the boy his name, and, as if somebody had thrown a bomb inside the tent, the boy would run away! Those who gave their stories gave cooked-up stories, you could tell . . . the details were fuzzy, the information didn't hang together. They had thrown their guns into the bush. They didn't want to be recognized. The braver ones admitted that they were scared, forced into the war, and were trying to leave, but were afraid of being "locked up by ECOMOG."

They were confessing.

And in those dreamlike moments sitting across the registration desk, I sensed a world of hurt in their eyes. I remember one boy who told my father that rebels had raped and killed his mother right in front of him. His eyes were yellow and glassy as he described how he was kidnapped. His hands and body jolted as if with electricity.

Hours later, my father took a break to wipe the sweat from his brow. I asked if we could go. "No, this is what I do, and this is what you wanted to do, Agnes," he said. I felt so ashamed. I felt that Tubmanburg Junction was a test and I had failed it. Looking around at the other aid workers, I worried that I had embarrassed my father. Exhausted and drained, I pitched in here and there while my tireless father worked for several more hours.

It was dusk when we finally left. I rode back in another Jeep with one of the aid workers. Driving along the jungle road, we passed hundreds of displaced people. Some lifted a weak hand to beg for a ride. Most just stared ahead as if they didn't see us or hear our Jeeps careening along the road. I asked the WHO driver what would happen to these people, but he didn't seem to hear me, either. I wondered if working a job where losing people is routine makes it harder to see the ones who actually survive.

As for the child soldiers in the registration tent and milling around the area, I did not know that I would meet one of them many years later. His name is Fofee Fofana, and he was there at Tubmanburg Junction that same soaked afternoon as I. He remembers similar sights: the suffering, the rain, the pregnant woman. Fofee remembers turning away when she delivered her baby. "To give her privacy," he says.

"But Fofee," I say. "Boys like you are the ones who *made* her suffer."

"That is true." He nods.

But to Fofee, this bizarre act of chivalry made sense at the time.

That is what war does to people: It transforms you completely into someone else—or something else. But every so often, you remember to be a human being, the person you were before.

When we finally got home, my father collapsed into a chair. I trudged into the kitchen and stared at the stove for some time. The soup I'd been making earlier was covered with flies. I scraped together what I could to make dinner. Neither one of us felt like eating.

4

I AM AN EX-CHILD combatant. Four years ago, I was abducted in a refugee camp in Guinea. Rebels attacked the refugee camp and captured fourteen of us.

In the beginning, I was excited about the whole thing because most of my friends had joined. I felt that by being a rebel with an AK-47, I would help my family. It was like a dream.

Because of my willingness to participate, the faction quickly trained me to shoot and made me a bodyguard to one of the most respected commanders. The AK-47 was heavy for me, but the commanders cut the gun's mouth to suit my size. I do not remember if I killed any civilians with that gun. Though I was enthusiastic about the game of war, fear really did chase me most of the time.

I was not a proper rebel at all. For that reason, my commander used to give me so many things to induce me. I smoked opium, hashish, and I was given an injection every week. I do not know what the injection was, but people said it was something called cocaine.

Now that I am demobilized, I am gradually putting the war behind me. I am learning carpentry, but I want to go back to school. I am trying to use the money they gave me when I disarmed to pay my school fees.

The school I want to go to is giving me problems, though. When I went to enroll, the head teacher recognized me as one of the rebels that intimidated her family. She refused to accept me and is

influencing her fellow teachers not to register me. I want badly to go
to school. Please help me, Aunty Agnes.

—George

<hr/>

I N LIBERIA, we say "The animal forgets, but the trap never forgets." I would never forget the experience at Tubmanburg Junction,
but I momentarily forgot what I had learned.

Back in Sierra Leone, I decided it was time to make something of
my future. While I would never be the doctor-daughter my father
hoped for, I was determined not to disappoint him. I vowed not to
come back to Liberia until I had made him proud.

I enrolled in secretarial school. Now, Monday through Friday, I
sat at a long wooden table with other enterprising young women and
learned to type, take dictation, and gossip. I liked it well enough. Not
the French lessons I signed up for, though. My head hurt trying to
remember the florid phrases and funny accent marks. My father
encouraged me: "The world is growing more complex," he opined.
"Language opens doors." He was pleased when I found an internship
booking airline tickets at a Sierra Leonean travel agency. "A future
cultural attaché?" he suggested. Then one day, a friend of mine told
me a radio station was opening in Bo Town. You should think about
applying, he said. Bo wasn't far. I had relatives there. I loved the radio
and knew a bit about music.

"Sure," I said. "I'll give it a try."

I was hired as a secretary at KISS FM. By the end of my first day,
I knew everyone in the office. After two, I'd learned their entire life
stories. Some, like me, had never seen any fighting. Others came from

villages the RUF rebels had razed. Everyone knew someone who had been affected by the war in Sierra Leone or in Liberia. They would tell me their stories in such moving detail that often, one or both of us would end up crying. In this way, I learned that even if you don't come from a place, it's possible to understand people who do.

"You really know how to talk to people," the station manager observed. "Why don't you try selling advertisements?"

"Why not?" I said.

Now, a couple of days each week, I visited local Sierra Leonean businesses. Sermonizing on the powerful public relations opportunities KISS FM offered, I sold business owners air time and even gave them ideas for their ads. Each time I made a sale, I got a commission. It definitely beat secretarial work! I would return to impressed nods from the station manager and with armloads of signed contracts.

One day, a deejay at the station approached me in the corridor. He said he liked my voice. Maybe we could work together? That sounded like a good idea, so we sat down and started brainstorming. We invented a contest and played new music from Kenya, Nigeria, and America. I would like to think that, in some small way, we provided people with an outlet, or even an escape from their suffering.

Not long after that, the station manager invited me to be a guest on a youth news program. I talked nicely on air, so he had me record promotional material for the station. I enjoyed it. I have a big, deep voice and most of my colleagues had soft, high ones. I still remember the script: "This is KISS 104 FM broadcasting from BO Town, Sierra LeONE!!!"

I got to know the radio personalities who delivered news bulletins and commentary between sets. They were charismatic people with big personalities like me, and we got along well. "Come on the radio, Agnes!" they urged. But I said, no. That was not my desire. I was restless and missed Monrovia. "Come back," my friends pressed. "It is better now!" Against my better judgment, I chose to believe them. Ignoring my father's entreaties, I returned to Liberia, even though the violence was escalating. Because I had been safe once, I believed I would be safe again.

I was shopping with a friend at Monrovia's Waterside Market when we decided to go to a nightclub on Eleventh Street and Tubman Boulevard. *Nightclub?* you are probably thinking. *But who was in the mood to celebrate, Agnes?* I tell you, you can't *imagine* the number of nightclubs that stayed open during the war. Every young person with a little bit of money went to clubs to talk, dance, flirt, and forget their hardships for a little while. So it was then, and so it is today: Youth goes on, no matter what is happening in a country.

I still remember that club . . . the thrill of walking into the dark, cavernous space, arm in arm with my friend. Inside, the big dance floor with modern music and young people glowing in white tank tops and jeans. My friend and I made our way to the dance floor and started grooving to Stevie Wonder in the traditional African way: twisting our bodies, snapping our fingers, and shaking our hips. We cupped our hands to our mouths and shouted over the music. "What boy do you like?" "Oh, him?" "No, that one!" "Yes, that one's good!" we giggled. Suddenly, I felt a sharp pinch on my shoulder.

"Ouch!"

A man was jabbing me in the back, trying to get my attention.

"Ay yah!" I shook him off.

"Do you know what is happening here?" he whispered.

I shook my head, steamed.

"Rebels," he hissed. "They are inside the club!"

My eyebrows all but joined my hairline. "What?" I snapped my head around. I scanned the club, but I didn't see anything suspicious. Believing the man was pulling my leg, I placed a disapproving hand on my hip and challenged him: "Rebels? How can rebels be inside the club?"

"That or robbers!" the man whispered. "I'd run if I were you."

He looked left and right, eyes bulging like a lizard feeling the swift rush of warm air that precedes a little boy's hand. Silly man, I thought. Unimpressed, I turned back to my friend.

"Suit yourself!" our informant said and bolted.

Crazy man, I thought. The club was not in a dangerous part of Monrovia. At least I didn't think so at the time. I'd heard stories about rebel factions that met in nightclubs. They brought guns. Something small would happen and they would start shooting everywhere. But this club didn't seem like a place where that sort of thing would occur. I shrugged off the little voice that began to bleat "danger" inside me and threw a bewitching glance at a boy I'd had my eye on. I grabbed my friend's hand and twirled her around. She started laughing, begging me to stop. So I stopped and let her twirl me. Soon, the club became a blur: a dark kaleidoscope of disco lights and smeary faces. Around and around I spun . . . I was losing my balance. Feeling sick and laughing, I gripped my friend's shoulders to try and steady myself. *I must be dizzy*, I thought, because when I looked up I didn't see any of the boys we had been dancing with. I didn't see the people we had been dancing next to, either . . . *That's curious*, I thought. In a heartbeat, half the club had cleared out. This is when I noticed the young men and boys mixed in with the people left on the dance floor.

It was a strange sight. An irrational sight. A mash-up of familiar elements in an unfamiliar scene. Children . . . in a nightclub? Your brain grips on to the parts it recognizes, but it can't make sense of the whole. I blinked. I closed my eyes and counted to three, but when I opened them again I saw more boys bobbing and weaving in and among the few oblivious dancers left on the dance floor.

My pulse quickened. I started breathing fast. I turned around and spotted more small boys hovering near the club entrance and at the door in the rear. *Oh my God*, I thought, flashbacks from Tubmanburg Junction flipping through my mind. Maybe the man was right. These boys weren't tall, many not old enough to be here. They were children, but they weren't holding guns. Had they left them outside? Checked them at the door? *Could* you check a gun at the door? Frantically, I looked around for an exit. Then I wondered what might be waiting there. Were there more boys surrounding the club, perched on the beds of pickup trucks manning tripod-mounted machine guns, like the pictures I'd seen in newspaper articles? One costumed hand on the trigger, the other pushing women like me and my friend onto the ground, pointing guns in our faces?

I fixed my eyes on a boy by the dance floor. I saw the bulges in his pants pockets. For a brief, paralyzing second, I forgot how to speak.

"Hey—" I said hoarsely, grabbing my friend and wheeling her around so she could validate what I knew I'd seen. *Guns*, I pantomimed with my thumb and index finger. When my friend realized what I was saying, her eyes grew wide like a person who rests her hand on a red-hot stove. I thought she might scream, so I quickly clamped a hand over her mouth. I put a finger to my lips to signal that we must be absolutely silent. Gripping her arm, I motioned toward the club entrance with my head. My friend nodded and dug her nails into my arm, sweaty and slick from dancing. We walked quickly. We kept our eyes down. We were careful to avoid eye contact with the boys. Looking at their feet, I noticed they appeared to be moving into some kind of formation. We moved toward the lighted sign at the entrance as if it were an angel guiding us from hell.

Not fast enough.

"ATTACK!!!" somebody shouted. Bloodcurdling screams emanated from across the room.

Chaos ensued. Shouts. Cries. Drinks sloshed, small tables capsized. The song on the speakers kept playing. Suddenly the club was a massive, writhing tangle of arms and legs. People were tripping over each other to try and escape. All I could think was, *Will we die here? Will my father ever know what happened to me?*

The next few seconds are dim in my memory. Somehow we managed to squeeze through the pack of screaming people and force ourselves through the bottleneck at the door. My last image of the club is of a small boy standing guard with his AK-47. The boy's eyes and his gun phosphoresced in the darkness. As he turned his head, I looked into his eyes. *Lifeless.* With our last energy, my friend and I tumbled out of the club and sprinted down the boulevard as fast as we could.

Past stores and dark apartments, ominous alleyways and gated houses we ran. We didn't look back. The sound of screams told us what was happening behind us. Eventually, the noise from the club died down. My friend was wheezing. My feet felt like stones. The shoes I had worn were cutting deeply into the sides of my feet, producing thin rivulets of blood. We slowed our pace. It was pitch-black outside. Crickets screeched. The air was sticky and moist. Sweat poured off us, attracting mosquitoes. Suddenly, my foot landed on something clammy. I tripped over onto my hands and knees and screamed.

"Help!!! Somebody!"

My cries echoed in the night.

"Shhh! What is it?" my friend cried, trying to quiet me down.

"I'm drowning!" I shrieked, dog-paddling through the bubbling goo.

"Agnes, no!"

My friend clambered into the brackish water after me. She clawed at my arms and feet. Thrashing and gulping for air, I took in muddy mouthfuls of water. It was probably only a foot deep, but in my terror, it felt like an ocean. Finally we extricated ourselves. We had reached a swamp.

"What do we do now?" I whined.

What could we do? We sat upon the shore, weighing our options. We had to get home, but the roads were too dangerous. That left the swamp or the nightclub, and we definitely weren't going back there. I took my friend's hand and squeezed. "We can do this," I said. Whimpering, we each dipped a toe into the mud. Then another, and another, until we had submerged our whole feet. It wasn't pleasant. I remember the sounds *Pish! Pash!* as we waded knee-deep through the ooze.

Screaming the entire way, we made it through the swamp as fast as we could. The swamp bordered a highway. When we reached the other side, I nearly got hit by a truck. "Agnes!" my friend shrieked. Vehicles were speeding by. I backpedaled toward the swamp, shaking hysterically from my second near-death experience that evening. Hugging my friend, I stood on the side of the road for a long time, unsure what to do. A few cars pulled over to offer us a ride, but we were afraid to jump in. They might be rebels! Did rebels drive cars? We didn't know! It was getting later and later. Tired and filthy, we walked for a long time, unsure where we were. Our feet were plastered with insects and blood. When the driver of a white Jeep pulled over and identified himself as a UN employee, my friend and I decided to take a chance. I asked the driver where he was headed.

"No questions!" he screamed.

Startled, I bit my tongue.

"Where can I drop you?" he asked more kindly.

He dropped us in Duala. We slept at a friend's house. I figured my father would worry about me, but what could I do? The phone lines had been cut. It was too late to find a taxi back to the Hotel Africa area where he lived. Lying on the floor of our friend's house, I thought back to the child soldiers at the nightclub, and the ones I'd seen at Tubmanburg Junction. This time, they had come too close.

Early the next morning, we hailed one of the few taxis on the road.

When I got home, I closed the front gate and quietly tiptoed up the path. No sooner had I snuck through the front door than my father, wide-awake, leapt from his chair.

"Where were you?" he screamed. "I drove all night looking for you! I thought you had been killed!"

Armed men were causing havoc all over Monrovia, my father said. Insurgent NPFL groups were announcing their presence as part of an effort to render the city vulnerable and cause chaos and fear. Did I have any idea? What was I thinking? When I hadn't come home, he had mounted a search party with two peacekeeping soldiers. He thought I had been shot at a checkpoint. Raped, mutilated, and lying in an unmarked grave! He didn't notice the muddy pair of shoes dangling from my hand, so I opted not to mention my own nighttime adventure.

"I'm sorry . . ." I mumbled, looking at my feet.

"It's time for you to return to Sierra Leone," my father announced.

I left the next afternoon. As it turned out, his timing could not have been better. The scene at the club was a prelude to Taylor's full-scale onslaught on Monrovia. A few days later, the NPFL launched a surprise attack in the early morning hours while most Liberians were still asleep. Taylor code-named the assault "Operation Octopus," because like an octopus, Taylor wrapped his troops around Monrovia and choked it.

Casualties were enormous. The destruction was severe. Many child soldiers were used for the attack. They cut across fields and through swamps just like the one my friend and I had waded through, and not all of them made it. Many were devoured by alligators. Others lost their arms and legs and became child amputees. Still others reversed course, using the swamp as an escape hatch from the combined forces of ECOMOG, the AFL, and the Black Beret, a military group organized by the Monrovia-based Interim Government of National Unity.

When my father called to tell me about Operation Octopus, he said he had never seen anything like it. Then he sighed and said he feared Liberia would see more, much more. "Now do you see why I told you to leave?" my father asked. His voice was tired and sad.

I had put off realizations and responsibility too long. This time, I would stay in Sierra Leone.

5

MY NAME IS BENATTA. I was captured in Cheesemanburg Market when I was selling fish. The fighters were shooting between themselves, and a twenty-year-old boy came and took me from the market to be his wife. I was forced to join him to save my life.

I didn't receive any training, but they gave me a gun. I fought in February, March, and April. By then, my stomach was getting big, so I fled to a refugee camp while my husband continued to fight. People pointed at me and said I was a fighter. They said I was one of the boys and girls who did wicked things.

I tried another camp but fighting broke out there, and the rebels said I should return to my own village. I went home and had my baby. There was no doctor, nurses, or anything. When my husband came to the camp, they pointed at him, too. They beat him severely and he ran away to hide. He came back, but we were thrown out of the place because we were fighters.

During the war, I captured other girls and brought them back to Bomi. They did it to me, so I had the intention of paying back. I captured girls, beat them, and tied them. At one point, I had forty-six girls under my command. Many girls died in the fighting. During World War I, I lost six girls, mainly because they were unfamiliar with the area and got captured. In World War II, I lost two girls in face-to-face combat.

Many girls were raped when they were captured, but once I had my own girls I wouldn't let that happen. The men didn't take my girls by force and rape them. They had to ask me if there was a girl they liked and wanted to take her. In many cases, I agreed and the girls went with them.

I N LIBERIA, when a female fighter says so-and-so was her first love, she is often referring to the first man who raped her. You hear a girl say, "My first love happened in the bush." What she means is somebody pinned her to the ground like an animal, climbed on top of her, and pointed an AK-47 at her head, ordering her to "Shut up or else!" There, in the mud, he forced himself and other things inside her vagina. He took away her pride. Many girls got pregnant this way. Only ten, eleven, and twelve years old, many were too tiny, too young, to have the babies. Without medicine or even a midwife present, the babies died. Many times the girls also died. Two children died on the same day.

Years later, I would call many of these girls my "daughters." Back then, I had no idea they even existed, or the terrible things that were being done to them. My own first love could not have been farther from their violent, horrific encounters.

It was four years after Operation Octopus. I was riding the Sierra Leone ferry to Freetown, and a soldier I knew was onboard. When we got to the other side, he said he was going on to Kissy, Sierra Leone, but that he had a friend who could take me into town. That's how I met Jeff.

We barely spoke that first day. He was sitting in the passenger seat, staring out the window. I was seated behind the driver and gazing at the back of Jeff's head. He was tall and handsome, wearing a military uniform with lots of bright, eye-catching badges. I wondered what army he fought for. When we arrived at my stop, I thanked the driver and turned to him.

"What can I call you?" I fluttered my eyelashes.

He smiled politely. "Jeff."

I asked Jeff what regiment he fought for. When he said ECO-MOG, I felt a surge of gratitude and respect. ECOMOG, you will recall, was the West African peacekeeping force formed to halt the carnage and bring an end to the Liberian war. Now, several years later, ECOMOG was fighting on two fronts, trying to save Liberia and also Sierra Leone from rebel onslaughts. ECOMOG soldiers were peacekeepers and peace enforcers who saved lives. In time, they would become a voice appealing to the rebel factions to stop using child soldiers.

In short, we saw them as our saviors. And so, as if this were a celebrity encounter, I reached into my purse and pulled out my personal organizer. Loneliness is pervasive in wartime, and Jeff seemed like a nice person. I asked for his number and took my sweet time writing down his rather short name: Jeff Umunna.

Weeks passed. One afternoon, I was flipping through my organizer and happened to see his name. Oh, why not? I thought. Let me give this guy a call. So I did. We talked every night that week. Jeff says I peppered him with questions. A Nigerian from the Ibo tribe, Jeff flew for the ECOMOG air force. I told him my father came from an ECOWAS country, Sierra Leone. It was one of the reasons we had fled. "Were you part of that initial invasion?" I asked. "Have you ever seen Charles Taylor?"

"Are you a journalist?" Jeff asked me at one point.

"No!" I laughed. "I just want to know everything about you . . ."

In time, I developed a crush on Jeff. Love had entered out of nowhere and suddenly the pepper flowers bloomed, and the bulbul birds sang in perfect tune.

I started commuting to the ECOMOG base on a daily basis. Soon I got to know the other pilots, and the names of wives and girlfriends they had left behind. I felt fortunate not to be like them: a picture in a frame. Friends warned me I was making a big mistake.

"He is an officer," they said. "They fight and come home in caskets!"

Blinded by love, I ignored them. I told them Jeff had a good star. That is what we Liberians call a person with a bright future. Someday, Jeff would become a captain, and I would be a captain's wife. I was sure of it. Then I got the news: I was pregnant. I was shocked, happy, and scared all at once. Jeff was certainly surprised and kept saying, "Wow . . . Wow . . . Oh my," but assured me we would figure everything out.

Did we consider the implications of bearing a child into a world at war? The conflicts raging in Liberia and Sierra Leone had defined our young adult years. We didn't know when the wars would end. Our love was strong, and I thought that was all you needed. To me, it seemed like things were falling into place at last. Everything was happening faster than Jeff and I had intended, of course, but we would prepare ourselves.

There are some things you can't prepare for.

Rebels' attacks against the Sierra Leonean government had been increasing. In May 1997, armed insurgents launched a coup. I was at the ECOMOG base with Jeff when it happened. We were in his room when all of a sudden, "Hey you!! Get up! Get dressed!" The base was thrown into a whirlwind of activity. I was scared but I wanted to be strong for Jeff. He raced out of the room and was gone for what seemed a long time. When he returned, Jeff told me the ECOMOG pilots had been ordered to suit up and fly the Sierra Leonean president to safety. Jeff, one of ECOMOG's best fliers, was to participate in this important mission. Because of me, Jeff had asked his commander to stand down. Chafed, Jeff's commander ordered another pilot to airlift the president so Jeff could "get his girlfriend off the base." I felt so guilty when Jeff told me this. Had I humiliated him? Cost him his career? Jeff didn't look at me, which was answer enough. I felt my stomach tighten.

"Jeff, I didn't mean to . . ." I started to say.

Gunshots interrupted my apology. "Get down!" Jeff screamed. He grabbed his pistol and was about to run out of the room when he turned back. "Don't go anywhere!" he said. "Lie on the ground under my bed. If someone tries to break in, stay down. There may be bullets flying."

He saw the terrified look in my face. Sighing, Jeff knelt beside the bed and took my chin in his hands. "Just try to get some sleep."

Sleep? I did not sleep. My mind ran marathons; my eyelids refused to close. If the Sierra Leonean rebels took the base, what would happen to me? Would they rape me? Kill me? After all, in the rebels' eyes, ECOMOG fighters were the enemy. Most women avoided the base for this very reason. Now rebels were taking the ECOMOG base, and my only protection was a mattress?

It was a nightmare. Thank God for daybreak. Jeff returned looking tense and tired. He told me the situation was dire; his squadron was preparing to evacuate.

"Evacuate?" I stammered. "When? Where to?"

"Now . . ." he said. "The rest is classified."

Classified? I felt as though the wind had been knocked out of me. I looked at him: my boyfriend, the father of my unborn child, and a man who came from Nigeria—a country known for male disappearing acts. What would happen to us? I was pregnant, but we weren't married. There was no tie of any kind.

"I am in love with you!" I begged.

But Jeff didn't want to talk about it. He left to find me a taxi. He said it was too risky for him to accompany me home, and his squadron needed him now. As the taxi pulled away, Jeff gave me a last, hurried kiss. I was beside myself. Lost and shaking, I boarded the ferry to Freetown and cried the whole way. Nobody even noticed. They were too focused on what was happening to their country. People running helter-skelter. The place swarming with rebels. Everyone shouting and crying.

"Stay indoors!" The rebels waved their guns menacingly and fired rounds at the sky. "There is more to come!"

For a moment, when the ferry docked, I forgot about my situation, too. Touching my belly, I looked around desperately. Where were the taxis? The police? How would I get home? At last, I found a hiding place, a small shop, and ran and cowered inside it. Touching my belly and trying to make myself small, I wondered if I would die in this place. The woman from Tubmanburg Junction bubbled up in my mind.

The gap that separated us was growing narrower. Two pregnant women: running, alone . . . The jaws of war dogged closer to her heels than mine . . . but for how long?

Suddenly I knew I couldn't die there. My life was not over. My baby's life would not begin that way. Careful to stay out of the rebels' sightline, I snuck out of the shop and looked around for an escape. A Sierra Leonean soldier who lived in my neighborhood saw me and ran over.

"What are you doing here?" he sneered. "Why are you coming from the ECOMOG base? That's where the Nigerians are! Are you dating a Nigerian?"

"I need to get home . . ." I begged. I didn't like the way he was looking at me. Rape, by soldiers, supposed friends, or men you trusted, was something we heard about all too frequently. "Can you help me or not?" I tried to sound desperate. It wasn't difficult. The soldier finally agreed. When he went off duty, he said he would drop me.

For three hours, I sat on a stoop watching people flee in all directions and thought about Jeff. I didn't know what had happened between us, only that it had not gone well. If your heart has ever been broken, if you have ever experienced the life-defining pain I felt in that moment, then my next thought might sound familiar: It's *amazing* how much two people can put into getting a relationship started and how quickly it falls apart. When an ECOMOG plane flew overhead, I glanced up and wondered if Jeff was looking down, or if he had forgotten about me already.

At last, the Sierra Leonean soldier appeared. Scared as I was to get into his car, I was grateful not to have to walk. When we reached my house, I hurried inside, secured the locks, and hid behind the door until the soldier drove away. At last, I made my way to my mattress. I felt as if I'd not slept in twenty years. I did not get up for several days, except to eat and stare longingly at photos of Jeff, hoping for a phone call that never came.

My stepsister, Regina, called, though. "Sister, get moving! I did not play the lottery so you could sit on your hands!"

Back then, there was an immigration lottery you could play. If you won and had enough money to pay for a visa and an airplane ticket, you could leave Sierra Leone and cross the border into Guinea to escape the fighting. There, you waited until your papers came through to go to America. Regina, who was already in America, had played the lottery for me, our mother, and my son, Reginald, and I had won. To someone not involved in a relationship, this would have seemed like a golden ticket. For me, back then, it felt like a prison sentence.

"Sister, get going," Regina pushed. "Not everyone is so lucky!" I sighed, trying to explain to Regina why I wasn't bouncing off the walls like her. Leaving Sierra Leone for Guinea meant a better life for me and my baby, but as for my future with Jeff . . .

"You have no future with Jeff," Regina said flatly.

My stepsister's words stung.

Eventually, I came to my senses. Jeff was gone. There was nothing left for me in Freetown. "You have a lot of choices," I told myself. "More than most. And if getting out of bed in the morning is a chore, then make another one." Resolved, I packed what I could carry and left. I had accepted my fate for now, and tried to smile for Regina when she called me to discuss all the things we would do together in America.

By the time we reached the Guinea border, I had counseled myself out of my misery and was looking forward to my meeting at the immigration office. But when I got there, the office was boarded shut. It was clear no one was getting to America. No one was going anywhere.

For eight months, I lived in a small house with a toilet that swarmed with flies. I was better off than most. Unlike the thousands of Liberian and Sierra Leonean refugees displaced to Guinean camps, I had a home and acted as temporary parent to children who had lost theirs and were living as street urchins. It was terrible hearing what some of them had gone through. Rape, violence, all kinds of abuse. Feeding them, I would hold my swollen belly and wonder what would become of my baby. How could I ensure that my child did not grow up like them?

Finally, a break in the clouds. The news the Liberian people had been praying for. The war was over. Peace had come. The newspapers blazed in large, block capital letters: CHARLES TAYLOR OVERPOWERS GOVERNMENT FORCES AND ENEMY FACTIONS. WEST AFRICAN PEACE- KEEPERS CLEAR COUNTRY OF LAND MINES AND ENCOURAGE REFUGEES TO RETURN BEFORE THE ELECTION.

We huddled around the communal radios, making sure that we had heard correctly. Could it be? Was the war actually over? Liberians had not voted since 1985. That was *twelve* years ago. Was it possible this was a new time? Was it real?

Oh it was real, people said. Taylor had an enormous war chest. Running on the slogan, "He killed my Ma! He killed my Pa! I will vote for him!", Taylor was traversing the country in his characteristic white suit and gold watch with his carved walking stick. He was greeted by grateful parades. Parades of people whose families he had *killed*, but who were coming out to root for this warlord turned whistle-stopper. After seven brutal years of fighting, I suppose these poor people made a quick calculation. In the name of survival, they saw giving Taylor what he came for as the best possible solution. That, and people said Taylor possessed a powerful charisma. One need only be in his presence for a moment to experience his awesome force.

Taylor's rival was a Liberian woman called Ellen Johnson-Sirleaf. She was an economist who had opposed President Doe, been placed under house arrest, and went to prison before serving a shorter term and going into exile. She moved to Washington, DC, and became the director of the United Nations Development Program's Regional Bureau for Africa. Initially, Ellen Johnson-Sirleaf supported Taylor but later she went on to oppose him.

It was a landslide. In the end, Taylor collected 75 percent of the votes, defeating Ellen Johnson-Sirleaf to become the twenty-second president of Liberia. Soon after, he charged her with treason. Despite allegations that Taylor's soldiers had helped illiterate voters fill out their ballots (some said the ballots were printed in disappearing ink), American election observers proclaimed the election to be free and fair. In a land of "jungle justice" like Liberia, diplomats shrugged and said the people had spoken. Maybe Taylor *was* the best outcome our people could hope for.

"I will not be a wicked president," Taylor declared in his inaugural speech. "But I have no intention of being a weak president."

Oh, if only the world had paid more attention. Congratulating the

Liberian people on a peaceful election, the UN Secretary-General Kofi Annan announced that Liberia had embarked on a new struggle for national unity, reconciliation, and democracy. The international community stood ready to assist Liberia, he said, but added that Liberia's success hinged on whether we could put our differences and wartime allegiances aside.

Taylor said we could.

I was skeptical at first. Suddenly, I, too, wanted to believe it. Have you ever been far from home when something important is happening? If so, you will understand my sudden, burning desire to return. To be there. To know that the peace was true. That, and I wanted to give birth in Liberia, my home, as opposed to Guinea, where I was a stranger. I missed my father. I missed Jeff, who was still flying for ECOMOG and based in Liberia. What more excuses did I need? Eight months pregnant, I looked at my belly in the mirror and wondered what Jeff would say when he saw me. His letters sounded alternately enthusiastic and hollow. I tried to call my father to tell him to expect me, but the phone lines were down. Maybe it's for the best, I thought. I had not broken the news of my pregnancy to him. With excitement and trepidation, I prepared to return.

6

I DO NOT KNOW if I killed people, but I fired a lot. I did not enjoy it, but I had to do it because I had nothing to eat. I was afraid, but when they gave me drugs I was brave.

When the war was over, I tried to find my family. I could not. I looked for my grandmother, but I could not find her either. I found a man and told him, "Oh, I am looking for somewhere to live. I do not have a home or anybody to live with." The man took me to his village. We reached his village at night.

In the morning, the man took me out to a big compound to introduce me to his people. It turns out he was the chief of that village. And as he was about to introduce me to his people, a woman came out of nowhere and bit my ear. She cut it off. She shouted that I killed her children and husband, and I should leave the village! And I did not know what to do after that.

—Wonlay

THERE WAS the prospect of returning to Liberia and then actually *doing* it. There is an old quote from Plato, "Only the dead have seen the end of war," and in Liberia, this proved all too true. No sooner had I decided to return than I wondered what I was really getting into.

Traveling alone was out of the question. With my enormous belly, I could go into labor at any time. Luckily, I had befriended a Liberian woman in Guinea who wanted to return to Liberia, too. She didn't have money for a ticket, but I told her I could pay. I bought three bus tickets for my friend, her baby, and me. We purchased water, juice, and roast meat for the car ride and ate a huge meal the day of our departure. The bus would stop, but my friend and I feared a rebel ambush. We didn't want to get out unless it was absolutely necessary.

The bus was unventilated and crammed with anxious travelers. Their belongings were heaped on their laps or extended over other people's laps, causing the usual tussles. The bus smelled like petrol, which turned my stomach. Its engine made a terrible racket. As the trip wore on, I hardly even noticed these things, though. Something far more distressing had captured my attention.

Child soldiers.

At checkpoint after checkpoint, boys dressed in coats and costumes like the ones I'd seen at Tubmanburg Junction stopped us and demanded to see our identification cards. "Those boys are bad. Don't look at those boys!" I whispered to my friend. Still, it was hard not to look. The boys' official orders were to prevent rebels from crossing the border. Instead, they harassed us with scornful questions and emptied our carefully packed suitcases onto the ground. Clothes, jewelry, family photographs—all carefully folded and stowed—were disemboweled onto the dirt road. The boys trampled on them. They took particular pleasure combing through ladies' underwear with their guns. I prayed that the babies in our car, temporarily hidden, would keep quiet.

There weren't only checkpoints between countries, there were checkpoints between counties, and Nimba County was one of the worst. This was the site of Taylor's "Christmas Eve Incursion." It was there that on December 24, 1990, Taylor invaded from the

Ivory Coast. You won't meet a Liberian who doesn't hear "Christmas Eve" and think "Charles Taylor" anymore. Eight years later, Taylor's boys were still standing guard. Fried on marijuana, cocaine, and opium, they shook their guns in our faces and screamed like banshees.

"Pay a tax for customs!" they shouted. "Or we will take your things!"

I didn't want to give those boys my things, but I kept quiet like the other passengers. "Give them what they want!" they whispered. "These boys mean business!"

Sure enough, the boys stole our food and belongings. They chastised us for leaving Liberia. "Where are you coming from? You were not here during the war! Go back to the country you have chosen!" Frightened, I bit my tongue, hoping this dressing-down would wrap up soon. But when the boys got to my suitcase and started smashing my things, I started to wonder. Was returning to Liberia really wise? Did we know it was safe? If the Nimba County checkpoint was any indication, it certainly wasn't.

I turned to my friend. "Should we go back?" I whispered, as if this was even an option at that point. She looked at her baby, then at me, and half shook, half nodded her head. I could tell she was as confused as I was.

It was late when we reached the outskirts of Monrovia, which was worrisome. It was not good to be on the road after dark. We had heard terrible stories about what happened to people after sunset: *Black magic! Human sacrifice! Cannibalism!* Gazing at the dark stands of trees quivering and shifting in the moonlight, I wondered who might be behind them and begged the driver to step on it. His head swiveled around and he snarled like an attack dog. Immediately, I regretted opening my mouth. After all, who was he? A rebel spy? How did I know he wouldn't reach into his glove box, pull out a knife, and splatter my blood across the backseat? In those days, you didn't know who anybody was.

At last, we pulled into town. I slept at my friend's house . . . or tried to. Earlier fears of an ambush gave way to new ones: *What will Jeff say when he sees me? Will he still have feelings for me? Will he want to be together?* All night, I tossed and turned. The next morning, bleary-eyed, I went to go look for him. I'd heard Jeff was stationed at the ECOMOG military base at Bong Mines Bridge. I sandwiched myself between passengers on a public bus, who rolled their eyes when I boarded. My huge belly filled up the car like a balloon. When we got to the bridge, I heaved myself out. I waddled over to a group of ECOMOG soldiers who were patrolling the bridge and smiled.

"I am looking for Flight Lieutenant Jeff Umunna," I wheezed, hoping that I looked respectable.

The soldiers stared at me. One whistled. I heard another one chuckle, "Umunna? Is this lady pregnant with Umunna's baby?"

Suddenly I felt very ashamed.

It was nothing compared to how Jeff felt, apparently. When he saw me, his eyes nearly popped out of his head. He quickly escorted me off the base, found a small café, and ordered us Coca-Colas. Jeff said he was glad to see me. But his eyes didn't look glad. I tried to make small talk, but Jeff kept checking his watch. He leaned back in his chair and seemed to wash his face with his hands, stretching the corners of the skin. At last, Jeff made a tent with his hands and sighed. He said his mission in Liberia was finishing. He had thought he would be in Monrovia another year, but it was not to be. Jeff twirled a toothpick in his teeth for a brief moment and placed it carefully on the table before dropping the final bomb:

"Besides," he said, "pilots don't marry foreigners."

I actively considered dousing him with Coca-Cola.

"Let me explain—" Jeff stopped my hands just in time.

For the second time in our relationship, my heart shattered on the spot. Eyes flashing, I told him he had thirty seconds. Nodding, Jeff quickly replied that he had thought long and hard about the life we might build together. At the end of the day, Jeff was an ECOMOG pilot. He might be called upon to bomb Liberia someday . . .

"Your family and friends, Agnes . . ." Jeff cupped his hands over mine. "Even *you* could be a target."

So that was it. Dating me, Jeff had failed in his mission. Military protocol meant we could no longer be together. I didn't believe him! I thought he was lying and had another girlfriend. Jeff hugged my shoulders and promised me he wouldn't leave me in the lurch. On the morning of my thirty-first birthday, he gave me one hundred dollars to cover the hospital delivery charges and flew back to Nigeria. At this point, single and miserable, I decided there was only one place I could go.

My uncle Tennyson lived on the Old Road in Sinkor. I figured I would use Tennyson as my litmus test: If he saw my belly and died, I might as well save time and put myself out of my misery. Strategically holding my suitcase in front of my stomach, I went to see him. When Tennyson took my suitcase, he almost fainted but checked himself in time and gave me a warm embrace. He said he had been worried about me. He hadn't known I'd gone to Guinea. "So many people have been killed in Sierra Leone!" he cried. "I thought you were dead!"

"I wanted to come back . . ." I shrugged. "But people said it was bad here."

Tennyson looked at my belly. "Were you scared to come home for a different reason?" my uncle probed.

I looked at the floor. Nodding and wiping away tears, I confessed that it was true. My father had gotten me out of danger and tried to help me build a future, and for what? I had money and opportunities and returned home pregnant and unmarried? My father would be so disappointed! "Be still," my uncle said and went to telephone my father. That afternoon, bracing myself for a tongue-lashing, I went to his house. When my father saw me, he broke down and wept.

"Why didn't you call?" He clasped my shoulders and looked at me as if I was a mirage. "You were in Guinea for eight months, and I didn't hear from you!"

I didn't have an answer, and my father didn't press me for one. He knew enough about war, and what it does to people, to realize explanations were often difficult to come by. He just sat there, shaking his head, hugging me and weeping to have me home. Not once did he ask about the baby. Only how I had survived and whether I was okay, and where I'd lived all this time. And I thought: *This is love. My father always loves me, even when I don't deserve it. Especially when I don't deserve it.*

When we finally got around to talking about Jeff, my father said he blamed himself: "It's my fault. You didn't have a true father's hug until you were thirteen." He apologized for not being around to provide a better example. I shook my head, no. I said I was bright and had money and encouragement but hadn't applied myself. Sighing, my father conceded that this was true. "Even if I had put you in a cage, you would have found a way to get out," he smiled.

A few weeks later, I was diagnosed with malaria. It was scary. Malaria is a common enough disease in Africa, but not something you want when you are nine months pregnant. Battling fever and chills, I sang songs to my belly and prayed that my child would be okay. As soon as I recovered, I went into labor. My father was on a trip in America but had helped me to arrange things before he left. As I rode in an ambulance to Monrovia Catholic Hospital, I stared out the window and saw a Liberian woman cradling her baby in the ghetto. I wondered whether this baby would go on to have a good life, or if it had been born with one foot in the grave.

Then I thought about the child soldiers: the boys who had harassed us and taken our things at the checkpoint. The boys who invaded the nightclub and played charades with their AK-47s at Tubmanburg Junction. People said they raped their sisters. Their *own* mothers. People said they cut pregnant women in half—for sport! Now here I was en route to a hospital, in a speedy ambulance, my bills paid. Safe, spoken for, and healthy. My mother was alive. My stepsister, Regina, was alive. My baby would be born into a clean, white room. What had I done to deserve this? To earn this? Nothing. When the smiling nurse handed me my daughter, wrapped in a warm blanket, I couldn't help wondering how many mothers and daughters weren't as lucky as us.

Jeff named our baby "Diamond." We were still in contact at that point. When he told me the reason for the name, and despite what had happened between us, I got a lump in my throat. When Jeff deployed to Sierra Leone, people had told him there were lots of diamonds there. Jeff, a poor pilot, left Nigeria believing he would return home a rich man. He didn't find any diamonds, he said, but he did have a child. Jeff said that was his Diamond.

I decided to take Jeff's last name. Although we weren't a traditional family, I felt my daughter would benefit from knowing who her father was from the start. This was hard for my father. He thought Jeff had deserted me, which was true. Eventually, I explained it to him, "I just think it will be simpler this way . . ."—and he said he understood but looked hurt. Quickly, I fetched Diamond and placed her in his arms. My father lifted her up, my precious, gurgling Diamond. He carried her around the house, singing lullabies and rocking her gently. Watching them, I felt that my heart could not grow any larger.

For so long, I had felt like a frustration in my father's life. Finally, I felt like I had done something beautiful. Children have that effect on us, that power: They breathe new life into our existence. They remind us how good the world can be. As I watched my father carrying around his granddaughter, his first daughter's first daughter, I felt peaceful. I felt like a mother at last. Then, as I watched my father holding the third generation, I wondered what kind of world my daughter would inherit.

7

I REMEMBER WHEN we killed people. We killed them because they refused to give us some of the rice they were pounding. Sometimes we slept in the midst of dead bodies. This was a method our commanders used to make us brave. It really worked. Human lives became valueless to us. When there was no life to destroy, we destroyed properties.

We burned entire villages, houses, clothes, crops. Sometimes we smoked to keep the cold off our bodies. We walked for miles to attack our foes. We did not hesitate to treat innocent civilians as our enemies. They were flogged, killed, raped, and parts of their bodies were cut off. The most wicked were elevated in the ranks and loved by our commanders. There were competitions and jealousy among us. We were eager to gain our commanders' favor.

—Orlando

W HAT SHOULD have been the happiest time of my life—a new baby, home at last, and with my father—was farthest from it. The feeling that someone or something was lurking around every corner, ready to grab Diamond in its cold clamp, was difficult to shake. Having been displaced for many years, I didn't know what peace was supposed to feel like, but it wasn't this. Whatever was governing Liberia definitely wasn't good.

My father wanted me to stay in Monrovia after I had Diamond. He felt it was safer for us there. Looking around, I wondered. It was not the homecoming I had imagined after these many years away. Charles Taylor had been in office for less than a year but warlords still cruised the streets with impunity. There was no justice, no rules, no discipline. When I left, the houses were standing erect. When I returned, everything was in a pile. Barbershops operated in the skeletons of government buildings. Large parts of the city had been weed-whacked to the ground. The place called the Monte Carlo where we used to go for treats and games had a strange smell inside. Driving around Monrovia, I recognized things here and there, but everything was scattered.

Theft was so prevalent that there was a place on Johnson Street where people used to go to buy back their own things. The merchants would yell, "Buy your own thing!" Meaning, "We have looted your things. Buy them back from us!" If you recognized an item that had belonged to you, you negotiated with the "store owner" for a price. Charles Taylor sanctioned this sort of behavior: He said it represented wealth circulation. Property was rotated among the haves and have-nots. I couldn't believe it when my father told me. "Go and see for yourself!" he said. That afternoon, I picked through bins of furniture, clothing, and valuables. Entire family histories dumped into wheelbarrows and hawked on the street.

"Buy your own thing!" the merchants clamored. And they meant everything. Nails, rods, the screws from your walls. "Pay for your *own* thing!"

Searching the stalls, I found a dusty crate of books. Browsing through it, my hands started to tremble. There were children's books . . . dozens of them . . . filled with numbers and lessons completed by tiny hands . . . 1988, 1989—right before the war started.

Where were these children now? What were their books doing here? *Why did they stop their lessons?* I felt like screaming at the shop owner, demanding answers, as if he would know something. Taylor was talking all the time now about putting computers in schools and increasing Liberia's literacy rate, but where were *these* children, the tiniest victims of the war he had started? Were they gripping AK-47s with the same small hands they had once gripped pencils and notebooks? Were they even alive? I thought about Diamond, napping at home, and hastened my search.

I tried another bin of books and came across a medical text, *Beginner's Anatomy. Maybe my father will like this,* I thought. Opening the cover, I gasped. His name and the medical college he had attended in America were written inside! Not even bothering to haggle with the shop owner, I thrust a wad of cash into his hand and ran.

"Look!" I shoved the book into my father's hands.

My father took the book from me and opened it slowly. Shaking his head, he turned the familiar pages from his school days, once lovingly cared for, but now streaked with stains and missing entire chapters. He ran his hand over the pages as if the book were an old friend or a vision that might vanish.

"Isn't it something?" I marveled.

"I told you . . ." my father sighed. "These are the things that happened during the war."

People did anything they could to make money back then. There was no electricity in Liberia, but my father lived in a house with a generator that was operational for several hours each day. Soon I started selling ice. I would wake up early in the morning, boil water in big kitchen pots, and freeze ice-cubes. I sold trays of ice in bulk and used the money I made to buy food and clothes for Diamond. At night, exhausted but proud to be supporting my daughter, I would snuggle up on a mattress with her, facing east according to Liberian tradition, and dream:

JOURNALISTS ABDUCTED!

NEW TALES OF TORTURE!

FORMER TAYLOR OPPONENT BEHEADED—EYES GOUGED OUT!!!

I had horrible dreams. Nightmares, mostly. Newspaper headlines blended with daily experiences to produce nighttime movies, frighteningly real. I was increasingly terrified to raise Diamond in this place. Many sleepless nights, I would lie awake, my mind reeling with chilling scenes. I would wake up in a twist of sweaty sheets.

Daily errands were becoming dangerous. In the old days, you could call a taxi. Now there were no cars to be found. To get somewhere, you had to go and stand in a particular place and wait for hours. Once inside the car, you had to lock your door and tell the driver to go quickly in order to avoid being kidnapped. Warlords occupied Monrovia's fancy hotels. Women were frequently grabbed off the street and taken to them as concubines. Sitting in traffic, I saw young girls nabbed right out of cars.

"Where are the police?" I shrieked when it happened the first time.

"The police?" the taxi driver responded, baffled. "Those warlords have guns. The police will not challenge those men!"

I told the driver to go quick, quick, quick.

One day, I was shopping at the Lebanese supermarket with some friends. When we finished shopping, we brought our items to the cash register. A tall, slim man in military gear had placed his groceries on the counter ahead of us but stepped aside to let us go first. Then he stood there flirting with us while the shop owner rang up our things: asking us our names and what we planned to cook for dinner.

"And where do you beautiful girls live?" he purred.

"Near the Hotel Africa," we giggled shyly.

"Hmmm . . ." he said, and seemed to make a mental note of the place.

When we reached into our pocketbooks to pay for our groceries, the man stopped our hands.

"I'll pay for these beautiful girls," he told the shop owner and winked.

My friends and I thanked the gallant stranger, who introduced himself as Isaac Musa. He said he would see us around. When I told my father about the chivalrous gesture, he was horrified.

"Why did you tell him where we lived?" he screamed. "Do you know who that man is? What he could *do* to us?"

Isaac Musa was Charles Taylor's military advisor and one of the most feared men in Liberia. Taylor accounted to no one, my father said, and his deputies like Isaac Musa killed at will. For the next few days, whenever I was alone in the house, I kept the doors bolted and jumped at the slightest sound, praying that Isaac Musa wouldn't remember my address.

Soon after that incident, Charles Taylor pegged my father as a spy. My father had set up a surveillance unit to screen for the Ebola virus in one of Taylor's strongholds. When the WHO transferred money to the site, Taylor's men accused my father of campaigning for Taylor's rivals. He was put on Taylor's hit list. He requested to be sent to Gambia until things calmed down. I could tell he was worried about Diamond and me, and I was nearing the end of my rope. If this was peace, and things like this could happen to my father, a humanitarian doctor trying to save people, what would become of Liberia?

Eventually, I left for Nigeria. I had to find Jeff. My father couldn't believe it. I tried to explain that it was complicated, why I didn't want to live in Liberia anymore. This country was no longer familiar to me. Jeff was. I still believed we had a future together.

After seven years of war, a dysfunctional romance *can* seem like an attractive option. That, and I believe some people are less rational about love. And if you are one of those people, you have my empathy. You who have been burned twice, or even three times, only to run back to the flame, you alone will understand my next move. For the rest of you, my apologies.

The same old story: I found Jeff. We dated for a while. I got pregnant. "Listen . . ." Jeff put his arm around my heaving shoulders. "I love you. You are a nice person. But there are rules. If I marry you, I must resign from ECOMOG. And it is not a good time for me to do that."

Confronted with a choice, to follow his heart or orders, it was clear where Jeff's priorities lay. Some things aren't meant to be, said my friends. Some lessons you have to learn twice, Regina scolded.

Although my situation was terribly black, there was a positive part to it. I got a job with a humanitarian organization in Nigeria. They hired me to work in a transit camp where refugees from all over Africa ran, armed only with the hope that whatever unknown thing awaited them there was preferable to the darkness they had fled. Unfortunately, once in the camp, these refugees confronted new dangers—including some they couldn't see. AIDS was spreading like wildfire. My uncle had been diagnosed HIV+, so I had some experience with the virus. The humanitarian organization hired me to educate refugees about AIDS and how to avoid contracting it.

It was a difficult job. Getting to the camp involved a three-hour commute over bandit-ridden roads. And inside the camp, life was very bad. People languishing in shanty houses. Shabby mud walls with only a scrap of aluminum for the roof. Zero protection from the oppressive heat and cold night winds. People were desperate and fights broke out. Saddest of all were the children who fell into prostitution. Nevertheless, I woke up each morning determined to do my part.

"Too many people are dying!" I said, handing out pamphlets and urging people to go and get tested at the clinic. At night, I cradled

Diamond in my arms—so tiny and unaware of what was happening inside the camp, and the horrors engulfing her own country.

Some people will do anything to get somewhere else. In order to qualify for relocation to America, many refugees had to prove they would be killed if they returned to their home countries. A great many refugees were illiterate, though. They couldn't read or write, let alone advocate for themselves as to why they met the criteria for resettlement. But there was one man, a refugee in the camp, who was a different story. He was an educated person from Liberia who spoke about human rights during the day and made up stories for other Liberians at night. Refugees would come to him: "Ah, I need to get to America! Write my story!" And he would . . . for a price. That man slept with so many girls in the camp, it made me sick—and with AIDS spreading!

"You have to stop," I said. "People are dying because of your actions!"

"Don't you want to go to America?" he purred.

"Not like that!" I said, handing him a pamphlet.

On the Day of the African Child, a major holiday in Africa, the organization I worked for decided to broadcast a radio program. They often transmitted public service announcements over the radio, important messages designed to prevent medical disasters resulting from the close quarters refugees found themselves living in: "Use a bed net, wear a condom, wash your hands after you go to the bathroom." As the Day of the African Child approached, I pulled some of the NGO workers aside. PSAs were all well and good, I said, but you know what would really be interesting? "Hearing from the refugees themselves."

I suggested we invite refugees on the air to talk about their hopes and dreams. What had brought them there? What challenges lay ahead? That way, people in the nearby host community would realize they existed and might even help them.

Nobody had considered listening to refugees before, or saw how it might be compelling. Most people in the host community prayed the refugees would just disappear. But on this day, I helped the NGO air a show about the people in the camp. I think it changed some people's mind-sets.

On November 3, 2001, I gave birth to my second daughter, Ogechi, in a Nigerian hospital. She was the last, beautiful product of an ultimately doomed relationship. Jeff had married another woman. She was a nice person, but for obvious reasons we couldn't be friends. Far from home and without a companion in the world, I soon grew lonely. I was barely making enough money to feed my babies. How would I pay for their school fees and doctor's visits? Had we lived in Liberia, it would have been different, but the prospect of transporting two babies across Nigeria and home was out of the question. Liberia had descended into war again. People called it "World War II," and it was as awful and terrible as the first one. Rape. Murder. Starvation. Rebel factions raining terror on innocent civilians. Apocalyptic violence was the order of the day.

In 1999, Guinea, Nigeria, the United States, and Britain had accused Liberia of supporting the RUF rebels in Sierra Leone in exchange for diamonds. A rebel group opposed to Taylor's government, the Liberians United for a Reconciliation and Democracy (LURD), launched operations. Fighting erupted along the Guinea border. Villages were shelled, and thousands of people were displaced. In 2000, Taylor launched a massive counteroffensive; in January 2002, he declared a state of emergency. When that happened, no one had food or water. Everybody was suffering. For a second time, Liberia became a living hell, a harrowing example of man's inhumanity. What kept people striving and fighting to survive was only this: the prospect that Taylor might be losing control. "He's done! He's finished!" people clamored. "We're going to have peace now, oh, we are going to have peace once we remove Charles Taylor!" But it was bloody and horrific to the end.

I went to Jeff to discuss the situation. "I am worried about our girls," I said.

We agreed that I should leave Diamond and Ogechi with him for a while. That way, our daughters would have a stable childhood. Meanwhile I would return to Sierra Leone and communicate as often as I could. Once things settled down, we would devise another solution. As difficult as it was to leave Diamond and Ogechi, I felt this temporary measure was best and thanked Jeff and his wife. Then I kissed my little girls good-bye.

I told them, "Mommy is going away to do something, so you will be proud of Mommy." But it broke my heart to leave them.

Back in Freetown, my principal home for the last fourteen years, I monitored the news reports. Taylor's regime was falling. Rebel factions were making significant advances. Attempts to negotiate a ceasefire between rebel forces and Taylor's government failed. Finally, the world woke up to Liberia's nightmare. International pressure for a peacekeeping mission grew. In June 2003, the UN indicted Taylor and issued a warrant for his arrest. The allegations: "bearing the greatest responsibility for war crimes, crimes against humanity, and serious violations of international humanitarian law within the territory of Sierra Leone." In July, President George Walker Bush called for Taylor to step down from office. As rebels battled for control of Monrovia, the ECOWAS countries agreed to supply peacekeepers.

The war that had separated me from my childhood friend, killed the woman at Tubmanburg Junction, brought me and Jeff together, separated us, then sent my father into hiding, and did far worse to hundreds of thousands of Liberians was drawing to a close. Still, memories of the last peace made me wary to return immediately.

In Freetown, I met an American woman who worked for the United Nations High Commissioner for Refugees (UNHCR) and was setting up a West African broadcasting service. It was a chance encounter that would change my life forever. As she described her plan to use radio as a vehicle of peace, I felt she was speaking in a language I understood. I remembered the powerful effect radio had had in the Nigerian refugee camp, and the joy I experienced working at KISS FM. I agreed with her: Radio might, in time, lead listeners to consider concepts they weren't now comfortable with. I nodded eagerly when she asked me to read a short script into the microphone.

"You have a good voice," she said when I was through. "You are a radio person!"

She recorded me reading UNHCR news bulletins. Then she edited them. When I listened to the edited versions, I got goose bumps. It sounded like something people might listen to.

"Do you hear this?" she asked. "Do you hear what you are capable of?"

I did now.

No one but my father had ever used that word *capable* to describe me. Just thinking about it—that I might be something, have a skill of some kind—was shocking . . . and wonderful. Maybe I could do something with my voice to help my country rebuild . . . and, in so doing, give thanks for all the opportunities I had been given. Become a role model to my daughters. I hugged the woman and thanked her for taking a chance on me.

On August 11, 2003, the news: Charles Taylor, warlord, diamond smuggler, and rebel dictator, had bowed to international pressure and agreed to resign the Liberian presidency. He would accept political asylum in Nigeria. Later, he would face a war crimes tribunal in Sierra Leone. The same people who had cheered Taylor on during the 1997 election now cheered with all of their might: *Get this man out! Get him gone!*

Like all things Taylor, it was a showdown until the end. "Today is a day of moving forward," Taylor opined on the eve of his departure, "a step that should bring relief to the people of this nation." Later, Taylor clarified his statement: "God willing, I will be back." In his final speech from Monrovia, Taylor declared: "History will remember me kindly."

Taylor's vice president, Moses Blah, was sworn in as president. As Taylor's plane lifted off the ground, we knew this thing was really through. At long last, Liberians could breathe easily again. And, when Liberians who had been living in refugee camps started returning to rebuild their homes, even I had to agree. It was a sign.

Not long after this happened, the UNHCR woman asked me to join her radio station. My heart leapt. But the next moment, I knew I could not accept her offer. I had finally found my purpose, but there is something more important than your purpose: your people. My own, dear Liberia was finally free but lying in a million shattered pieces. More than anything, I wanted to help my country. I, who had been so fortunate, and who had never suffered half the torment my people had, wanted to be a part of the solution.

The UNHCR lady was disappointed but said she understood. She offered to write a recommendation letter on my behalf. I was moved, and when she addressed it to the head of public information at the United Nations Mission in Liberia, I was speechless. These were the powerful people restructuring Liberia. The lady said they were hiring. Maybe I could join them? Maybe, I nodded in disbelief.

There is no way to prepare for a journey like the one I made to Liberia. The extermination. The ruin. The loss. No way to gird yourself for the level of destruction our ex-president, multiple rebel factions and sub-factions, and splinter rebel groups had wreaked upon our country. Warlords and their armies completing their errands of death. For as long as I live, I will not forget that journey home.

We were five in number: four other displaced Liberians and me. We were returning to rediscover the country of our childhoods. What hadn't been killed or destroyed, that is.

Powerful rebel groups still controlled large parts of the country. People like us traveled in groups for protection and support. We had heard about the "checkpoints" child soldiers had erected. These weren't the checkpoints you crossed during the war: quasi-legitimate governmental attempts to collect a tax. These checkpoints were the brainchild of Liberian child soldiers, established to shake down returning refugees for their money. "They aren't killing anybody anymore," people said. "It's just for show." As if that made any difference. "Watch your back!" people said. These boys were disturbed drug addicts. Capable of anything. Lords unto themselves. They weren't killing now, but who knows? *Those children can turn on you.*

"Be sure to go to the bank," people said. "If you don't have money, those boys will take everything else!"

Cars weren't allowed on the bridge between Sierra Leone and Liberia, so we had to walk. When our small group got there, boys wearing wigs and black face masks (like the ones you wear to costume parties) materialized out of nowhere and started running toward us. They were an ominous sight . . . an unruly band of masked gunmen. Gun children. AK-47s dragging down their shoulders, the rest armed with knives, machetes, and iron rods. They were tall and thin. A few wore women's dresses over their black blue jeans. These were boys who didn't want to be identified, that much I knew. These were boys who had done wicked things.

"Give us your money!" they snarled. "Or you die!"

Trying to stop our badly shaking hands, we paid the tax. Once we did, a boy lifted a long, leafy tree branch he had hewn and lain across the bridge to let us through. "Hurry up!" the boys screamed at us as we hurried through the checkpoint. We walked a distance of some meters before reaching another one. "Give us your money!" the second group of child soldiers manning the "exit gate" roared. "Or else!" We gave them our money, they lifted the pole, we walked a few more meters, and did it again.

This absurdity was nothing compared to what greeted us on the other side. I clutch my heart remembering the gruesome wreckage. In the rural areas, charred remains of huts. Animal carcasses. Burnt fields screaming with the violence that had lately taken place there. Schools were desecrated with unprintable words, warlords' names and scribbled stick figures depicting torture and rape. Gigantic, overturned trucks cremated by gas fires rusted on the side of the road. Traffic inched around them like a somber funeral procession.

In the towns, I saw apartments riddled with bullet holes running the entire length of the buildings. Store fronts streaked with blood. Worst of all were the people . . . zombies. Adults grief-stricken and dumb with silence. Some bandaged, others crying on the ground or picking at their gaping wounds. *Oh my people*, I remember thinking. *What has happened to my people?*

Now I saw what fourteen years of war could do to a soul . . . to a body, a face, a mind. War broke bones. Spirits. It demolished fields and homes and counties. A country is its people, and until the Liberian refugees began to arrive from Guinea and Sierra Leone, these broken people were all that was left. I will never forget those faces. There was at once so much to look at and nothing at all. The saddest welcome home in the world. And then, as we pulled into Monrovia, it started to rain.

8

MY NAME IS MAYUPLEH. Well, I was affected by the war. I have three children. I don't have anybody to help me. So that is what bring me here. The people that are helping the women that disarmed. And I one of those.

I fought for Chief Blessing. LURD. After my father was killed, and my mother, that what made me to join the people. My mother was dead by a stray bullet. That what made me to join. Myself talked to myself: I say I will join, and I joined. I toted armor to get a little food for my children.

When I be behind the armor, I only looking for survival for my children. When a certain time came, I ran away. I saw dead bodies. When I saw the bodies, I felt bad. Even I get sick from it. That thing, I not used to. It can affect the body.

Nobody raped me. I was having my husband. He was a fighter. He was one of the top men. They kill my mother, they kill my father, and that what he fighting for. He one of the fighters for Charles Taylor. He do bad. But he reconciled before dying. Plenty thing fighting, he killed, he killed his enemy.

I feel bad! I will say sorry. That the war. Well, that just the sorry I can give. If the people come up to say, "Your husband killed my children and I want to kill your children," I will tell them sorry. Because we have to reconcile. We have to move the country forward. That's why the president came to us. To move the country forward.

THERE IS A TERM for what I experienced in the car pulling into Monrovia: survivor's guilt. Although my people were still alive, they were not entirely alive. And I was. And I felt guilty for it. It took time for me to make sense of things . . . the horror, and what my contribution might be. Eventually, I found a place in the pain.

"Good afternoon," I said to the soldier in the security booth at the United Nations Mission in Liberia's (UNMIL) military base. It was August 2004. The war had been over for eleven months. The largest UN mission in history had been launched the previous September to bring order to the catastrophe that was my country. It was headquartered at the German Embassy, which was determined to be the most secure place. In addition, UNMIL had established a military base and a radio station at Bong Mines Bridge, where I had gone to see Jeff. Battling nerves and waves of nostalgia, I shifted my bag on my shoulder, left my ID with the soldier, and entered the gate.

I had bought a suit, my first, the day before. I tied a purple sweater (my lucky color) across my shoulders and carried my resume and rec-ommendation letter in a bag across my chest. I looked more profes-sional than I felt. Walking in the direction the soldier had pointed, I tried to step like I knew where I was going. Hundreds of diplomats and UN peacekeeping soldiers scurried around madly, clutching clip-boards and walkie-talkies, and not noticing me in the slightest. They were there to fulfill UNMIL's mandate: Support the ceasefire, disarm combatants, destroy weapons, and ensure that, this time, the war was really over.

As I approached the office of UNMIL Radio, I rehearsed uncon-vincing lines as to why I should be allowed to join their elite company.

I had a few radio shows under my belt but no real skills, unless you counted passion and heart. Neither the person whom my recommendation letter had been addressed to nor her deputy were around, so people advised me to try the UN Radio chief. Kojo Mensah, wearing a blue shirt, black pants, and shiny cuff links, was elegantly sipping a cup of coffee and smoking a cigarette when I arrived. I told him who I was. He looked at me as if I'd landed from the moon.

Kojo Mensah set me straight. "The deputy is in America. You can visit him on Monday." Little did I know I had just met my future boss.

On Monday, I visited the UNMIL Public Information Office and met the deputy public information officer, Patrick Coker. Patrick was a dapper man, a retired Nigerian navy officer. Like Kojo, his fashion sense clearly defied whatever circumstances he confronted. Patrick told me there were no more jobs for Liberians, but he might consider giving me a short-term contract depending on what I had to say. Or, as it turned out, what Patrick had to say. My secretarial training came in handy that day.

"Take a pen," Patrick instructed. "Write down these ideas I have for Liberian radio."

By now, you probably have a sense of the key role radio played during the war. It's what brought us news of invasions, of the fighting, and of the peace. The same was true in those post-war days. Drive down any major boulevard in Monrovia or backwater road in Liberia's rural areas, and you would see groups of Liberians clustered around small radios, taking a break from their labors, checking in on Liberia, and making sure their efforts were worth it. Only very rich people owned televisions, which is still true today, so radio was the principal means of getting information out.

Proper, regular information dissemination was a key component of UNMIL's strategy in Liberia, Patrick said. He told me the day peacekeepers set foot in Liberia, UNMIL Radio had begun broadcasting from a satellite van. They moved to an emergency studio facility before relocating to Bong Mines Bridge. From there, UNMIL kept Liberian citizens apprised of critical steps in the peace process. Its staff worked hard to defuse misconceptions about who had done what to whom. "Go here to give up your weapons," they might say. Or, "Remember, violence is never the answer." In those early days, everyone feared the war would resume, and UNMIL wasn't taking any chances.

Patrick was responsible for shaping UNMIL's message. Going forward, he said, he wanted to discuss the challenges post-war Liberia faced, specifically HIV/AIDS. During the war, rebel soldiers on all sides of the fighting had raped and terrorized women and girls. Many were infected. They were giving birth to babies who were HIV+. Liberian clinics were overcrowded and poorly equipped to handle the crisis. Anti-retroviral drugs weren't available.

"How will society deal with this calamity?" Patrick asked, waiting for an answer I didn't have.

Instead, I told him about the Day of the African Child and my work with refugees in Nigeria. He was moved. But he was even more pleased with the notes I had taken. He made a couple of corrections and told me to bring them to Kojo. I thanked Patrick and returned to Bong Mines Bridge, holding not a recommendation letter this time, but pilot concepts for UNMIL Radio.

Kojo was sitting at his desk smoking a cigarette when I arrived. "Everybody is talking about HIV/AIDS!" he roared. "That is not what I want!"

"That is not what I want either . . ." I agreed, believing it was wise to do so.

"There is so much else to talk about!" Kojo gestured like an orchestra conductor. Cigarette smoke lingered behind his every flourish like a jet-stream trail. An employee who had been sitting there before

I arrived hurried off. Kojo took a long drag of his cigarette. He peered at me closely and asked me to repeat my name. Agnes, I said. Well, Agnes, he said, it was time to talk about *emotional* life. How Liberians would deal with the past and embrace the future, and how difficult it was for most people to conceive of doing either one. Moving forward did not mean winking at the past, Kojo said. Many people witnessed their entire families being slaughtered. The memories were still fresh in their minds. "We need to talk about what happened . . . *in detail!*" Kojo spoke as if an audience of people was seated in his office, and not just me in the room.

People suffered, Kojo said. Women were raped, their husbands were killed, rebels kidnapped their children. Let's talk about *that*. Let us investigate where Liberians stand on these issues *publicly* and *in private*. "People have wounds," Kojo said. He punctuated each word with a cigarette stab. "We must talk about them before they scab over."

His eyes glittered like jewels.

"Get up!" he ordered.

I did. Kojo grabbed me by the arm and hustled me into the hallway.

Like a benevolent dictator presenting his kingdom, Kojo introduced me to the team of Liberians manning various desks and doing his bidding. He led me to a desk at the back of the room and introduced me to a woman with a proud face and a shiny cap of braids, named Patience Goanue.

"Goanue, this is your student!" Kojo put a hand on my back and pushed me forward.

Patience extended a demure hand. Pleasantries exchanged, Kojo ordered us to get to work.

"Write something! Do something!" He gesticulated in the air. "Help Agnes write a script!"

From that day forward, Patience took me under her wing. She taught me everything about the radio. What made a story newsworthy, which questions sparked vibrant conversation, and how to make guests feel comfortable on the air. She put a pair of headphones on my head and let me sit beside her in the control booth while she read UNMIL's daily news bulletins or recorded promotional material:

"If you're just joining us now, I'm Patience Goanue and this is UNMIL Radio—your one-stop guide to peace!"

In the afternoons, Patience let me look over her shoulder while she developed story concepts. When she was done, she helped me develop story concepts of my own. Patience was a wonderful teacher, and I was an insatiable student. When I wasn't shadowing her, I walked around the office, peppering UNMIL employees with questions. I think some people gave me bad advice for fun, but it didn't matter. I wrote down every piece of wisdom that was offered to me, whether it was right or wrong. Long after everyone else left the building, I stayed behind and did research on my colleagues' computers.

Eventually, Patience decided that we had enough ideas to launch a program. Now we needed a title and theme music. Patience liked a song by the Canadian musician Bryan Adams called "Straight from the Heart." We could start each program with the first verse and sprinkle the rest through the broadcast. We might as well name our program after the song, too.

At last it was time to bring Kojo our idea. I'd had time to observe the boss in action for a couple of weeks and braced myself for the worst. "Like a father," UNMIL Radio colleagues praised him in public. "Like a porcupine," they snickered behind Kojo's back. "Too bitter to swallow, too greasy to throw away." In truth, I know they all secretly loved him.

Kojo took one look at our ideas and whistled.

"Well?" Patience said.

I cringed.

"You are ready!" Kojo banged his knuckles on his desk, laughing.

Patience and I recorded a promo for the show before I even signed a contract. I had assumed the whole program was going to be recorded, but Kojo said no, your voice is good. *Straight from the Heart* would be a live, one-hour show airing at 3:05 p.m. on Thursdays with a repeat broadcast on Sunday nights at 11. The reason for the second broadcast was that the BBC's *Focus on Africa* program aired on Thursdays at three p.m. A David and Goliath scenario, if you will, but Kojo had no other slots available.

As for the format of the show, Patience and I would record stories from survivors of the war. We would invite guests, ranging from human rights advocates to psychologists to transitional justice officers, to weigh in on the stories. Liberian listeners could phone the studio and share their opinions. Based on their reactions, we might tack left or right in an effort to respond to our audience's needs. Would people be brave enough to share their stories on the air? Dig up the past and divulge painful things in public? We weren't sure.

Looking back, it was an even bigger gamble than we realized. Liberia was an angry and divided country. Many times people would ask me, What's the *point* in talking about the past? Aren't you aware of the *dangers?* Our show was about reality, you see. Deep-seated hatred and painful memories, which many people, including politicians, wanted to push past as soon as possible. But we weren't going to do that. We weren't just going to talk about Liberia as it ought to be, but Liberia as it *really was.*

"Reopening old wounds will be painful," Kojo kept saying. "But in the end, the scar will be smaller." But what Pandora's box were we opening? There was nothing like this going on in Liberia. There was no authority to say, yes, honesty after darkness is the proper path to peace. Quite the opposite, in fact. People were living in silence, prisons of paranoia. And now, after fourteen years of war, a radio show was going to dig up all the lies and hate? *That* was our solution?

Kojo looked at Patience, and Patience looked at me.

"Welcome aboard, Umunna." Kojo smiled.

—◆—

9

MY NAME IS IBRAHIM. I come from Lofa County, ZorZor town. I joined the war during the year 2000. I was given arms and told to go on the frontline to fight, because I was an able-bodied man. That is how I joined the revolution.

We fought with a warlord who was the deputy chief of staff. He was a very wicked man who executed two of my brothers right in front of me, because one refused to follow an order. He killed the other boy for taking three luncheon meats from his wife. Because of that, he beat the boy to death. It hurt me badly.

We did all kinds of things in different areas, but all I did was because I was forced to do it. There were so many massacres during the war, some of which took place simply because of women business. I killed [with a gun, like this] un un un un unh. Nothing I did came from my heart or willing mind. Now that the war is over, it is time for us to reconcile our differences and live together as one people.

W E DEBUTED in November. All day, Kojo paced up and down the hallway hovering over Patience's desk and bursting into the control room seconds before airtime to give us last-minute directions: "Remember to do this!" "Whatever you, don't do that!" "Be natural!" "Don't mind him," Patience said, as she patted my hand. She said the most important thing was to remain calm. Calm? With Kojo around, I said I didn't see how that was possible.

That first time, we agreed that Patience would do most of the talking. She would introduce the show, play the recorded testimony and promo, and then open things up to our studio guests. I would function as first mate and concentrate on the more administrative tasks: saying a friendly hello when Patience introduced me and recording callers' names and telephone numbers so we could follow up if need be. I was happy with this arrangement—it meant less pressure for me. I wanted badly to please Patience and Kojo, but was having trouble commanding the butterflies in my chest to settle down and fly in formation.

I recorded our first story from an old woman I had met a few weeks earlier. On the show, we called her "Grace" to protect her identity. The United Nations High Commissioner for Refugees was repatriating Liberians who had fled to Ghana, and Kojo suggested that I meet the refugees when they arrived.

I got to Robertsfield Airport as the plane landed. I stood in the baggage claim area watching the sea of refugees pour out. These were not well-dressed people anxious to disembark and get somewhere. These refugees were full of fear: the adults hanging back, the young people looking years older than they actually were. Except for the tiny children who didn't remember Liberia, and for whom riding in an airplane had been a big adventure, the faces of this ragtag group were masks of dread. The refugees put their feet on the ground as if the earth might cave in.

For their relatives waiting in the baggage claim, it was a different story. They had endured the war but not experienced life in refugee camps. They greeted their family members with hands clamped over their mouths. Seesawing embraces. Speechless slaps on the back. Some refugees allowed themselves to be hugged but seemed to have forgotten how to return them. Many people had not seen each other for fourteen years and barely recognized the lean bodies and heavy eyes that met them. I saw unbearable stories written on those faces. People struggling to remember joy, calculate the lost years, recall times spent together before the tragedy set in.

Everyone had someone waiting for them. Everyone except this old woman, Grace. She stood in the baggage claim area with a fraying "Ghana Must Go" bag at her feet. She was ancient, with skin like bark. With her headscarf tilted sideways on her head, she reminded me of a tree that had survived a storm but lost all of its branches.

I watched her scan the crowd for someone she knew. I saw her eyes follow the small departing groups until there was no one left in the baggage claim. Her face was blank, but I could sense how desperate she felt. I could read her thoughts: *What do I do now? Where do I go?* Finally, I couldn't stand it anymore. I walked over and said, "Can I help you?" Grace didn't speak. She looked at me as if trying to place me in her memories.

"I'll carry you to my house," I said, picking up her bag. Her name was written on the luggage identification sticker. "Tomorrow we can search for yours."

Grace followed me out of the airport. Driving home, I pointed out places she might remember, depending on when she had fled. Her eyes struggled to make sense of the scenes, and I felt sorry for her, imagining the bad shock she must be experiencing.

When we got to my house, Grace took a bath. We ate dinner and I made up a bed for her. She went right to sleep. She slept through the night. All this time, Grace was silent, but I could tell that there was something there. The next morning, I made her breakfast and offered to drive her to her house. What was the address? Grace still hadn't spoken. We got into the car and she used a frail, feeble hand to guide me.

Down this street, down that street, a right turn, then a left. It was the dry season, and the Harmattan winds had kicked up the Liberian roads and turned them into a dustbowl. At last, Grace motioned for me to stop. I pulled off the narrow road, parked my car, and removed the key from the ignition. I stared at the property in front of us: a big, gleaming house that had recently been renovated, which is when I really felt sorry for Grace. During the war, many people had fled. Others took advantage of the abandoned properties and moved into them. They refurbished the damaged structures, raised families. After the war, the original owners, refugees now, returned to Liberia to find themselves homeless. Looking at Grace, her thin frame barely occupying half the passenger seat, I felt certain this is what had happened to her.

Poor Grace, I thought. Returning home to find no home! She got out of the car slowly. She proceeded up the walkway to the front door, as if heading to a burial. Grace paused before knocking. I braced myself for a melancholy scene. Imagine my surprise then when a pretty young woman opened it and squealed with delight.

"People said you'd been killed!" She threw her arms around Grace.

"People said many things!" Grace clasped the young woman tightly. Her voice was low and joyful. She was crying and laughing at the same time. It was surprising to hear it . . . after those many silent hours. Grace had not spoken until this point.

"I saw you running!" the young woman cried. "I didn't know where you had gone!"

"Praise God!" Grace threw her hands heavenward and pressed the young woman's tear-strewn cheeks to her old, dry, leathery ones.

The woman of the house was Grace's daughter. She was alive. Grace was alive. It was a miracle. I shook my head in disbelief, feeling as if I was part of their family for a moment—I felt such love and relief for them. Never in my wildest dreams had I imagined a reunion like this would occur. It was one of those moments when you think, *The world is really an amazing place.*

We entered Grace's house, a beautiful, refurbished home filled with new furniture that the Liberian shops had only recently started selling. Overcome with emotion, Grace introduced me to her daughter as the kind woman who had taken pity on her at the airport. "Oh, it was nothing." I brushed aside the compliment. "It was everything!" Grace protested. She was an entirely different person now, laughing and buoyant.

We sat down in the living room. Grace took her daughter's hands in her own and started asking her questions about the war. Grace told her daughter that rebels had killed the girl's father and three sisters, and of her narrow escape to Ghana. Her daughter shook her head for the family she could barely remember and told her mother how a man had saved her life from the rebels that wanted to rape and kill her. She told her mother he had been a wonderful, loving person, kind and considerate, who took care of her all through the war.

"Oh Mommy . . ." The young woman shook her head. "It was terrible! This nice man helped me, though. We got married! We have two children."

And, oh? Grandchildren?! Grace drew her hands to her heart in ecstasy. She asked where her daughter's children were. At school, her daughter gushed. They would be home soon. They would be overjoyed to meet Grace. So would her husband. And where was this man, this heroic husband? Oh, he is at work. He's so handsome, Mommy! He does this and that, the young woman chattered. "Well, bring me pictures so I can see!" Grace cried. She was excited, giggling and crying at the same time, really over the moon.

So Grace's daughter got up and went to fetch a picture of her family. When she left, Grace placed a frail hand on my knee and smiled as if to say, *Can you believe my good luck?* After all that she had been through, Grace had found her daughter, her daughter had a family, Grace had grandchildren, and she would not die alone. Grace could live out her final years as an old woman should. "That is *very* good," I said. "Sometimes these things have a way of working out."

Grace's daughter returned, holding a frame. She polished the frame with her dress before handing it to her mother. Grace, beaming, took the photograph and held it at a distance, squinting with her old eyes at the handsome young family dressed in their Sunday best. "Now let me see . . ." Grace said, scanning the faces. The next instant, her smile faded. She flinched. She dropped the frame as if it were covered in acid. It clattered to the floor. Grace started rubbing her hands with the folds of her dress as if trying to put out a fire. The light in her eyes went out like a snuffed candle flame.

"We should go," Grace said to me. Her voice was cold and flat.

"Go?" I said. I wondered if I had heard her correctly.

Grace stood to leave. For a moment, I wondered if she was experiencing a delusion. Had the war affected her mind somehow? Besides her earlier silence, she had seemed sensible. Baffled, I got up. Grace's daughter bent to pick up the photo, which was lying facedown on the floor. What was going on? Did she say something wrong? Do something? Her mother had just arrived! Didn't she want to meet her grandchildren and son-in-law?

"Let me cook for you, Mommy!" Grace's daughter begged.

But Grace was walking toward the car. Her daughter, running behind her, looked as if she was about to cry. Was it the house? Memories surfacing from the war? "If so, let us leave, Mommy!" she cried. "When my husband gets home, he will join us at the nice woman's house!" Grace wouldn't even look at her. I had no idea what was happening, only that something was wrong, and I pitied this girl. I wanted to help her. And so, once I had put Grace in the car, I pulled her daughter aside and said I would be in touch. I needed time to get to the bottom of things.

We drove home. Grace was mute. The atmosphere inside the car was charged, as if angry words were being hurled back and forth. I didn't know Grace, and now I didn't know what to do. Grace didn't eat or sleep as she had the previous evening. The next day was a Sunday, and in the morning I asked her if she wanted to go to church. I wasn't sure it would help, but I felt Grace needed a higher word than mine.

I brought my Bible and the passage they read that day was the story of a man who worked for twenty years to win his wife, motivated only by a belief that God would someday answer his prayers. The moral of the passage is: Keep praying. When I handed Grace my Bible, she studied the verse intently. She listened attentively during the sermon. Her face had softened by the end. When the service was over, we drove back to my house. I was replacing my Bible on the shelf when Grace cleared her throat.

"Do you know what my daughter has done?" She spoke so softly I almost didn't hear her.

I went and sat down next to her on the couch. "No," I said, and took her hand. "But I would like to."

Then Grace told me the story of what had happened to her family.

"It started out as a typical weekend morning," Grace said. She told me her husband had worked for President Doe. They lived in that house we had visited. Her family of six was up and getting dressed for the day's activities when news of the war broke.

"We had to flee for our dear lives," Grace remembered, with a quavering voice. Grace, her husband, and their four daughters fled. Along the way, one daughter went missing. When the rebels caught up to them, they demanded Grace's three daughters. Grace's husband pleaded with the rebels, offered all of their valuables. He pleaded in the name of God.

"But the more we pleaded," Grace said, "the angrier the rebels grew." The rebels' only concession was this: Either they would take turns raping Grace's daughters or her husband had to.

Of course, he refused. "They are my children!" he cried. "I cannot lie with my children!"

"Do it!" the rebels cried. "Or we will do it for you!"

Grace's husband couldn't do it. So the rebels tied her husband to a tree and made him watch as they raped his three daughters. They forced Grace to watch, too.

Her voice faltered. "It was too much, too much. . . ." Her little girls screaming and bleeding. The rebels raped her daughters and then killed them and her husband in cold blood.

Somehow Grace managed to escape. Believing she had lost her entire family, she fled to Ghana. "I felt dead," Grace said. She had memories she couldn't wash away. Years passed. Finally, the war ended and Grace returned to Liberia. She said she couldn't believe it the day before, when, arriving at home, she met her youngest and only surviving daughter at the door. "What a grand and happy reunion it was," Grace said. "We cried, oh! And when I heard of their marriage, blessed with children? My joy knew no bounds."

Grace hesitated. She took a deep breath. Leaning forward, she continued as if in great pain. "I wanted to see my son-in-law. But upon seeing his picture, I received the shock of my life. I immediately recognized him as the man who killed my husband and three daughters."

When Grace was finished, her whole body was shaking. I was speechless. For a long while, we just sat there. Finally, I asked Grace what she wanted to do. Return to her daughter's house? She must be very confused, I said. But no, Grace said, she didn't want anything to do with her daughter. "Are you sure?" I said. "Give it some time . . ." But no, Grace had made her decision. She didn't want to see her daughter. She could never face the man she had married, or think of that man and her daughter sleeping together in the house where her father and sisters had been killed. In Grace's memory, going forward, her entire family *had* died that terrible day, and nothing I said would change her mind.

This is the story we played on the first program of *Straight from the Heart*. We obscured some of the details, so that if Grace's daughter heard the interview, she would not know it was her mother speaking:

What am I to do? Tell my only child her husband whom she loves killed her father and three sisters? Tell her the truth even if it destroys her marriage? I can't . . . She was too young to know, too young to realize. But also, not telling her will cause me to carry the guilt all my life. I don't know what to do. I don't know how things like this happen in this world.

It was a tragic story, but only the beginning.

I didn't do much talking that day. Neither did Patience. What advice could we give? In time, I would learn that people like Grace don't expect you to give them advice. They know there aren't words to change what has happened to them.

I spoke with Patience afterward. "What do you make of that story?" she asked. I said I believed Grace didn't want to destroy her daughter's happy life. She knew what losing everything meant and didn't wish the same fate on her child. Grace loved her daughter enough to keep on living a lie. "Maybe so." Patience nodded. "It was a very sad story." Still, perhaps it would open doors. Help other people to open up about their own impossible experiences. It was a first step, the first of many.

I kept in touch with Grace. For a while, I believed I could help her reconcile with her daughter. I offered to find a priest or an elder from their tribe to talk with them. In the end, I was not able to convince her to do either of these things. Grace's story, and how she copes with it, are her sacred rights. It is not for me to tell a person how to feel, or when it is time to forgive. Like my father said, war is senseless. And how people deal with it doesn't always make sense either.

I have collected many stories since Grace's, but I still don't know how to respond when people ask me: "What will telling my story do? Will it bring my husband back? Restore my child?" In these instances, I take their hands in mine and shake my head no. The gaping hole you feel can never be perfectly filled. And yet, maybe there is a way to live with your sorrow. You can't blame your daughter for doing something she didn't understand. And this man, he killed your husband and three daughters but he saved your fourth daughter's life . . . maybe that counts for something? Or, maybe he was drugged and can't be held entirely accountable for his actions. I try to show people the benefits of reconciliation. But in Grace's case, blocking out the past is all she is comfortable with.

It will take time. That's my belief. I still encourage Grace to go to church. Maybe one day she will hear another Bible passage that speaks to her. One that helps her make up her mind that memory is long, but life is short, and the war won't change the fact that this woman is still her daughter.

10

WHEN CHARLES TAYLOR launched his menace upon this country, my father was a prime target because of his wealth. All our properties were looted, and my mother and only son were killed. We were so harassed that all of us ran away to neighboring Sierra Leone and Guinea. Living as refugees was not an easy thing, so we returned to Monrovia after the first peace accord. On our arrival, we met squatters in our houses, most of whom were rebels. We tried to retrieve our houses, but it was impossible.

One particular rebel used to harass us. The man commonly called "Colonel Bush," who killed my son before we ran away from the country. He was the very man that was occupying our house! And one time, when I confronted him to leave, he ordered his boys to torture me. I was severely beaten and released when the boys thought I would die. Because of the torture, I became impotent. Now I am a good Christian and a pastor in my church, and this man came to our church to be a member. I have a problem. I have all the memories of what this man did to my family and me. I cannot pray as I used to pray for the church.

I do not want this man to leave, but I am confused. I talk about reconciliation, but I cannot see myself reconciling. Please Aunty Agnes, help me, but when you are giving your advice, bear in mind that:

1. I lost my father and mother and my only son.

2. I lost my pride and all my properties.

3. I became impotent.

I SAW LITTLE beyond the walls of UNMIL Radio that fall and winter. With the few free hours that remained, I rebuilt my father's house, one of two that had been destroyed during the war. He lost the first house, the one he built in Paynesville, in 1990. NPFL rebels torched it to the ground when they invaded Monrovia and left behind a heap of ashes. The second house, the one he built near the Hotel Africa Road, survived the war but not its aftermath. LURD rebels looted it on their retreat from Monrovia. Only a plank or two remained. My father was devastated. Once I tried to raise his spirits by making a joke: "You have bad luck, Daddy. NPFL from one side. LURD from the other."

It fell flat.

My father was one of the last UN employees to remain in Liberia during the war. By the time he left for Gambia, he had been robbed, brutally beaten, held at gunpoint, harassed by powerful warlords, and placed on Taylor's hit list. But in many ways, I think seeing the home he hoped to grow old in obliterated was the worst shock of all.

I have pictures of this second house from before the war. It was located high on a hill and powered by a large generator. Once, it functioned as a landmark for Liberians driving in and out of Monrovia. "When you see the lighted house on the hill, we are just behind that!" my father's neighbors would say. He adored that house. It was his temple. He loved to return to it after a long day at the

WHO or the medical college, and rest his feet on a stool, with a hot bowl of pepper rice. When I came back and saw what was left, my jaw dropped.

"When they loot a house in Liberia, they rob it wall to wall," my father lamented. "The iron rods fresh from your walls."

It was true: The windows had been chopped out, the wiring uncoupled, the generator stolen. Crumbs of pulverized furniture littered the floor. Grass grew where the carpet had once been. Even the nails in the walls were gone. The well-lighted house on the hill was now a shell of darkness. My father turned to me at the end of this depressing tour.

"Please, Agnes," my father said. "Please take care of this house for me."

I didn't know what to do. It's not as if there were companies specializing in post-war clean-up and reconstruction. My father's wife had moved to America to be with her family, so I couldn't ask her for advice. With my own two hands, I cleaned and painted. I bought new doors and windows and hired contractors for the more complicated tasks. We rewired the electricity, installed new plumbing and carpets. When my father returned from Gambia and saw what I had done, he was speechless.

"There is light shining in my house again!" he wept.

At UNMIL Radio, I was busy collecting stories. It was at once thrilling and painful work. Patience and I kept asking people to bare their souls to Liberians in their living rooms, and for what exactly? Discussion was cathartic but couldn't bring back the dead. After the initial feeling of relief, the emotional takeaway seemed rather small.

When I expressed my concerns to Kojo, he said he understood but believed we were doing something good for Liberia. Most shows were interviewing politicians about their plans for the future. *Straight from the Heart* gave ordinary Liberians a forum to discuss the past.

Meanwhile, at the national level, major changes were afoot. In November 2005, two years after the war ended, Ellen Johnson-Sirleaf, who had lost to Charles Taylor in 1997, ran and won the Liberian presidency. "Ma Ellen," as we called her, made history by becoming the first African female head of state. As president of Liberia, she immediately started doing good things for our country. Today, Ma Ellen is restoring electricity and running water to many parts of Monrovia, helping Liberia grow and sell its own food, and fighting corruption. Still, if you ask me, her most powerful legacy is Liberia's Truth and Reconciliation Commission.

We called it the "TRC" for short. Back then, rumors were swirling about what it would be and do. People remembered South Africa's landmark Truth and Reconciliation Commission. Chaired by Archbishop Desmond Tutu, that commission offered apartheid chiefs and freedom fighters amnesty in exchange for information about their violent acts. Apparently, Liberia's was being modeled after it. Unsurprisingly, we had questions: Would Liberia's truth commission offer amnesty for information? Would the country's victims have a voice? Would TRC Commissioners sit down with the people one-on-one, or would it be more like the United States' Supreme Court, with nine judges sitting on a bench? Finally, how was Liberia going to pay for it?

Many of these details were still being ironed out. In the meantime, Kojo said *Straight from the Heart* was greasing the wheels and paving the way for a countrywide conversation. Patrick Coker had a different theory. According to him, *Straight from the Heart* was a means of endearing the UNMIL mission to the Liberian people. It was important that UNMIL be seen as a grassroots organization; if our program could generate interest in the TRC, all the better.

Patience and I hosted two more programs. After the third one, Kojo stopped me in the hall. He jerked a thumb toward his office door.

"Close it!" he bellowed.

My knees were knocking. "I am sorry about the dropped calls, Mr. Mensah. We are still working on the static issue."

Kojo waved this away as he might a mosquito. This was just a friendly conversation, he said. "Relax. Sit down."

"A friendly conversation?" I was confused.

Kojo chuffed like a lion. "Relax, Umunna!"

He lit a cigarette and exhaled slowly. He placed his hands behind his head and leaned perilously far back in his chair. The chair creaked, and I held my breath, hoping he wouldn't fall over and trying not to sit ramrod straight in my own. It was impossible to be at ease in Kojo's presence.

"Agnes U-MUN-na . . ." Kojo stubbed out his cigarette languorously. "You are getting big."

I demurred.

"Possibly famous." Kojo cocked an eyebrow.

I blushed. Compliments from Kojo were a rare treat, something you felt compelled to chew a small bite of, then rewrap and slip into your back pocket and savor later on.

"I am taking Patience off the show," Kojo announced. "From now on, you will host *Straight from the Heart* by yourself."

It took me a minute to register this volcanic piece of information.

"What? No, Mr. Mensah!" I sat bolt upright in my chair, knocking over Kojo's ashtray and displacing several manila folders from their tidy rank and file. Kojo frowned but quickly reproduced his devilish grin.

"You're great," Kojo said. "Possibly a natural. Anyway, I have made up my mind. You have to do it."

Unlike the diverse range of opinions Kojo encouraged on the air, clearly only one mattered backstage.

"But Mr. Mensah—"

"Final answer!" Kojo thrust an index finger in my face like a game-show host to a paralyzed contestant. "Final answer, Agnes U-MUN-na."

I left Kojo's office in a daze. Colleagues who had been listening behind the door, or tipped off to what had happened, teased me. "Oh Agnes! You're going to be *alone!*" They laughed. "What will you do without Patience Goanue beside you?"

I raced down the row of desks to find Patience. To my surprise, she was aware of Kojo's decision, hardly angry, and secretly relieved. Now she could return to doing the news broadcasts she loved.

When I entered UNMIL Radio on the day of my first solo broadcast, colleagues removed their headphones and looked up from the stacks of paper they were reading to wish me luck. Scanning their doubtful faces, it felt more like I was marching to my doom. I thanked them but didn't stop to gossip or crack a joke as I normally would. I was terrified.

I watched the hands on the clock tick twelve o'clock, one o'clock, two o'clock p.m. At two thirty, Kojo came over to tell me my guest had arrived. I was so nervous, I don't even remember who it was. I greeted whomever and we waited outside the control room while the announcer read the afternoon bulletin. When he was done, I showed my guest into the studio. I expected Patience would be waiting there. Up until that moment, I didn't believe this was actually happening.

But no, I was going on the air alone. Patience's seat was empty, and mine looked very large indeed. Trembling, I adjusted the height of the chair and put on a pair of headphones. Extracting my carefully written script from my pocket, I set it to one side just in case. I checked my watch: 3:03 p.m. I looked up at the sound technician for my cue, but the face behind the glass was Kojo's. He was sitting directly across from me and waving. Kojo never sat in the booth during shows! It made him jumpy. It made his radio hosts panic.

"What are you doing?" I mouthed through the thick pane of glass.

"You can do this," his twinkling eyes telegraphed. "You can do this, Umunna!" I read his lips.

I grabbed my script and held it in front of my face. Kojo hated when we read directly from the script. But that day, I was too nervous to meet his eyes.

"It's time," the technician signaled by knocking on the glass.

I remember what I visualized that day: the Liberian people . . . putting down their hoes and fishing poles, cell phones and brooms . . . pulling up dusty crates and buckets, or pulling over to the side of the road and turning on the radio. Somehow, picturing my people listening, I forgot my fear.

Hello, and welcome to another edition of *Straight from the Heart* on UNMIL Radio, 91.5 Monrovia, Harper and Zwedre, 90.5 Gbanga, 97.1 Voinjama and Greenville, and 95.1 Sanniquellie. *Straight from the Heart* is an hour-long phone-in program specially designed to air your true-life stories. The stories discussed on our program, and your views and pieces of advice, help to solve the problems in the stories or serve as a form of encouragement to those who are involved. Stay with us if you can. My name is Agnes Umunna.

I did all right. Not one hundred percent, but all right. I kept asking people to reduce the volume on their radios. I lost a few callers. At one point, I think I might have sneezed. Kojo met me in the hallway afterward. He told me to take the rest of the day off. For a moment I thought I was fired.

"Enjoy it!" His face broke into a broad smile. "You did well today."

Each of us has strengths and weaknesses. Sooner or later, we face our weaknesses and find our strengths. My strength was that I remembered another, more peaceful Liberia. Listening to survivors for whom the war wasn't a memory but the nightmare that continued to define their lives, maybe I could help them remember that Liberia too. A Liberia that was far from perfect but was at least peaceful. Just like looking at pictures of my father's house and remembering what it had been, I could help people envision what Liberia could be someday.

11

CAN YOU IMAGINE? Hunting for your fellow human beings? Like as if the person did something unforgivable to you, or has something you are looking for? Those guys are evil guys ... I don't even want them to live to see the sweetest part of this world. They raped me when I was sixteen. A girlfriend of mine ... fifteen men came and raped her. Can you imagine? She died on the scene. Fifteen men at the same time, and she *died*. If you people want people to reconcile ... it's not easy to see somebody killing someone in front of you! Or taking a plastic bag and putting it around a human being's head—just for nothing! Just for nothing and they do something to you ... They just *feel* like hurting. And you ask me to reconcile with that person?

—Dorothy

I WAS SHAKY at first but improved as time went on and eventually developed a rhythm. I entered the studio as the Bryan Adams song was playing and briefly introduced listeners to what I would be speaking about that day. Next, I went to a music break: Tracy Chapman, Tina Turner, Bob Marley, or the Temptations. There seemed to be a song for every story, and I was particularly pleased when the music complemented the interviews I had done.

Then I welcomed whatever guests I had on and reminded the audience about my aim: to air true-life stories. The material was raw and often very painful, and I asked difficult questions of people who had already been through so much. *Do you believe there are some things too terrible to be forgiven? What would you say to those who hurt you if you had the chance?* After the stories played, I would invite counselors, human rights workers, and others to weigh in on these emotional subjects.

Next, after each guest had his say, I invited listeners to call the station. The end of the program was my favorite part. I would share lessons and stories of healing from other countries and cultures. I talked about the Holocaust, apartheid in South Africa, and the plight of the Native Americans in the United States. I might say, "Here is what those people did." Or, "I know it is difficult for us, but I want you to be like Nelson Mandela." Finally, I bid my listeners good-bye: "Wherever you are, I am highly delighted to know you, be good to yourselves, and take care until I see you next week."

The show was getting popular despite the fact it aired at the same time the BBC program did. I started receiving fan mail, and Kojo had me open an e-mail account. I was surprised and flattered when letters started pouring in, including some marriage proposals! When Christmas came, I encouraged my listeners to send letters to people who had hurt them. Patrick had worried that my slight Sierra Leonean accent might alienate me from Liberian listeners, but it proved to be an asset—giving me a neutrality and independence that other UNMIL Radio hosts lacked. Still, no matter how many hours I logged at UNMIL Radio, some things weren't getting easier with time.

I tried not to cry when victims told me their stories. I reasoned that if they were strong, enough to come and tell them, I owed it to them to be strong, too. But as soon as a victim had left the studio, or later on at home, I wept and wept. I could not believe the horrific things my people had endured in the war.

I met a woman who had sent her seven-year-old daughter to stay with her sister. The little girl met her death at her uncle and auntie's hands—tortured and killed by the very people who had promised to help her! Her uncle was a leader in a rebel faction who "needed a child to sacrifice."

I met an eighty-year-old woman who was raped alongside her daughter and granddaughter. All three got AIDS. Another mother with four children, all girls. Rebels killed her husband. They tied him up, beat him, and murdered him, and two sets of rebels raped her four girls and her. Now all five women were HIV+.

I met an AFL soldier the rebel soldiers mutilated. They chopped off his lips, ear, and nose, leaving only a grisly mound of flesh. The rebels had taken turns beating him with hot metal, saying he was a "bad omen" who must suffer and die. When the AFL soldier's wounds began to rot, the smell was so bad, but the rebels refused him any treatment. "I felt spiritually dead," the man said. In hopes they would kill him, he decided to insult the rebel commander. Instead, the commander ordered the rebel soldiers to cut off his hands. "I wish I could be born again," the AFL soldier said, showing me his stumps. "It hurts me to see my reflection because of the way I look today. When my wife saw me, she found it hard to see me as a human being. She just felt very, very sick."

Everybody had a story. Tales so unspeakable it was hard to believe they had actually occurred. A woman who slept in a toilet to hide from the rebels; ten men raped her. Another woman was forced to stare at the sun until she went blind. One woman told the rebels she was cold: "So they set my hair on fire!" Another woman, who, waking up, found her child's dead body lying next to her and her husband's body being eaten by dogs. More and more, worse and worse. Could human beings be so cruel?

Equally astounding, maybe more so, was their resilience. *How do people manage to survive these things?*, I found myself asking over and over again. The mutilated soldier's wife who hadn't left him. She said her child needed a father; the child she was carrying in her belly "was for them." I interviewed a woman who gave birth to her rapist's child and she said she hated the child. But then another woman with a similar experience who was listening called in to console her: "I am the mother of my enemy's child, too. And I felt the same way you do when I got pregnant. But then I realized, my child is innocent! He had nothing to do with what happened to me!"

In time, I started to wonder about the people I actually knew. Were they suffering in silence, too? Shouldering similar burdens? What didn't I know?

One day, a colleague named Esther approached me as I was leaving the office. "I am a victim," she said.

"Esther, please," I said. Esther liked to joke around and make light of difficult situations.

"Big Sister . . ." Esther called me by my nickname. She is descended from the Americo-Liberians and a beautiful woman, too. She grabbed me by the soft part of my arm. "Big Sister, it is true . . ."

I was running late and needed to finish my work.

"Okay, Esther," I sighed. "I believe you."

That next week Esther showed up for her recording session, and I remember thinking, hm, Esther doesn't seem like her usual self. Her ordinarily fluffy hair was pulled back in a tight braid. Esther has a voluptuous figure that she likes to flaunt, but that day she was wearing a conservative, floral dress.

"I am ready," Esther said. "Press the button."

It was August 1990. We were living in Paynesville. My family fled to the Old Road when Taylor's troops advanced. We had to run from our homes and leave everything behind, because Doe was about to throw missiles into the area. We got as far as the airport and saw where they had tied people to poles at the end of the runway. They were about to execute them, and the soldiers warned us not to look.

My uncle remembered he had a friend on Fifteenth Street. He said we could take shelter there. So me, my mother, my grandmother, and the rest of my family went to this house, which was owned by a former telecommunications director.

My cousin and I were playing Scrabble. While I was shaking the Scrabble bag, some of the Scrabble seeds fell onto the floor. I bent over to pick them up when I heard vehicles stopping outside the gate. And I said to my cousin, "Oh! Something's going on! I see vehicles with army people parking in front of the house!" And he said, "Are you sure?" And I said, "Come and see!" Sure enough, soldiers were coming. They started banging loudly on the outside gate.

My uncle told us not to panic. He would go downstairs and talk to the soldiers. So he went downstairs, but the soldiers insisted they needed to search the premises. As they were marching upstairs, two of the soldiers dropped bullets on the stairs, and another soldier who was behind them saw it. He said, "Oh chief, I found something! This is enough evidence to prove these people are rebels!" My cousin tried to say no, it was the soldier who mistakenly dropped the bullets. But they didn't pay him any mind.

They came into the house. They searched the rooms. And like I said, this residence was owned by a former telecommunications director. He had a room full of old handsets and communications equipment. And when they entered that room, ah! They started saying my uncle was communicating with Charles Taylor! We were rebel spies! And no, no, no, my uncle tried to explain that this was not where we lived. We fled from the Old

Road when the soldiers started bombing the area. But they just screamed at him, "Get downstairs! Get downstairs! Take him and put him in the back of the car!"

They took my uncle away. Then they turned and screamed at us: "All you people put your hands up unless you want to die!" My family and I were taken to one side. But then a soldier came over and pointed right at me. "No, you can't take her!" he said. "This one going to be my wife!" And he took me and my girl cousin away, and they took the rest of my family downstairs. And we started crying, begging him to let us be. I was only fifteen years old. My cousin was just fourteen.

They did whatever they could do to us . . . They took away our pride. Our womanhood. After that, they ordered us to go downstairs. And there's this man, I won't call names, but there's this man here in Liberia. He holds a high position. I see him in the papers. I watch him on TV. Hear him on the radio. After he took my womanhood away, he couldn't stop there. He used his gun and hit me in the face! It broke my teeth. I dropped to the floor. I was bleeding heavily.

Fortunately for us, the soldier they left behind to watch us decided to let us go. "Run!" he said. And we did. We stumbled out onto the street, bleeding and crying. It was then that I remembered what my mother had said: In case we ever get separated, get to the Ghanaian Embassy. That's where we'll meet.

My cousin and I could barely walk. We were bleeding severely. Finally, we found my family. We stayed for a while. But then what happened? I was pregnant. A month passed, and I didn't see my cycle. The following month, it didn't come. My mother took me to the clinic. When the doctors did the test, they found out I was carrying. And ah! How could I conceive that child? That was the most unbearable thing for my mother . . .

So she talked to the doctors and asked them if they could do an abortion on me. But the doctor said a lot of damage had been done. "We are afraid that if we do the abortion, maybe this child will not be able to conceive again," the doctor said. But my mother said, "I don't care what you people do, she can't give birth to this child. Take it out."

So they did the abortion. I stayed in the hospital for a long time. Later on, I left Liberia.

I've come home now. And after so long, I see the very people that did this thing to me. I see these people holding high office. They're in places of authority, making decisions for our country. And, would you know, one day this man had the nerve to come to where I work, and ask me out on a date. He waved a hundred-dollar bill in my face, as if I was a prostitute.

How can I forgive and forget that face? That man? For what he did to me? It's hard . . . Inasmuch as we all want to reconcile and put the past behind us, he took something away that can never be given back. I can forgive, yes, forgive is not the point. But how can I forget? How can I bury my past? I ask you, Agnes. This is my question.

Stunned, I just sat there looking at Esther with tears streaming down my face. Esther, who had remained calm throughout most of her story, started to choke up. Together we sat there sobbing for her loss and holding each other tightly. Or maybe Esther was holding me. Finally, drying my tears, I asked Esther how she had coped all these years, hiding this terrible secret.

"It's not the coping I'm concerned about," Esther said. "It's the way that people *look* at you."

Esther had never told anyone about her rape, not even her husband. The stigma and shame were too great. When I asked Esther why she had finally decided to open up, she said she believed that God wanted Liberians to reconcile. That He had good things in store for her. "If someone does bad to you, God means well for you somewhere else," Esther explained. But she looked like she was still trying to believe it.

When it came time to air Esther's story, we decided to call her "Mary" so as not to unmask her. We altered her voice with sound effects, but Esther has a distinctive voice and everyone knew it was her. Colleagues approached Esther afterward, saying, "Esther, oh Esther . . . ," asking what they could do, praising her courage. "If only we'd known . . . ," people kept saying, as if they could have prevented her rape.

When I went to play Esther's story, I started sniffing on air. I tried to pull myself together, but my voice was plugged in my throat. Kojo raced into the control room and started banging on the glass.

"What's wrong with you? What the *hell* is wrong with you, Umunna?" he demanded.

He told the studio technician to go to a music break. Then he entered the sound booth, grabbed my shoulders, and started shaking them. This only made me cry harder.

"Relax, Agnes!" Kojo ordered. He instructed me to take a deep breath and count to ten. Kojo said he knew the story I was airing was good.

"It's not good!" I cried. "It's terrible!"

"Well, we can't just play music!" Kojo said. Where was my professionalism? My integrity? I owed it to Esther to keep going. Wiping the tears from my face, I agreed to go back on the air, but the lines I had written felt pointless and shallow. I was grateful when my guest did most of the talking.

After the program, Kojo called me into his office. It was an interesting approach, he said . . . the host breaking down instead of the storyteller. He asked me to explain. And so I told him, "Esther is my colleague. She is like family and I never knew. I ignored her!" Who else had I worked with, side by side, oblivious to the terrible things in their hearts stamped "confidential"? I told Kojo I had no idea what I'd agreed to.

"And you're not finished," he said. "You haven't done anything yet."

Too tired to think, I collected my purse from Patience's desk and left UNMIL headquarters feeling numb and drained.

With my eyes glued to my feet, I almost ran into a woman balancing an enormous jerry-can on her head. "Oh excuse me," I apologized and helped her rebalance her jerry-can. She stared at me with eyes that looked like Esther's.

I started looking around me . . . I started looking at every woman I passed, wondering what had happened to her. What burden was she carrying? That one in the shawl? The lady with the bunch of plantains? I went home and thought about the women of Liberia. Three-quarters of them raped, carrying those stories around and clinging to memories of the people who had hurt them? I thought of Esther. "Until you let go of your story, you are owned by the people who hurt you," she had said. Esther had freed herself. Could I help other women free themselves?

We have a saying in Liberia: "You can fall seven times and get up." I got up the next morning and marched back to UNMIL Radio. Esther was in her seat, looking tired but somehow stronger. I told her I was proud of her. She didn't need me or a microphone to tell her story. She just needed to be ready in her heart.

"Maybe we can do something this weekend?" I suggested.

I have learned that the human mind is an amazing piece of engineering, but it does not have the ability to forget at will. You can't just skip to the part where you feel better, and I feared it would be difficult for Esther. I wanted to be there for her as she entered the next stage of her recovery.

Then I went to Kojo's office. I said I'd done some thinking. I wanted to talk to women—as many as I could—and see how I could help them. Apparently, Kojo had done some thinking, too.

"Agnes," he said. "Is it only victims who suffered in the war? Is it only women? What about perpetrators?"

I looked at him, confused.

"Child soldiers," he said. "Go to the ghetto. The boys are there. See what happened to them."

I was silent.

Then I started to laugh. "Oh, Mr. Mensah . . ." I chuckled. "You really had me."

Only it wasn't a joke.

"I live by the ghetto where they go," Kojo interrupted me. "Those boys won't kill you."

He rose from his desk. He started walking toward me. Kojo Men · sah, star-maker, mentor, and madman, placed his hands on my shoulders. In a soothing voice, he reminded me I was a journalist. Hadn't I signed a contract?

Then he produced two bottles of Coca-Cola from a small refrigerator beneath his desk and toasted my "new assignment." I left Kojo's office, not quite remembering the last five minutes of my life or what, if anything, I'd agreed to do.

As usual, my office mates had been listening at the door. "Those fighters? Those unruly fighters?" they jeered. "Those boys will *kill* you, Agnes!"

Now I was terrified. I did not know if I wanted my job anymore. I had to find some way to talk Kojo out of this. Some way to convince him that he was *absolutely* insane. I wanted to cry. But then, MacDonald, one of the men I worked with, came up to me. "Don't worry," he said. "Those ex-fighters are all right." He offered to go with me if I liked.

If I liked?

"It's a date," MacDonald said.

And this is what gave me the courage.

12

MOST OF US had turned into walking skeletons. I saw the sad faces of once happy friends, and sorrow filled my heart. Why were we suffering like this in our land? There were three of us. We were twenty years of age. We had to cover seventy-two kilometers on foot.

That wasn't our worry, but rather our safety. We walked in silence, afraid our voices would attract attention. At one place in the bush, we came across rotting bodies. By now, their children would be crying and wondering when their parents would return.

Suddenly, we heard *Pop! Pop!* And ah! What was happening? We were in rebel leader Charles Taylor's camp! Immediately, we dropped under the bushes in an attempt to hide. But it was too late. The soldiers jumped on us and beat us. They accused us of spying for the enemy, of being recruits in the late president's army. I was just an ordinary citizen. I wasn't sure about my friends.

We were thrown in jail. The jail was a dark place in the middle of human bones. I was sure if they kept us there for a week, we would die. Every morning, we were brought outside and offered green cassava leaves to eat. They made us drink from human skulls and bury dead bodies.

Here, I began to feel I would be set free by the Almighty God. I am not sure how I came to have such a feeling, but it was there. While lying down one evening, I heard a silent voice call my name. It commanded me to rise up and walk away from my captors. I obeyed and walked past the sleeping guards and onto the main road.

—Daniel

P ICTURE HOW YOU WOULD FEEL if someone asked you to visit a maximum security prison. An *unguarded* maximum security prison, full of the most violent offenders, who were free to do anything they wanted to you. That is how I felt when Kojo handed me my "new assignment."

Child soldiers. Go to the ghetto. The boys are there. See what happened to them.

What *happened to* them? Didn't Kojo mean what they had *done?* And what did he mean "boys"? I don't know about you, but I wouldn't call a killer a "child." I wouldn't call a boy who cut off my radio guest's genitals a "boy." I would call him a demon. A devil. I was worried Kojo had lost it and let this truth and reconciliation business go to his head. Talking to victims was one thing. But perpetrators? What was Kojo thinking? Besides, who would want to listen to them?

Of course, Kojo has a way of persuading people to try things they don't want to try.

But how to do it? These boys were killers, addicts. Many still carried weapons. You didn't just book an appointment to *talk* to them as if they were normal human beings with feelings and valuable perspectives.

And if you did, what then? How did you talk to a child soldier? I hadn't a clue. If my experiences until that point had taught me anything, it was this: *You didn't.* I thought back to the boys in black masks manning the Liberia–Sierra Leone bridge. The checkpoint guards in Nimba County who smashed our things and nearly refused to let us pass. The disturbed boys at Tubmanburg Junction. These days, when I saw boys on the street who looked like fighters, I averted my eyes or crossed to the other side as if they didn't exist or had a fatal disease. Everyone did. Just seeing a child soldier slink past a shop or along a boulevard, weaving among cars stopped at traffic lights, was enough to make you double-check your purse, rearview mirror, and locks. They moved like cats and shook their upturned palms as though absorbing feedback from invisible AK-47s. They were monsters, murderers.

You have to remember: 250,000 people had been killed, nearly 75 percent of Liberia's women were raped. The only people who would go near child soldiers were the relief workers called in to clean up disasters many hadn't lived through. Of course there was the UN's National Commission on Disarmament, Demobilization, Rehabilitation, and Reintegration. This was the program where, for a limited time, soldiers could trade in their weapons and receive cash and counseling. It sounded promising. Unfortunately, the UN failed to account for a postwar reality: residual loyalties. Warlords still commanded allegiance from their child fighters. Obedience from the older soldiers and from the younger ones, something approaching worship.

Child soldiers brought their Kalashnikovs, grenades, and mortars to designated weapons-collection sites. There, they gave false names, grabbed the cash, and ran right back to their commanders, who spent it on drugs, women, food, clothes—whatever they wanted. Often, child soldiers sent proxies (younger siblings or cousins) to the collection sites to avoid being identified and derailed. UNMIL collected only 35 percent of the weapons thought to have been used in the war. The child soldiers who were taken to demobilization centers confronted well-meaning humanitarian workers who struggled to deprogram them and get them involved in skills trainings, but the programs lasted only a couple of weeks, not several months as originally intended. Attempts to de-brainwash ex-combatants often disintegrated into violence and anarchy.

Child soldiers had to go somewhere, but where? How do you welcome monsters back to your city? Your village? The last thing tribal chiefs struggling to stitch families back together wanted was the boys who tore them apart. Many communities refused to embrace child soldiers because of what they had done, or *might* do. No one wanted to hire former child soldiers. Would you trust your cash register with a boy who sprayed bullets from a gun? Only very few were doing anything meaningful with their lives. And these boys were *still* causing people pain. I interviewed a woman who ran a school before the war. She was raped by rebels. Now, one of the child soldiers who had raped her had shown up at her school, demanding to study there.

Many ex-combatants ended up hustling on the street and committing petty robbery to survive. You'd be stopped at an intersection when suddenly, "Old Ma! Old Ma! *Ehhhhh* . . ." Red eyes, dirty fingernails. "Roll up the window! Quickly, oh!" you would scream. Finally, even if you had never met a former child soldier face-to-face, which was rare, you had heard stories about them. No one wanted them in Liberia. If possible, everyone wished they would disappear.

Everyone except Kojo, apparently.

Finding the boys wasn't difficult. Everyone knew they haunted the neighborhoods of Monrovia we were taught to avoid. I was brave, but not foolish, and knew I needed an escort to accompany me. MacDonald suggested I approach Amos, a boy who volunteered at UNMIL Radio and lived near the area where Kojo said I should start.

"I know a place," Amos said and described an eviscerated location in Monrovia's Sinkor ghetto. "It's a bad place . . ." He whistled. "A real bad place."

I told him I imagined so, and to please spare me the details. I asked him to book an appointment for me. He looked confused. "Please," I said. "This might sound strange to you, but here is something I have learned: People respond to courtesy. I don't want to go, but if I have to, I will do it right." My plan was to visit the ghetto safely, quickly, and most importantly . . . once.

And so, Amos went and delivered the message I had dictated to him: "There is a woman who hosts a radio program and wants to visit this place. What do you people think? Can she come?"

I felt sure that the child soldiers would refuse my offer, prayed for it in fact. Amos returned and said they would be pleased to see me anytime.

We left in a taxi, me, Amos, and MacDonald. As the UNMIL base receded in the distance, I looked at my traveling companions and wondered if I had really thought this thing through. I was a relatively young woman with three children and her whole life ahead of her. Amos was tall but scrawny, practically a teenager. MacDonald, my security detail, was in his twenties and far from intimidating. Who would protect me if things went south? There is no "911" emergency number to dial in Liberia. As we approached the ghetto, I noticed that the only vehicles going near were cars I wouldn't want to get into.

We turned off the main road and down a narrow street, then veered into an even narrower alley. When we stopped, I paid the taxi driver and wondered if I should ask him to keep the engine running. "Come," Amos said, and led the way down a dirt path lined with flimsy buildings and houses Swiss-cheesed with bullet holes. Men leaned in shadowy doorways. Filthy children played in the street, or sold things. "Why aren't you in school?" I asked a tiny girl selling scratch cards from a battered cigarette box. Others thrust packs of batteries or recycled plastic supermarket bags filled with cold water—"*Coh wota! Coh wota!*"—in my face. Young girls with matted hair and bright lipstick slouched on the hoods of parked cars. They flashed looks that didn't match the fearful expressions in their eyes. Then we came upon a corridor.

"This is it," Amos said.

"This is what?" I wondered. I saw a pile of bricks. A few freestanding walls shedding their paint like snakeskin. Amos motioned toward a courtyard that had clearly been some sort of structure before it was leveled. The stench of poverty and decay was everywhere. We came upon a clearing. And there they were: ten young men and women sitting on a crumbling wall beneath a spindly plum tree.

They looked like any other gathering of young people: slack, indifferent, killing time. Only then, as I looked closer, I noticed how thin they were. Broomstick-thin. Their shoulders slumped despite their young ages, and the scars . . . their legs and forearms were engraved with them.

They weren't talking when Amos and I arrived, just staring into space. A few of them smoked. One girl scratched absently at her hair, clearly unwashed. She had muscles, and I was not used to seeing girls with muscles. She turned her head and stared at Amos with glassy eyes.

"Hey people," Amos said. "This is the woman I told you about."

I lifted a weak hand and waved. They didn't wave back. I stowed my hand behind my back in the uncomfortable silence.

Nothing happened. *Now what?* I thought. I didn't know what to do. What magic words were they waiting for? I looked at Amos and MacDonald, but they were looking at the fighters. I cleared my throat. Attempting bravery, I smiled awkwardly and said, "I am Agnes. Thank you for letting me come." I said this a little too loudly.

Nothing. I put my hands on my hips and sniffed the air. Marijuana. *At least* marijuana. The smoke, their bloodshot eyes. Eyes like cartoon characters who plug their fingers into electric sockets. Most probably bombed.

I noticed they were poorly clad: dressed in mud-caked jeans and T-shirts with terrible slogans from America. The shirts swam like tents around their bony bodies. Most were barefoot. A few wore sandals so busted the soles had practically peeled off altogether. *Someone needs to help these people*, I remember thinking. *Somebody really needs to do something.*

Sensing my discomfort, Amos started to speak. He began telling them about my program at UNMIL Radio. Alarmed, I looked at Amos. I knew I had to jump in. I didn't know what he would say.

"I'm here to talk to you about my work," I interrupted Amos, and suddenly I had a brainstorm. "But first I would like to get us some refreshments."

That's all it took. The fighters seemed to wake up. A few of them smiled. One of them, a boy with a bald head that was shiny as a pebble, rose from the pile of bricks and came over to shake my hand. He was extremely tall. I noticed he was wearing a button-down shirt and pressed pants, so different from the others in their T-shirts and jeans. He had intelligent, suffering eyes. He introduced himself as Ebenezer.

"Hey, Sister." He smiled a kind smile. "We have been waiting for you."

Ebenezer fetched the one piece of furniture in the place, a badly cracked chair, and offered it to me. I thanked him and sat down, hoping I wouldn't break it for good. Fishing a couple of bills from my wallet, I suggested that one of the fighters go out and buy beer and soft drinks. They said they wanted hard alcohol. "Okay . . ." I looked around, wondering if that was a good idea. Rummaging through my purse, I found more bills. Almost immediately, they started arguing over who would handle the money. It wasn't much, but each fighter wanted to hold the change in his hand. I sat there quietly, watching them bicker. *Okay,* I thought. *Now I know the type of people I am dealing with: people so desperate they quarrel over touching money.*

Finally, the one called Ebenezer spoke up. "Get a hold of your-selves!" he said. His voice was authoritative, and they listened. "Please remember, Sister Agnes is our *guest.*"

That's what he called me: Sister Agnes. He delegated the errand to a young man named Folley, who had been sitting quietly on the jagged wall. Folley grabbed the money from my hand and ran. I wondered if I would ever see him again. Soon, Folley returned with a crate of dusty bottles. He handed me the change, and it seemed to be the right amount.

"To you," I said, lifting a bottle of beer from the crate. I didn't drink alcohol then, but felt I needed to in order to win their trust. Bracing myself, I swallowed a bitter sip.

"To you, Sister." They raised their beers. Glad smiles replaced previously blank expressions. They chatted. Laughed. Told stories about people they knew: stories about boys in Sinkor and girls hustling in the Red Light district. At last, they turned to me.

I wanted to keep things casual, so I stayed where I was. I introduced myself as a Liberian woman, first, and as an independent journalist, second. "I come from the UN, but I am not UN staff. Scratch it from your heads," I said, making sure that each one heard me. This was a tactical move. The UN paid its full-time employees hefty salaries. These fighters were poor, and I didn't want them to get the wrong idea and think I was rich and come and rob me. Also, I imagined that many of them held little regard for UNMIL due to the disarmament fiasco.

They sat there silent, glum. They were so thin, hard-up, and obviously depressed . . . *Somebody really needs to help these people,* I kept thinking. So I thought, *Well why not, while I'm here, let me get to know them.*

You never start with a hard question. Any journalist knows that. So I asked them their names and ages, their tribes and counties. Then, eventually, I wound around to what I really wanted to know (what Kojo wanted to know). "I am only asking in general," I said in a measured tone. "Did you fight, and if so, will you tell me the truth about it?" I said I knew they had reasons, and I wanted to know those reasons. I was interested not just in the bad things they had done, but also the bad things that had been *done to them*. I wanted to know how they felt and, I paused, lived with their actions. I said I knew how most Liberians felt, but that I believed things might improve if we found a way to talk about the war. No one had heard from ex-fighters yet—not in any meaningful sense.

"I have come to give you a platform," I said, surprised at the words coming out of my mouth. "If you're interested."

One fighter whistled. Most stared at the empty bottles in their hands. Aside from Ebenezer, who was looking at me, their eyes began to dart around the area. Had I been too blunt? Moved too quickly? Had I hurt their feelings or insulted them? Then I checked myself: These are *child soldiers*, Agnes! I wasn't telling them anything new! They knew what they had done. Still, without knowing why, I felt guilty.

The girl with the muscles stared at me with a strange intensity. It was off-putting. She was obviously high, and I wondered how many of the boys she had slept with. One boy lit a cigarette and started rocking back and forth, his eyes blinking rapidly, no longer seeing me or hearing anything but the roar in his head. For a brief second, I can't explain it, but I could hear the roar, too. *What is happening?* I shook myself. *What am I doing here?* A few silent, uncomfortable minutes elapsed. Finally, Ebenezer stood up. "Okay," he addressed the crowd. He gestured toward me. "You have heard what this lady has to say," he said. "What do you people want to say to her?"

Arms shot up. "Miss! Miss!" Fingers snapped in the air in the traditional way we Liberians use to get someone's attention. It surprised me. They had questions, so many questions. Who would hear the stories? Would they be paid for their stories? Where would the stories go?

"Calm down." Ebenezer fielded the inquiries like a football referee. "Let Sister Agnes speak."

I cleared my throat, stalling for time. I really hadn't thought this thing through. I did my best to explain—invent?—the process. Those who were interested could give me their names. We would record their stories individually. I would broadcast some of the stories on my radio program, *Straight from the Heart*. Liberians would listen to them. Some might call in. Others who were listening might hear the stories and think, "Hm, that's interesting. That's good."

Of course, people might say other things. I didn't need to explain. Those fighters knew what I was talking about. One boy stood up: "I 'na give you people my story!" he shouted angrily. "That my story! Not you people's!"

His tone made me uncomfortable, but I kept my cool. That was fine, I said. I wasn't forcing anybody to talk to me, and no one should feel obligated. "If you want to give me your story, give me your story," I said, looking from one fighter to the next. "If not, don't. If you lie, I won't air your story. And another thing," I said. "I don't pay for stories." I could transport them to and from UNMIL Radio and give them lunch, but that was it.

Whether it was the food or something else, I'll never know. Immediately the fighters started shouting, "Ah! I have a story! I have a story! I have a story to tell!" And this is when I really gulped. The prospect of bringing ten fighters to UNMIL Radio and recording their stories, only to turn them away, was unpleasant. Because we would have to turn them away. . . .

Suddenly, I felt like I needed to rein this thing in before they got too excited. Before they started to trust me, to *like* me. But how? And should I? After all, *Straight from the Heart* was a show about truth and reconciliation. Was I a hypocrite for not wanting to talk to them, the "other side" of the war? Until now, I had only interviewed victims. I supposed collecting fighters' stories couldn't hurt. It might even be interesting. They had given me their time, and I supposed I owed it to them.

"I can't promise things will get better if we do this," I said. But nobody heard me in the chaos. They kept shouting their names at me and moving closer: "I am Edwin!" "I am Moses!" "I'm Jimmy from Congo Town!" Where had all these boys come from? Had more arrived? I counted eleven, twelve, thirteen . . . A boy in a white shirt that had not been white in some time leapt right in front of me, too close for my comfort. He smelled so bad my eyes watered. "You record my story now, oh!" he cried and shook his fist in the air. "Now, oh!" Startled, I put up my hand and began to back up several paces. "No, not now." I shook my head. I told him I couldn't record his story just then. We would need a recording booth for that. His face fell. His shoulders sunk. Extreme disappointment. Clearly, he had nothing else going on.

As calmly as he had before, Ebenezer quieted the group and advised the fighters to be patient. He turned to me and volunteered to compile a list of names.

"I will make it easy for you, Sister." He put a hand over his heart. "I will gather the information personally and make sure that each and every thing is correct." He tied a bow in the air with his fingers.

I thanked him. I knew I'd found an ally in Ebenezer. I gave him my cell phone number and bought him a calling card so he could phone me when the fighters were ready to speak. Then I opened my wallet and handed Ebenezer money to buy them food. The ex-combatants cheered. When it was time to leave, they escorted Amos, MacDonald, and me back to the main road and kept us company while we hailed a taxi.

"When you coming back?" they pressed. "You sure you're coming back, oh?"

"Why the doubts all of a sudden?" I wondered.

"Old Ma . . ." they complained. "Foreigners took our stories. They promised things that never happened. They took our stories and left!" The fighters told me about journalists and filmmakers who had poured into Monrovia after the war, established intimacies and then disappeared without so much as a thank you.

I felt my cheeks flush. This had been my plan exactly, but now . . .

"Slow your breath," I said. And all of a sudden, I can't explain it, but I wanted to be there, help them, and do what those other journalists hadn't. Amazed at the words coming out of my mouth, I told them I was a Liberian woman, not a foreigner, and would not be the same old song and dance. If they would commit to me, I would commit to them. I said all of this in pidgin English, which they knew, and not the crisp, clear English I used on my radio program.

"Okay, okay!" they clamored. "But what you give us? What we get for our stories?"

My smile faded. Again, I clarified my position: "I can't pay you and I'm not making a profit. I am doing this for Liberia."

And, "Okay, okay, okay . . . That sounds good. That sounds good, Old Ma . . ." they said.

With that, Amos and MacDonald and I left.

"Well?" Kojo asked when I returned.

I dodged his questions. I avoided my colleagues' questions, too. All I would say was something big was under way. Early the next morning, Ebenezer telephoned. I was still asleep when he called. "Hello?" I answered groggily. He had shared my proposal with the group, he said. Some had questioned my intentions. Others wanted cash for their stories. A few had harassed Ebenezer, because I appointed him chairman.

"Chairman?" I raised my eyebrows. *Oh well*, I thought, *okay . . .*

Happily, Ebenezer reported that after a long and heated conversation, the group had reached a consensus. They liked me well enough to give this thing a try. "We will work with you, Sister," he said.

"That is really good news," I said. "Which boys and girls will speak to me?"

Ebenezer said he had drawn up a list: Of the more than two hundred former child soldiers who frequented that ghetto, most were interested.

"Two hundred?" I nearly dropped the phone.

A drop in the bucket, Ebenezer replied. Did I know how many child soldiers fought the war? He would be glad to tell me. I was speechless. We scheduled the first interview for the following day. As I hung up the phone, all I could think was: *What have I done?*

13

HEY PEOPLE, I'm very sorry to say this. We were very small at that time. Now I'm twenty years. Oh, we bother with people. Really. We bother with people.

The people, they say, "You have to sleep with women, so if you get hit by a bullet you don't die from it." But you see, people die from it...

We fought the war. I don't kill people, I kill people, yeah. I told you they killed my people. They killed my father, they killed my mother, my brother. There was nowhere for me to go. So they forced me. And how can I live if I not be with them?

Me, I never did any bad in the war, you know. I did not do any bad. People who were bad were going around killing people. Killing people, start eating their own friends—human beings! Well, you're not supposed to be like that.... The war is over and everybody crying and praying for forgiveness. For me to say, "I took a weapon and killed my friend, you know, but I never do it intentionally."

—Musa

IN LIBERIA, WE HAVE A SAYING: "There is no bad bush to throw away an ugly child." This means that no matter what a child has done, or how unconscionable his actions, the community always has a place for him. It is an old saying created by our ancestors, but sometimes as I listened to the fighters' stories, I wondered what our ancestors would say if they were alive today. And then, what they would think of me.

In retrospect, it was strange I had paid so little attention. Just like every other guest on my program, these fighters had endured terrible things during the war. Still, like most Liberians, I had divided our country in half: victims and perpetrators. Good and evil. Us and them. It took me a while to see how the categories blended, and one became another, sometimes on the very same day. I had been living on one side of a one-way mirror and was about to step through.

They were not children. They had never been allowed. But they were not adults, either. They were something else entirely—something uncategorizable.

At first, I refused to visit the ghetto alone. Once I'd gotten used to the idea of entering and returning alive, the prospect became less frightening to me. It's like anything in life: Sometimes the fear of something is worse than the thing itself. Of course, in other ways, what I experienced in the ghetto was far worse than I could have imagined.

I was not prepared for their stories. It had been bad enough hearing the victims' tales, but now right in front of me, in the studio, speaking into my microphone, were the boys who had done those murders and rapes. What do you ask a murderer? A rapist? A boy who ate the heart of a small child for a rebel sacrifice? When a boy who fought for the NPFL was sitting there, I would immediately think of Grace. When a boy from LURD sat down, I thought of a man I met whose own nephew, a LURD fighter, had executed his daughter. I envisioned what that man or Grace would ask these boys—"Why? Why? Why?"— with vengeful tears. I was a journalist, and I had to remain neutral. Kojo was always very firm about that. "Fine," I'd reply, not seeing how anyone could remain "neutral" in this situation.

"Tell me how you were taken . . ." I used to start my interviews with the fighters. Many had no education, so in plain language, I asked them to describe how they were abducted or recruited. "When you were young, when the rebels came to carry you, how did they come?" I would say. And suddenly, I was there. Experiencing death from the other end of the gun barrel.

I'm very small. Eight years. People came to our town. They killed my brother. Killed my mother, my father. Came to our town, started killing, forcing here and there. And I got wounds, different different. Break my legs. Forced me to do things I did not want to do. Say, "Get up! Gun!" People forced me. Took me. Where I don't belong. And gave me gun. I started fighting here and there.

We were all hungry. We couldn't find any food. My friends told me to join them, and the four of us went into the bush. We arrived at Robertsport and ran into one of the rebel factions. They told us only soldiers could pass. If we did not join them, they would not let us through. So we joined. I was only ten years old. We had to go fight on the front. The days we fought, we ate. If we did not fight, we were not given anything.

The boys had many unfortunate reasons for joining the war. Some were taken when they were as young as two. Most were older. Ebenezer was in his early thirties when he was forced to perform services for the rebels, and no less traumatized. They are between twenty-two and forty-five years old now, but I started calling them "boys." Then eventually, "my boys." They seemed to like that. There were a few women who fought or served as rebel concubines, but I didn't get to know them until later.

Ebenezer, now thirty-seven, served as my intermediary. He helped me organize and transport groups of two and three boys to UNMIL Radio. You should have seen the looks on my colleagues' faces when the boys visited for the first time.

"Your children are here!" Kojo announced, enjoying the nervous ripple his words created among the staff.

Male coworkers shot the boys suspicious glances. Ladies removed their handbags from their desks. Everyone huddled in tight clusters by the watercooler, whispering and craning their necks to steal surreptitious looks at the fighters. Work stopped suddenly and completely. Kojo quickly told me to take the boys into a conference room. When I did, the boys grew uneasy. Had they ever sat in real chairs? Where was their "war room"? In what dark jungle enclaves had their commanders incited their troops before battle? They were like fish out of water at UNMIL Radio, sitting down gingerly as if the seats might be booby-trapped. I interviewed a few of them, so they could see how it worked. I didn't get a lot of information that first day, but I didn't expect to. At the end of the afternoon, I showed them to the gate.

"Bye Old Ma, bye Old Ma!" they called as they left. (Old Ma is what people call women over a certain age in Liberia.)

"Okay, bye eh!" I responded in Pidgin English.

My colleagues didn't relax until the boys had disappeared. "You and your rebel people!" they groused each time another group came through. They walked around them in wide circles. I found it amusing until my colleagues started avoiding me. They looked at me as if I'd crossed a line or become dangerous.

In retrospect, my transformation was rather quick. The former child soldiers had no one else, no one outside their group, and I pitied them. That, and it has always been easy for me to get lost in other people's stories. It was the same with these boys. It was easy to get wrapped up in their stories—their lives, however monstrous, coming through my microphone. Natural enough in the emotion of the moment to nod my head vigorously. "Yes, yes, I see, I understand." Only then, a boy like Wamah would say something and I would no longer understand:

> I joined the war in revenge of my mother's rape. I joined voluntarily and did a lot of things more than revenge. I killed an unspecified number of persons, opened sporadic shooting into a crowd, killed indiscriminately, flogged a couple of people in public after I arrested them in bed. I did it to have people be afraid of me. I became more wicked when my father, a critic of the NPFL, was killed. They chopped off his body parts. My emotion toward my father's death put me over.

I wondered if a boy like Wamah had even known what he was doing at the time. Forced to be a soldier when he was too young to know right from wrong, told to do wrong, told the wrong was right. Forced to kill friends who fell out of line during training, killing "enemies" who had been captured, or killing their own parents. What happens to a child in that situation?

Closing my eyes, I tried to imagine these boys coming after my parents and children. I couldn't! Or seeing my son, Reginald, now twenty-five, approach me with a gun. Screaming at me. Forcing me to the ground. I shut my eyes, willing the sickening images to disappear.

Sometimes the boys seemed almost proud of their pasts. At UNMIL Radio or back in the ghetto, they debated battles and gory figures.

"Hundreds died!"

"You are a liar!"

"That boy was a coward!"

"When they cried, we felt proud!"

I couldn't understand it. But then, just as quickly, their faces grew morose, their voices contrite. It was clear they had no idea how to feel or make sense of their situations. For some of these boys, war was all they knew.

In the beginning, most of the boys tried to sway a little bit. To say, "I saw the fighting, but I didn't participate." Or, "I wasn't a perpetrator. I was a victim. Yes, that's it. I was a *victim* of the war." When they started to bend, I would say I knew they were victims, but hadn't they done things, too? I'd say, "You know, at ten, going to the battle, I can't imagine. Were you scared? And you had a gun in your hand, how were you feeling?" Then, I would stop and let them fill the silence.

I listened and nodded encouragingly as each began to divulge his personal role in the war. It didn't happen overnight. With deeply emotional stories, it never does. You bide your time and chip away with a gentle hammer until something *gives*.

Even Ebenezer hesitated at first. He would list all of the good things he had done, or the bad things he had refused to do. But when I asked him to come clean about the rest of his experience, he would repeat a story, or smile and tell me I was digging too deep. I wanted Ebenezer and the others to admit what they had done and to acknowledge that it was wrong. To say, I am a victim because I did not choose to kill, but I am also a perpetrator. People wronged me, but what I did was also wrong. Ebenezer was one of the most difficult boys to crack.

"What do you want from me, Sister?" Ebenezer and the others would say.

What did I want from them? The same thing all Liberians did: an answer to an impossible question.

"Why?"

He said, "You got to be a soldier, or we kill you now." Then he ordered some people to do me wrong. They gashed me seriously! One of my veins was cut! Then he say, "There is only two options." Either I join or die. I joined. I have a mark on me today from the people who forced me to join their revolution.—John

I would say this to people: We started moving with the people who were freedom fighters. Roaming around with these guys. They came and organized us in the bush and carried us to the war. All we knew was we were born in the bush and grew up there. There were plenty of children roaming around. We were trying to seek survival. They supplied our food, started helping us, said: "Stay here and nothing will happen to you."—Abdullai

When I come back from our farm, I see my grandmother laying down on the ground, already dead. And my sister and her little son, too. The rebels surrounded our house. They started burning it. There was a mattress in the house. My uncle wrapped it around himself and tried to escape. People firing on him! I told my brother, I say, "Let's go in the bush. This is nowhere for us to stay." But we ran into some people there. They say, "Where you people going?" We told them we were going to the bush. But they say, "You people are not going anywhere. Take ammo so you can fight." That is how they claimed our heads.—Willis

I was fatherless and motherless. My throat got cut. After they cut my throat, my throat was wide open. Blood flashing! I was in the senior class. I was feeling bad. I was not born like this. I did not see myself slaughtering.—Musa

When the boys told me how they were recruited or taken, I got so angry at the people who had done it. "Adults!" I would spit. "And who was your commander?" I would say. "Can you identify the people who killed your family?"

I asked some boys how their mothers and fathers had reacted on first seeing them with a gun. But many had none by the time it happened.

Recruited or captured, the boys did the very same things to other people that those warlords had done to them. "Did you ever think it was wrong to join the war at your age?" I asked.

It was choosing between life and death, and I choose life, which meant I was to become a rebel.

I 'na mean it. It was the devil that fooled me! Our minds were disturbed.

And as a child they put you on the big drugs: cocaine, PCP. Drugs I don't even know what they were!

How I feel? The first time I taste it, I was looking away. But you get used to it, so you just start doing it. They give you the opium, you do it, you get the "coffee cup." In one week's time, you do it every day.

They drank medical alcohol stolen from clinics. Sniffed gasoline from bottles. Snorted cocaine mixed with gunpowder and stuffed down their gun barrels. They were tricked into it, forced to do it, and eventually chose to do it. It made the war disappear. Then, blunted or in a wild frenzy, they fired indiscriminately at men, women, children, animals—even graves.

"We killed people for cigarettes," said a boy named Sam. They shot to prove themselves, to feed themselves. Otherwise, they scrounged for leaves, snakes, or bush meat. They went for days without sleep. Many of their friends died from malnutrition and dysentery.

Returning to camp, they drank to dull the pain or to celebrate. I met a fighter whose regiment played soccer matches with human skulls. Many boys were told their families were dead, so why not join the rebels, their "new family"? Some were told the people they were fighting were the ones who had *killed* their families, and if they didn't join, the same things would be done to them.

We were desperate. Forced to possess the full demon. Forced to do bad, bad things.

My conscience is not clear, and will never be . . . Inside I feel terrified of what I have done, and I regret it deeply. The nightmares haven't started yet, but I can't stop thinking about what happened in the bush.

And those who didn't fight? "What happened to them?" I asked. And oh, there were some . . . They got hacked to death by other child soldiers—by their friends. The action came first, the remorse set in later. "When the drugs wore off," they explained.

"And how do you feel now that the war is over?" I said. "Is the war over inside your hearts?" And they would say yes, yes, yes, they desperately wanted to reconcile. They hoped Liberians could find a space in their hearts to forgive them. "I live with the consequences of my actions every day," said a boy named Dolo. "I know what I have lost in terms of inner peace. If I were able to relive that moment again, I know I would do things differently." "Once we were normal," Ebenezer confirmed. "Then we were fighting the war. We never knew our dreams."

I didn't broadcast all the stories. There were far too many of them. I aired only the most compelling ones, and those I could fact-check. Many boys came willingly. Some feared the consequences of talking to me. Would the warlords, their former commanders, hunt them down? Would they go to jail?

"They're going to catch me and put me in a cell!" cried a former fighter named Dwe. He was a quiet boy until he talked about the war. Then his face stormed over, his words became flammable. It turned out Dwe was related to Charles Taylor's vice president, a powerful warlord. But those high connections meant nothing during the war. "Are we safe? What will happen to the people whose names we call?" Dwe asked me. I could almost hear the earsplitting feedback pounding inside his head. So I told him that he could give his story anonymously, or we could alter his voice with sound effects. He would be doing a good thing by sharing his story with the Liberian people, I said. Eventually, Dwe came on *Straight from the Heart* and told listeners what had happened to him:

Rebels killed my brother and chopped him up into little pieces before my eyes. When they asked me if I wished to fight or suffer the same fate, I joined them. I never saw the rebels who killed my brother again.

It was difficult to sit with Dwe and the others day after day and hear the grisly details of how they had become killers. Some weeks I was unable to sleep just thinking about everything. It made the heart hard. I lost my appetite. I would wake up screaming: "No! No! No!" I had to force myself to remember what had been done to them, and stretch my brain to imagine myself as young as they were when gunmen came. What was the trauma associated with such scenes, of children being forcibly taken away and recruited as fighters?

When things proved overwhelming, I went to Kojo.

"Yes, it's difficult," he said. "But you have to shake it out of yourself, Umunna." Kojo would make me sit down, take a deep breath, and repeat ten lines of inspirational words he called a "mantra." I wish I still had that mantra.

Of course, this is Kojo Mensah we are talking about. Most days, he grew impatient. "Agnes!" he would scream, exasperated. "This is the job you signed up for. Do it or get the hell out of here!"

14

I'M LIVING IN A GHETTO, sleeping in a ghetto. I lie on a piece of cloth. When the rain falls, it falls on me. I don't know where is my father. I don't know where is my sister. I have nobody in Monrovia Town. Up to now, I got nowhere to go. Nothing to do. We tell people we no longer want to go back to stealing, harming people. We are really looking for help in this country! I'm asking you, God in heaven, to be able to do something.

—Lansford

A GREAT RIVER had torn Liberia apart. At first, I was afraid to wade in. Then one day, I looked up and I had crossed the river. I was on the other side.

They would tell me their stories. And I couldn't just send them away. How would they eat? Where would they sleep? These questions became deeply concerning to me. Ebenezer would tell me which boys were really traumatized, and which were hanging in there. It turned out many were homeless. Five months of rain were approaching. They had nowhere to go. Ebenezer told me I needed to do something. And soon, what had started out as an assignment for my radio program turned into something else altogether. I became "mama." They became "my kids."

Take Lansford, for example. His mother had been raped and killed right in front of him. As a small boy, he started carrying arms for the NPFL. During Operation Octopus, Lansford escaped. He hid inside a schoolhouse. In exchange for cleaning the school's toilets, the school let him sleep there. Then the war ended. People took over the building. Lansford was evicted. A grown man now, and homeless, Lansford spoke about his mother, father, and little sister as if he was still a small child. It was as if seeing his mother raped and killed in front of him had split his mind in two. I would look at Lansford, so damaged, and feel as if he was my own son.

But where to start? I didn't have much money, but I promised Ebenezer I would try my best. I went to Patrick and described the ghetto the boys were living in. He agreed that we should do something. Give back to the community that had given to us. Building the former child soldiers a center seemed like a good idea.

Patrick donated $350 U.S. to the cause. Kojo gave us $500. I reached into my pocket for the rest and asked Ebenezer to give me an estimate on what building materials would cost. He consulted with the boys and came back with a figure. I believed those ex-combatants overcharged me, but I didn't mind. If it cost me my last dime and ounce of energy, I was determined to see this thing through.

We bought building materials. Ebenezer organized the boys into teams. Some cleaned up the area, some sawed wood, and others laid bricks. It took us two days to complete the center: a wood and tin structure with a common area, a bathroom, and a kitchen. When we were done, the boys stood gazing at their handiwork, whistling and patting each other on the back. They had torn many things apart during the war. For the first time in a long time, they had built something.

Next, I took my salary and bought them food. Basic things: rice, red palm oil, cubes of Maggi. I hired a local woman to cook meals for them. She prepared *gari*, a local dish made from cassava, in the morning, and dry rice at night. The boys ate like lions, and I wondered how long it had been since they had eaten a proper meal. I told them to slow down, that more would be coming. But they didn't believe me and kept thrusting fistfuls of food into their mouths. In this way, I knew how bad it had been for them.

Sometimes there were quarrels. Boys accused other boys of eating "double shares." Boys would come late and the food would already be gone. Ebenezer complained that he was making peace on a daily basis. Soon he came up with a solution. Ebenezer would act as monitor, staying at the center until everyone had eaten. No matter how late you were, Ebenezer made sure something was kept on the fire.

When I could, I purchased salt, sugar, and vegetables to give the boys nutrition and variety. Another week, I bought plates and cutlery. Some of the boys didn't know how to use the silverware, but they enjoyed holding it in their hands. They returned the forks and spoons to the washing place as if they were priceless jewels.

"If you have small money, kick in," I told them. "If not, no problem."

I used my whole salary on those boys. When I started running out of money, I went to Patrick and Kojo for more. "The rice and *gari* are really helping them," I said. "To keep this place going, we have to keep cooking." They grumbled and said that I was always after them for money. "Money looks for money." I shrugged. "If you sit on it too long, how will more come?" And okay, okay, these goodly Nigerians nodded. Let's do the calculations. Somehow, somewhere, we found it.

Only then, there was no place for us to sit. "We should not be sitting on rotting chairs," I said. Because it was "we" now, me and the boys. And "Yes!" Ebenezer and the others agreed. "We need good furniture, just like every other house."

I bought six rubber chairs with GOD BLESS YOU stamped onto the backs of them. Next, I purchased a table and a blackboard so we could hold meetings. I bought the boys dice and playing cards to pass the time. (I considered these healthier pursuits than marijuana and drinking.) Kojo furnished a football and gave us money to print jerseys. The boys played games in an open space near the center and even competed against local teams.

Finally, Kojo gave us generators and we had power. Humble as it was, the boys took care of the center as if it was a fine place to which only they enjoyed VIP access. They dusted the chairs, swept the floor. When they informed me they had decided to name it the Straight from the Heart Center, after my radio program, I was really touched.

We started holding meetings on Sunday afternoons. I invited various speakers to come and talk to them, including guests from my program. Some were scared to come initially but always warmed to the boys by the end. Usually, the person would give a speech; the boys would ask questions. Sometimes, the speaker would leave behind a little money or a bag of rice. The boys would take the rice and thank the benefactor, as if he or she had just bought them a new car or motorbike.

When I could, I took groups to the local market to shop for clothes, or brought them used garments from my father and male friends. I preferred it this way. I didn't like the way the shopkeepers glared at my boys. I could tell it embarrassed them, but I said they shouldn't mind.

I was visiting the boys every day now. When I entered the ghetto I would shout, "Hey!" And they would shout back, "Our mommy is here! Our mommy is here!" And I would laugh, "Eh, my children!" And they would hug me, these grown men, and often, I would forget the things they had done to other women.

Eventually a few of the boys expressed interest in going to school. They wanted to "reset their educations," as a boy named Jimmy put it. To "become better people." I offered to pay for a few of them to take entrance exams. They studied hard and helped each other to prepare. A twenty-three-year-old boy with a sixth-grade education might help a thirty-three-year-old boy with a first-grade education brush up on his letters or math. One boy named Nelson even enrolled at a local elementary school. Now a couple of days a week, he sat on a wooden bench beside his small daughter and son.

As for Lansford, the boy who had slept in a school? He had more education than most. And one day, Lansford told me he wanted to go to college. "I will support you," I said. But I was anxious because Lansford did a lot of drugs, and I worried he would overdose before the exam. As the test date approached, I said, "Lansford, I hope you will try." He said, "Mommy, I will try." I took him to a barbershop to get his hair cut. We ate lunch at a café. Before he entered the exam building, Lansford thanked me for believing in him. He said nobody had ever treated him like that. I waited outside the testing center, praying he would pass. When Lansford emerged, he was smiling ear to ear. But when the result came, my heart was pounding. I opened the envelope and Lansford had failed. He was crushed. I told him not to give up, and I tried to get him a tutor, but his heart was not in it. This tendency to give up easily was a battle I would wage over and over again with my boys.

I let them use my cell phone to find jobs. One boy called Musa replaced his tough clothes with a smart blue-and-green shirt and a baseball cap. He started selling gasoline in glass bottles on the road. Others washed cars to make money. Patrick and Kojo were pleased. They advised other boys to start small businesses. "Do not look outside for the leader. It could be you!" Kojo said when he visited the center. "You don't need the world to start something," Patrick agreed. "Your first car will lead to your next." One boy said he wanted to be a priest. He started leading the group in hymns and delivering sermons—fearsome and long!

Not everything was on the up-and-up. Moses, a former NPFL fighter, walked to UNMIL Radio one day to ask me for help. I was shocked when I saw him standing at the gate. It was a long distance from our center. "I want a job," Moses said with such emotion I got tears in my eyes. "I want to be somewhere, Mommy."

"I will try my best," I said. Eventually, I found Moses a job working as a security guard. He was so happy and proud. But soon after Moses started the job, thieves broke in. He had only been there a week, and despite recent neighborhood burglaries, the family blamed him. I tried to reason with them. I said I knew Moses was a trustworthy person. But they didn't believe me, and Moses disappeared.

Then there were the boys' habits . . . difficult to break. Sometimes I had to do what they were doing to get their attention. I would beg them not to smoke, but when they rolled their eyes and whined, "Oh, Mommy . . ." I would say, "Fine. Give me a cigarette. If I die, you die. And while we're at it, let's have a beer!" I think they respected me for living as they did and not trying to change them overnight. I wanted them to see that I understood what they were going through and wouldn't desert them. "You must never discourage anyone who continually makes progress, no matter how slow," someone wise once said. And it's true. Still, I made it clear my goal was to help them move past these things. "You can do this, but you can also leave it. It's *worth* leaving."

Meanwhile, we were airing their stories on *Straight from the Heart*. It was an interesting experiment. My listeners couldn't believe some of the things these boys had done. "They are wolves, not sheep!" some cried. "Send them back to the bush where they belong!" Or, "Who is this Liberian woman? Is she *really* a Liberian woman?" They questioned my sanity, called me a traitor. They told me I was wasting my time. They talked about my boys as if they were the lost cause of Liberia.

I tried to keep things civil, while maintaining my neutrality. "Yes," I would say after a boy had told his story. "It's horrifying, but wouldn't you rather know what happened during the war?" Or, although Moses or Lansford or Wamah has done terrible things, we must also take into account his life circumstances. Or, while we could send them back to the bush, they might turn into the very people who took them in the first place. They might do the same things to other children. The clock was ticking for this lost generation, which was, of course, the next generation.

Obviously, I got threats. Some people called to congratulate Jefferson or Willis or Momo for finding the courage to admit what he had done. But others wanted to grab and choke my boys and they wrote me nasty letters, or telephoned the station directly. If, for instance, a former child soldier came on the air to tell his story, and a concerned citizen was listening, he might call in and say, "What are they talking about on this program? It is a stupid idea! They have killed our people! Why are you encouraging them to talk? They have to be prosecuted! You ought to be killed yourself!" I would look up from my script to see the studio technician holding the telephone at arm's length, while someone upbraided him on the other end of the line.

The first time it happened, I got flustered and hung up the phone by accident. That was a mistake. When a caller is talking, no matter how heated he gets, you can't cut him off. The first time I did, Kojo said, "No, don't argue with these people or raise your voice. They are talking in a stupid voice, saying stupid things. Eventually, they will finish." So the next time it happened, I let the person talk. And when he had finished, I thanked him for sharing how he felt and suggested why we couldn't have revenge in Liberia. "We can't say, 'You killed our people, so I will kill you,'" I said. "Because then we would be committing the same crimes."

I liked to played devil's advocate, but I am human. Sometimes I got defensive. "Who is behaving more uncivilly?" I wanted to say. "These boys or you?" It hurt my feelings when people questioned my morals and ethics. "Concentrate your fire, Umunna," Kojo would say. Then he would help me write some peaceful lines before I went back on air. Lines like:

What comfort is revenge? It is such an ugly word. You know what my boss said? Just this: "Revenge is a dish best not served."

Sometimes I got scared, but not often. I knew my child soldiers would protect me. I don't mean they would *harm* anyone, just that they were nearby and listening. Later, when I started interviewing warlords and the conversations spiraled out of control, this became especially important. I would return to the center visibly shaken, but my boys would say, "Don't worry. We know that guy. We'll talk to him."

Sometimes I got suspicious. "What are you going on about?" I would say. But the boys reassured me they meant no harm. I had taken care of them. And in their own way, I think they wanted to take care of me.

15

IT WAS DURING the year 1990 when I used to hear about the "guerilla fighters." I used to think they were animals—gorillas—because of their name.

They entered on a Friday morning and began to loot our town. I had a young baby. When they entered our house, my baby was taken from me. They throw my baby on the ground and left it to die. I was forced to bury my child in an hour's time. When I took too long, a rebel hit me with the bottom of his gun.

These guys took us with them to Lower Bong County and made us do their work. I was arrested by Taylor's supporters. They commanded me to look at the sun for more than an hour. Because of this, I am half blind. I really regret the past but am willing to reconcile with those who hurt me. I am prepared to captain the boat of national reconciliation.

—Harriet

IN AFRICA, we have traditional ways of getting past our conflicts. Method varies according to ethnic group and religion, but dialogue is the bottom line. In South Africa, "chiefs' courts" assisted local communities struggling with life after apartheid. In Rwanda, *gacaca* courts helped Rwandans recover from the genocide.

Perpetrators and survivors sat down to talk about what had happened, and why it couldn't again. You might wonder how this helped when 800,000 men, women, and children were brutally murdered in less than 100 days—what solace it could bring. Or how blacks could forgive forty-six years of racial persecution in South Africa. And all I can say is that's Africa: a place of immense tragedy but even greater miracles.

In Liberia, when two parties have a disagreement, we call it a "palaver." Warring parties sit down in a palaver hut with a mediator, before a council of elders, and talk until they find common ground. Afterward, a kola nut is fetched. The kola is a bitter-tasting nut that grows in Africa's tropical rain forests. In Liberia, warring parties split and eat the kola nut and take an oath they will not harm each other. In more elaborate ceremonies, they sacrifice a cow. Then the whole village gathers and everyone feasts. Palavers are how many Liberian communities got over the war.

On a national scale, we had Liberia's Truth and Reconciliation Commission, or TRC. It was a body firmly rooted in dialogue, too, but vested with special powers besides. Created in May 2005, the TRC was given two years to investigate and report on human rights violations committed in Liberia between January 1979 and October 2003. That's two years to investigate not twenty-four days, not twenty-four weeks, but *twenty-four years* of atrocities. The commission was not a court. No court could handle the caseload in Liberia. It was similar to what happened in Rwanda. If you put all the criminals on trial, the work would never be done. Instead, the job of the TRC was to decide for the record what the record of our nation's history really was. It did so by conducting public hearings and private statement-taking sessions. Some people thought it was wonderful. Others called it a waste of time.

The TRC operated out of the old Public Works office downtown and later moved to Ninth Street in Sinkor, on the coast. It occupied a three-story building in a place where mansions and beachfront hotels gave way in the space of a few streets to slums and trash-strewn lots. Colorful murals were posted outside the building. They depicted what types of crimes the TRC would investigate in unapologetic detail: graphic representations of murder, theft, and rape so clear that even illiterate Liberians— 50 percent of our population—could understand. In nearly half of the paintings, the perpetrators pictured were young boys, which goes to show you how many children were caught up in the fighting.

IT WAS MAY 2006. The TRC would launch in one month. A ceremony was planned at the Central Pavilion in Monrovia, and I wanted my boys to be a part of it. I went to see Councillor Jerome J. Verdier Sr., the chairman of the TRC, and a prominent Liberian attorney and advocate whom President Ellen Johnson-Sirleaf had appointed along with eight others. She called the commissioners "the people's hope." As chairman, Jerome's job was to oversee the proceedings, break deadlocks among them, and ensure the operation ran smoothly. When Jerome was appointed, I called to congratulate him and said, oh, by the way, I need to ask you something. Can I drop by? Jerome is a busy man who makes time for other people. He had listened to my radio program and knew about our center for ex-combatants. Yes, he said. Drop by anytime.

"How are things?" I asked when I arrived at TRC headquarters.

"Proceeding." He smiled the weary, fulfilled smile of a man working hard for noble ends.

"Is everything on track?" I asked him.

Jerome nodded. "It is a new time for Liberia."

"To have a good report, we'll need a balanced story," I said. "You can't just interview victims. What about the boys?" I asked. "They are part of this country too."

Interviewing victims of the war and the warlords who had carried out the fighting was obviously critical. But if you were going to have a good report, it only made sense to interview the soldiers who committed the individual atrocities. They needed to talk. They could shed light on important events. And, really, I told Jerome, perpetrators were also victims.

"Many were small when they were taken and offered a 'choice': kill or be killed." Given that choice, what would Jerome have done? What would I have done?

I shared a particularly heartbreaking story from my center. Varlee was just nine years old and living with his grandmother when the rebels came. They threatened to rape and kill Varlee's grandmother unless he joined them. "Don't kill her! I will go with you!" Varlee cried. To save his grandmother, Varlee took up the AK-47. He fought for fourteen years, the entire duration of the war. Varlee grew from a boy to a man in the rebel army. The only thing that sustained him was his hope of returning home.

"And do you know what happened?" I asked Jerome.

He shook his head.

Varlee escaped with a group of boys. They walked for two days in the bush without food or water. They found themselves at a government soldiers' barracks. The soldiers interrogated them. Miraculously, they did not kill them. Instead, they sent the boys to a humanitarian organization. Later, Varlee found our center. He didn't speak at first. He was high, but I could tell there was something going on. It wasn't just the drugs. So I encouraged Varlee to come for meals and meetings.

I tried to talk with him, but every time I started to ask about the war, Varlee vanished. Then one day, I parked my car on Randall Street to do an errand. (Randall Street is where many ex-fighters hang around and beg for money.) Varlee was there and he must have recognized my car. When I came back, he was washing it. It startled me, and I guessed Varlee wanted to be paid, but he refused.

Varlee brightened. "Oh, just for you, Sister." He grinned. "I get water just for you, Sister . . ." And then I handed him small change and we started talking about the war.

Later, I encouraged Varlee to record his story. He said he was terrified of what he had done. He feared his conscience would never be clear. Varlee had joined the rebels to save his grandmother. He had fought and taken drugs to forget, but they didn't entirely work. It was clear that Varlee was really suffering and needed a home, more of one than Straight from the Heart could provide. At the end of our recording session, I encouraged Varlee to write a letter to his grandmother. I advised him to let her know that he was alive and ask to come back. Varlee was unsure, but he wrote the letter. He didn't hear from her.

"Perhaps she does not want to see me because of what I have done." Varlee looked pained. Don't lose hope, I urged. I asked Varlee where his village was. He told me.

"Good," I said. "Then we will go there together."

It was a long journey to Zwedru, Varlee's town. As we approached the small cluster of mud huts that Varlee had pointed me toward, I stole glances at him. He seemed incredibly anxious. When we got to his grandmother's hut, Varlee exited the car as if in a dream. He took in the path, the small garden, and his grandmother's house as if he wasn't quite sure whether they were real. I wondered if he was remembering it as a child before the war, or the day the rebels came and took him at gunpoint. Varlee ran a hand over his shirt and pants, which looked cleaner than I'd ever seen them. I followed him to the door. Varlee knocked. Nothing. He tried again. Still nothing.

Then I tried. I heard a rustling. Footsteps. With a slow creak, the door opened and an old woman appeared.

She greeted me coldly. She did not look at Varlee.

"Hello," I said. For a moment, I wondered if we had the right house. Had Varlee made a mistake? Had the drugs scrambled his mind? But then I looked at Varlee and knew we had found it. Somewhat disconcerted, I introduced myself to Varlee's grandmother and suggested we all sit down. Varlee's grandmother offered me a seat in the traditional porch area where some Liberians entertain guests. She did not offer one to Varlee.

"What about your grandson?" I said. "Where will he sit?"

Varlee's grandmother shook her head and said Varlee was not welcome here. I blinked. Had I heard her correctly? "This boy is your blood. He saved your life. And he has come back to ask for forgiveness," I explained as if she didn't recognize Varlee, or hadn't understood our mission. But her face was unyielding.

Noises came from outside. A group of men and women appeared in the doorway. They were different ages and dressed in rags. They recognized Varlee and stared at him with their mouths hanging open. Varlee's grandmother acknowledged their presence by offering them places on the porch. I glanced at Varlee, cowering in a corner, looking so lost and miserable.

I started to speak, but Varlee's grandmother interrupted me. She seemed to draw strength from these new people's presence. She said: There were boys who went with the rebels and did not kill. But her grandson, she looked at Varlee for the first time that day, he had *killed*. Pursing her lips and with a voice like steel, she explained that Varlee had killed in their village. *That* made him the enemy.

I was surprised. Angry. I wanted to shout at Varlee's grandmother and go over and hug Varlee, but I didn't. I didn't look at him, because I needed to stay focused. I had to change her mind. I was about to say something hostile, but then I noticed the bracelets on Varlee's grandmother's wrists. Putting two and two together—the bracelets, her age, the group of people—I realized Varlee's grandmother was a village elder. She was making a political statement by banishing her grandson. She was sacrificing Varlee to save her status in the village.

I tried to stay calm. "Varlee did not join willingly . . ." I said. "He was dragged to fight the war. Drugged out black and indoctrinated. He did it to save you!"

Her face was like stone. Mine was more flustered with each passing second. "Perform a ceremony!" I pleaded. "You elders have *ways* to cleanse him." I was groveling at this point. "Take him back or don't take him back." I begged Varlee's grandmother, "but please forgive him. Not to forgive him is just something I don't understand!"

Varlee's grandmother refused. She evicted him. Even though this boy, her grandson, had saved her life over fourteen years ago. . . . I could understand the complicated situation, but not her pride. I realized she didn't want to lose her power, but is that any reason to reject your family? We left the village empty-handed, Varlee broken-hearted. I didn't know what to say as we drove back to Monrovia.

"And now?" Jerome asked. His face was full of concern.

Now Varlee drifted in and out of the center. The drugs were getting worse, I said. I was worried about what he might do to himself. I feared that one of these days, one of these days . . . but I couldn't finish the sentence.

"This is what my boys are dealing with," I sniffed.

Jerome was quiet for some time. At last, he took a slow, deep breath and nodded. "Yes," he said. "Varlee's story is a shocking reminder of the victimhood and re-victimization that is occuring in Liberia." He agreed to give the boys from Straight from the Heart Center a slot at the TRC launch. He advised me to select a former child soldier to deliver some remarks. I felt like cheering. I hurried back to the center.

"Hello Sister," Ebenezer greeted me when I arrived.

"We have this speech to give," I told Ebenezer excitedly. "And I would like you to do it."

16

PEOPLE WHO USE VIOLENCE see things only from one angle. They don't see that if you use violence, you encourage revenge and hatred in others. You end up with a never-ending cycle. Some people can't forgive, but that doesn't mean they are weak or will be consumed by bitterness or anger. It just means that, as human beings, they have been hurt beyond repair. And who are we to say they should forgive?

—Sidiki

ONE TIME I ASKED Ebenezer why he came to Straight from the Heart Center every day. Unlike most of the boys, he had a home. "Because I have nothing to do and nobody." He shrugged. "These boys are my brothers." I nodded, because after the incident with Varlee's grandmother, I understood.

Ebenezer had a different story than most of the boys. He had never held a gun. He was a grown man when the war started. His childhood was tragic in its own way, and I think it gave him empathy and an ability to understand the other boys' experiences. This, and the fact he had played a key role in helping a former child soldier–recruit escape.

As a little boy, Ebenezer was chastised for being a bastard. He lived with his grandmother, who didn't want him. He then lived like hired help in his father's house. Ebenezer used to eat the scraps from his stepsiblings' plates and wash cars on the street for a dollar apiece to buy his school uniforms. Somehow he managed to rise out of these dismal conditions. He sat for a national teaching exam. He came in first. Ebenezer became a teacher, and later a school principal. When the war came and Taylor's NPFL forces invaded Liberia, they said Ebenezer must join them. A deeply religious man, Ebenezer adamantly refused. Then the rebels tied him with a rope, kicked his head, and stabbed him. They poured boiling water infused with hot peppers into Ebenezer's eyes. He had cuts all over his body. "Like an animal." Ebenezer showed me the scars. Astoundingly, he wasn't crippled. At this point, commanders of another faction formed to defeat Charles Taylor caught up with Ebenezer. They identified him as a "person of promise" and hired him to be a secretary civilian representative. Ebenezer didn't want to do it, but the rebels said he didn't have a choice. Besides, the job was "purely administrative." With a heavy heart, Ebenezer consented. "Anything to get myself free from the gun," he explained.

Like all rebel groups, the one Ebenezer worked for terrorized innocent civilians. Sometimes Ebenezer was called upon to identify NPFL spies. "It was terrible for me," he said. But mainly, Ebenezer's job was to serve as a liaison between the rebel fighters and the civilians who lived in Taylor's NPFL-controlled areas. Also, to prevent villagers from escaping. While many civilians supported the NPFL, many more lived in occupied areas but were not necessarily associated with the rebels themselves. Although a rebel soldier was supposed to ask for a civilian's identification card before doing anything to him, soldiers often skipped this step and harassed villagers for nothing.

All of the rebel groups did this, and Taylor's boys were especially cruel. They would invent charges against people. Such as, it is a crime to work for the government! It is a crime to be well-groomed! It is a crime not to speak the dialect of the ethnic group you claim to belong to! If a child soldier asked you to speak your language and you failed to do so fluently, there was a penalty: Death. Not that they knew what language you were speaking . . . they just needed a reason to kill you.

Several times, Ebenezer intervened to prevent rebels from exacting violence on innocent villagers. "I would place a call to the rebel leaders and say, 'These people are citizens of this place, and you have to calm your soldiers down! If your soldiers come on so harsh and cruel, these people will leave and join your enemies.'" Sometimes it worked. But not always.

Over the years, Ebenezer came to understand why the rebel group was intent on keeping villagers in one place: They needed child soldiers. Mothers and fathers got to know Ebenezer and begged him to intercede and prevent the rebels from taking their children. Ebenezer used to fast and pray to God to guide his actions. One day, the rebels took a young boy Ebenezer knew. The boy wouldn't stop crying. Even when the rebels threatened his life, he wouldn't stop crying. Ebenezer knew he had to do something. Mustering his courage, he went to his commander and, lying, said the boy had a fatal disease. If he went to the battlefront, the enemy would surely kill him. "My heart was beating fast!" Ebenezer said. "But God was controlling my voice that day." Ebenezer's commander listened. He told Ebenezer to help the boy escape. "Keep him inside," Ebenezer instructed the boy's mother when he delivered her son. "If the rebels come again, tell them he is sick. We will find a way to get him out for good."

It was one child in a thousand, but it made a difference. Many years later, Ebenezer would see this same boy on the streets of Monrovia. He called Ebenezer "Uncle" and told his friends how Ebenezer had saved his life.

When I first met Ebenezer, he was working as a janitor. He was ashamed of the work and did not want the other boys at Straight from the Heart to know. How could I not love this boy? No one had given him a leg up, yet still he worked so hard for them, and for me. When I asked Ebenezer to give a speech at the TRC launch, his eyes lit up. "I'll do it, Sister," he said. But when he asked me for suggestions, I shook my head. I knew he would be fine on his own. It gave me joy that Ebenezer could compose something for this important event and let his intelligence shine. I wanted the moment to be Ebenezer's alone.

On the day of the TRC launch, June 22nd, I hired taxis to take a group of boys and girls from the center to Monrovia's Central Pavilion. The TRC had given us T-shirts designed in blue and red. Security was tight. The event organizers wouldn't allow everyone inside, just Ebenezer and me. Ushers showed us to our seats in the back. Ebenezer recognized several warlords sitting in the front rows. I waved to people I knew, members of the press and guests I'd had on my program. They waved back, but really they were looking at Ebenezer: *Is that a former child soldier?*

Ebenezer was nervous. Every few minutes, he removed the speech he had written from his pocket. At one p.m., the master of ceremonies asked everyone to quiet down. Jerome and the other Commissioners took the stage. From our seats in the back, we listened as the MC introduced dignitaries there to endorse the TRC's mission. There was President Ellen Johnson-Sirleaf, the United States ambassador to Liberia, a representative from the African Union, UNMIL, the European Union, and the directors from several Liberian civil society organizations. We listened to speech after speech. I liked Ma Ellen's speech best. Flanked by bodyguards wearing dark suits and sunglasses, she encouraged every Liberian to support the TRC. "The future and the stability of our country will remain in doubt unless we face ourselves as a people," she said with real feeling. "Unless we tell the truth of what we did to ourselves and to our nation."

When Jerome took the stage, he promised the TRC would work hard to produce a fair, unbiased report and "give a voice to the dead." He said the TRC's efforts would be conducted "without fear or favor." No Liberian, he added, looking around the room, would be immune from the process. At last, the MC turned to us. She looked straight at Ebenezer. "I call on the perpetrator from Straight from the Heart!" She raised her hands in welcome. "Perpetrator, give your speech!" This was Ebenezer's cue.

Ebenezer is tall, as I have said. Even in his homely pants and TRC T-shirt, he is the kind of person you see and think, there goes some-one. People craned their necks to see Ebenezer as he made his way up the aisle. Ebenezer kept his eyes on his feet the whole time. When he reached the stage, Jerome shook his hand. He looked about as ner-vous as Ebenezer did! Of the twenty-nine truth commissions that had been established worldwide, none had involved child soldiers in the way Liberia's was proposing to do. Jerome said something private to Ebenezer. Ebenezer nodded. His hands shook as he unfolded his carefully folded speech and laid it on the podium. But when Ebenezer spoke, his voice was steady and true.

I still have his speech. It was a great speech, even if I did not un-derstand every word of it. I suspect that Ebenezer might have con-sulted a dictionary for certain parts but will let you be the judge.

We have experienced the most bloody historical transformation of our political structure involving 90 percent of our youth, who were used as agents of death and destruction by unpatriotic citi-zens of this country for fourteen unbroken years. With the new government headed by our intelligent, farsighted, illustrious, honest, sincere, and hardworking mother, Ellen Johnson-Sirleaf, president of the Republic of Liberia, we would like the word to go forth that the youth of this country will never be used to kill and destroy our beloved citizens and country again.

What we as youth would like to see happen in this country is for us to reconcile our differences and become united to ensure that the youth of this country are empowered academically. Over the years, instead of positively permitting . . . youth of this country . . . to improve their academic status, they were indoctrinated by a so-called godfather who had a high degree of acidity for power and instigated fatality on the peaceful loving people of Liberia, which has been very pernicious to human survival . . .

Our goal now should be set at equipping the youth of this country for future leadership, and to develop the sense of national greatness as we strive to restore the pre-war pride and dignity to this noble country, Liberia . . . The TRC being the best framework in achieving lasting peace in this country, the youth are prepared to help in making this organization successful by giving it all the necessary information needed to make it successful, since indeed, 90 percent of the youth of this country were involved in the execution of the war. It is our understanding that the purpose of the TRC is to investigate and establish the root cause of the conflict that took away thousands of lives and destroyed millions of properties. If we help in making this noble undertaking a success, we can assure you that the youth will take its useful place in the nation-building.

I thank you.

You could have heard a pin drop. The great hall was silent. When Ebenezer looked up, the people broke into the loudest applause I have ever heard. Ebenezer was spellbound. I could read his thoughts: *These people really cheering for me? A child soldier?* He was beaming! He stood there drinking in the incomparable and unfamilar feeling of acceptance.

As Ebenezer left the stage, people leapt into the aisles and leaned over to shake his hand and pat him on the back. *Well done! Well said! You are really something, boy!* Even Ma Ellen approached Ebenezer.

"You have spoken and made a point, and I will definitely take that point into consideration," Ebenezer remembers her saying.

She hugged him. So did the U.S. ambassador. People were telling Ebenezer that they had never heard a speech quite like it. I wanted to run up and hug him too, but I stopped myself. Not because I didn't want to embrace Ebenezer, but because I had a mission: to watch the warlords in the audience and gauge their reactions. The look on their faces when Ebenezer finished speaking was, "Now what have we got here?"

Ebenezer represented a threat, you see. His bravery indicated there might be other former child soldiers like him. Children who would talk and implicate them. These warlords were scared of that, although they tried to hide it, clapping in their ringside seats and fine suits with smug looks on their faces. They reminded me of crocodiles sunning themselves on riverbanks, seemingly asleep, their jaws wide and ready to snap. A few warlords shook Ebenezer's hand as he made his way back to his seat, which intrigued me. Were they doing it for show? Or warning him?

Ebenezer clearly thought it was the latter. His smile faded and he became frightened. "See that one looking at me?" He trembled. "That guy is staring at me, Sister!"

I patted his hand. "Don't mind them," I said. "They made you guys suffer. We will expose all of them."

As the ceremony drew to a close, I started getting nervous. I had a show that afternoon but no idea how Ebenezer and I would get out of the busy pavilion. I flagged Jerome, who was supposed to be my guest on the program.

"My show starts in five minutes!" I mouthed, pointing to my wrist. "We need to leave now!"

I had to drag Jerome and Ebenezer out of the pavilion. "That was good! That was *something*!" the mob kept shouting.

We made it to UNMIL with moments to spare. Kojo was sweating profusely. "Cue the music!" he cried. I had written an introductory monologue but delivered it from memory. Jerome talked about the TRC and the challenges that lay ahead. After the show, he thanked UNMIL Radio for assisting the TRC's launch and helping Liberians understand the commission in a straightforward way. Jerome confessed that he had been worried Straight from the Heart might *compete* with the TRC and was happy to see we could be partners in this endeavor.

I showed Jerome out. As he was getting into his car, he turned to me.

"That boy's speech." Jerome paused. "It was wonderful. I have just one question for you."

"Feel free," I said.

Jerome looked at me. "Did you write it?"

I chuckled. "How could I write a speech for a perpetrator?"

Jerome was impressed. Up until the moment Ebenezer started speaking, he feared the boy from Straight from the Heart would disparage the TRC.

"On the contrary," I interrupted him. "My boys are behind you."

Back at the center, I found Ebenezer. He was still carrying his speech in his hand, recounting details from the launch for the boys who hadn't been able to attend. I asked him how he felt. Ebenezer shook his head and grinned broadly. "There was no fear in me," he said. "If I died today, I would die with pride, Sister."

Some days later, Jerome reappeared on my program with another boy from the center. The boy said he was a victim who became a perpetrator. He was up-front and honest about his actions and pleaded with society to forgive him. Jerome praised the boy for his candor and encouraged him to take his story to the TRC. I asked: "What is the TRC going to do to encourage these boys to tell their stories? What value is there in someone going to the TRC? If a boy goes to the TRC, will he have protection?" Jerome did his best to answer these difficult questions.

Basically, he said, if a boy spoke truthfully, he would likely be granted amnesty and could go on and do something good with his life. Reconciliation would not come by itself. It would require structures and processes. And it was time to start the process.

And I thought, at last, we are getting somewhere. Liberia had a choice: to confront our past by pointing fingers, or to face it together, looking toward the future. Happily, more and more people seemed to be choosing the second route.

17

I JOINED THE WAR in 2003 because of disadvantage. Some guys used their weapons to threaten my life. They took away my belongings. So I joined and was assigned to the Beer Factory near Monrovia. I was not a frontline fighter, but I was a great looter. I was usually the hit-and-run type.

My education went backward. I'm an unprofessional person. Sometimes I feel bad about my wasted time and doing nothing to better my life. I was neglected by society, because they think I am no good to them.

I am willing to sit in class to learn so that I can be a better person. It really hurts me, the way people take us to be. They think we are criminals, but some of us are not.

—Melvin

IT WAS OCTOBER 2006. Soon the TRC would start taking statements. Jerome invited me to work as a citizen statement-taker for the TRC, which meant I would do exactly what I had been doing, only this time I would collect stories for the TRC's final fact-finding report. I was honored. Concerned, too. Despite the warm reception Ebenezer had received at the TRC launch, many Liberians questioned why child soldiers deserved to participate in the process.

Even my close friends who had stayed in Liberia during the war told me I was insane.

"Agnes, these boys will kill you!" a girlfriend pleaded with me. "I know some of them. I saw what they did during the war!"

Unlike me, this friend had stories from the war: The day rebels barged through her front door with the butts of their AK-47s, and she had to lock herself in the bathroom with her mother. The warlord who used Monrovia harbor as target practice: He would wait until the food ships pulled into port and the hungry people ran out with baskets and buckets to greet them, and then "Pow! Pow! Pow!" Now my friend works at a major telecommunications company. She has a car and nice clothes and is married to a good man and recently had a baby. Like all Liberians who saw what our country is capable of, she welcomes her success but wears it with caution.

Then there was my schoolmate. Now he is a student at the university. He was in the lecture hall one day when he recognized the new student in his department as the rebel who ordered his hand to be severed! My friend is a good student. This ex-combatant was having difficulties. When the school master asked my friend to tutor the former fighter, he stared at the school master in disbelief. How much were Liberians supposed to take? "I realized this fighter did not even recognize me," my friend said, looking at the place where his hand used to be. "But I hate this man with a passion."

To some of my friends, my work with the boys must have seemed like a betrayal. These fighters had savaged our country, killed their friends and families. Why was I *choosing* them? They didn't deserve it! They didn't understand when I said I wasn't choosing sides but trying to work for unity and peace.

Back at the center, Ebenezer's speech had raised everybody's spirits. Ever since the launch, more boys had approached me with ideas on how we could help. We put some of their ideas into action. On the

International Day of Peace, my boys joined the UN Special Representative for Liberia and carried out a citywide clean-up campaign. They continued to tell their stories on *Straight from the Heart*. Many were scared but considered it their patriotic duty. I was proud of them and wanted to showcase their commitment to reconciliation.

Brainstorming with my boys one afternoon, we hit upon a plan. We would organize a parade to celebrate the start of the TRC's statement-taking process. The boys would make signs. I would silk-screen T-shirts. It would be a powerful way to make an important statement: that if you are the kind of person who wants someone to forgive you, you must go the extra mile.

"We are doing something big," I told my friends and pointed to the silk-screened T-shirts, drying on a clothesline. "Something important!"

"What is more important than your safety, Agnes?" they cried. "You are getting in too deep!"

I ignored them. "Wait and see . . ." I said.

On the appointed day, I chartered buses to transport the boys to one of three designated meeting spots: Paynesville, Central Monrovia, and Bushrod Island. Our plan was to walk from three points of a triangle, meet, and cross the bridge at Broad Street. From there, we would march as a group to TRC headquarters.

That morning, hundreds of ex-combatants took to the streets of Monrovia in the name of truth and reconciliation. In place of shouting, my boys sang. Instead of the costumes they once wore, the boys had on baseball caps and T-shirts emblazoned with TRC and STRAIGHT FROM THE HEART in red and black letters. We waved banners. The boys held signs they had made with Magic Markers and construction paper: THE TRC IS HERE TO HERE TO HEAL WOUNDS! their posters read. And, ONLY UNITY CAN BUILD ANY NATION, YES!

People left their houses to watch. They peered out of shop windows. They could not believe what they were seeing: Young men who marched for rebel warlords marching for peace? Some of them joined us. I called my friends on my cell phone. "Ah! We are almost at your place. You hear us? Come out and march!" Busy as I was, I didn't even notice the fancy young man in the shiny shirt and shoes, carrying a slim book in his hand.

"Who is in charge of this parade?" he approached our group and asked one of my boys.

Later, this boy told me he had eyeballed the newcomer suspiciously. "Our ma," he finally said and pointed at me.

"Your ma?" The boy in the fancy shirt raised an eyebrow.

"Sister Agnes." The boy pointed me out in the swarm of people.

I was waving, working the crowd. When the fancy young man tapped me on the shoulder, I hardly paid him any mind. He said he wanted to talk. Great, I said. Let's talk. "Now?" he asked. "No, not right now. We are marching!" Fine, the young man said. He would march with us. And he did. In his fancy shirt and shoes, the boy marched beside my boys in their TRC T-shirts and busted sandals. I forgot all about him in the chaos.

When we arrived at the TRC headquarters, Jerome and several of the TRC Commissioners greeted us. They praised the boys from Straight from the Heart Center and applauded their commitment to reconciliation. "You are not disparate elements of rebel factions anymore," they said. "You are a unified force for national peace." People gave speeches. The press snapped photos. Some of my boys got their pictures in the newspaper.

I'd completely forgotten about the fancy boy until he reappeared later that afternoon. We were stashing the signs and stacking T-shirts, laughing and chatting about the day's events. All of a sudden, I felt a tap, feather-light. I turned to find the fancy boy from earlier. He was short and slim with skin as smooth as satin, not a scar on his face. Whereas my boys and I were soaked in sweat, he looked cucumber cool as he had that morning. He was still holding the book in his hand.

"Hello again," I said, wiping my brow. "What can I do for you?"

The boy studied me for a moment. His eyes were filmy. He looked to his left and right before leaning in close and cupping a hand to his mouth. His breath was soft and humid as he whispered in my ear.

"I want to be a part of these boys . . ." he said. "But these boys don't know anything."

I cocked my head.

"They are *small* boys," he continued in a strange, hypnotic whisper. "They tell you things everybody knows." He glanced around. "I can tell you things *nobody* knows."

Is this boy high? I wondered. He didn't seem to blink. His voice maintained the same register. I looked to see who was left at the center. Confirming that a few boys were, I turned back to the stranger.

"Things like what?" I challenged him. He curled his lip and smiled. "Do you know Alhaji Kromah? Prince Johnson?" he murmured. "I know where the powerful people go."

At this point, he had my attention. He was calling out warlords' names. I hadn't met any boys with that kind of access. I wasn't sure I wanted to. Still, it was impressive, and I said so.

The boy nodded. But I didn't want to seem overeager in case he was bluffing.

"Maybe you can tell your story on my radio program in a few weeks," I suggested casually.

But no, that boy was determined to tell me then, now, *yesterday!*

He said he could bring me boys who fought the war. Those who *really* knew things, *really* fought. His eyes darted from side to side. He spoke so urgently that I thought, *hm*, this boy has something he needs to tell me, and we can't do it here. "Just a minute," I said, and turned to one of the boys who was helping me clean up. In my native language,

Mende, I said, "This flashy boy says he knows everything. Should give him a chance?"

But the fancy boy didn't wait for an answer. He laughed. And then in Mende, he replied that it was true. He *did* know everything. And I was surprised, because I didn't think he could speak Mende. He didn't look like he came from a place where people did. The boy smiled as if he had won a contest of some kind. Then his face darkened.

"I am afraid . . ." he whispered.

I asked him why. And oh, he said. He was afraid because he had such stories, such secrets. If he told me these secrets—

"You don't have to," I replied matter-of-factly.

"I must!!!" he cried.

Suddenly, I didn't want to be around this boy anymore. He was smooth one moment, rattled the next. He made my skin crawl. Besides, if he was a fighter, where did he get those fancy clothes? And what was that book he carried? The boy leaned in. His lightless eyes bored holes through my own. "I talk to rebel leaders who can organize a rebel army with a phone call." He snapped his fingers, eyes gleaming. "Like that!"

Despite the hot afternoon, I shivered.

Still, it was the end of a long day. I was exhausted and implied that I would be going home soon. The strange boy nodded like that sounded fine to him. But I didn't want this boy to know where I lived.

"If you give me your contact information, I would be happy to talk to you tomorrow, Mr. . . . ?"

The boy introduced himself as Mohamed Ismael Sheriff: senior commander of Charles Taylor's anti-terrorist unit.

I blinked. I processed the magnitude of what he had said. In the calmest voice I could manage, I asked the boy to wait a minute. I went and got a piece of paper and wrote down the address of UNMIL Radio. When I handed it to him, he smirked. "I know the place," he said as if he had been there several times, watching what went on, the people who entered . . .

He took the slip of paper and turned to leave. I watched him slink toward the door, still holding the mysterious book in his hand. Even staring at his back, I felt that he could see me watching him. He moved like smoke. Aside from a slight limp, he seemed to glide. Right before he left, the boy turned and saluted. Something told me I had just met my new chief informant.

18

---◆—

HONORABLE CHAIRMAN of the Truth and Reconciliation, Commissioners, all NGO's, instructors, students, distinguished guests, ladies and gentlemen ...

When of the particular attentions, which I have never ceased manifesting to this nation, and in my profound belief for crystal clear transparency in the Truth and Reconciliation Commission for Democracy and the Democratic process ... I am again saying the truth, nothing but the truth, so help me God, with no fear or favor ...

In Greece, they say "Laboramus Expentantis" (labor and expect). My brothers and sisters who were in the arms struggle, fasten your seatbelts for we were loaded on an ungrateful vessel, now we have landed in a regret wharf. Let's also put on the coat of seriousness before the dry winds go away. Or else we have nobody to blame but ourselves.

Friends, we were left out like the ashes from the coal of a fire, more pain no gain, no day, no pensions, no encouragement, it was all a fruitless endeavor, the leaders keep enjoying the fruit ...

Again and again I say sorry to the people of this nation, let them forgive me and forget about all that I did to whosoever. I ask for pardon, and I continue to be under the umbrella of Truth and Reconciliation Commission. For I was not conscious, for I was just twelve years old ...

—Testimony of ex-general of the National Patriotic
Front of Liberia (NPFL)
Mohamed I. Sheriff

MAYBE YOU HAVE experienced something similar: Your life is bumping along just fine, when suddenly someone sidles up to you at a parade. They are magnetizing. Really, they are meant to derail you. You get taken in. But by the time you realize it, you are on your knees. This is how I would describe my relationship with Mohamed.

Up to this day, I still don't know everything Mohamed did. Or how he came to learn those elaborate Greek phrases. Or what, if anything, is true. I suspect that most things are, and what he told the TRC is a matter of public record. But in Liberia, there are thousands of stories. Every story has a thousand competing angles. Depending on where you lived or stood, or what someone told you at the time, or what you thought you had to believe, you might think A when really it was B or C, and just the opposite was true. It's a confusing introduction to Mohamed, but the best I can provide.

What is certain is that Mohamed had a story unlike any I had heard before. He had fought for fourteen years, the entire duration of the war, and in many different capacities. He fought for the Liberians United for Defense Force (LUDF), for the rebel group ULIMO (the United Liberation Movement of Liberia for Democracy), and for the rebel faction ULIMO-K. Then he crossed over to Liberia and fought for Charles Taylor. Back and forth, back and forth, and in many major battles. When I finally got him to sit down and record everything, he told me he was just twelve years old when he was abducted from a Sierra Leonean refugee camp.

All throughout 1990, Liberians fled to camps in Sierra Leone and Guinea to escape the rising hostilities in our country. There, veterans of the Armed Forces of Liberia and other refugees formed the LUDF, led by a former defense minister named General Karpeh. As they strategized on how best to infiltrate Liberia and recover control, the government of Sierra Leone was losing power to dissidents, including some schooled at Moammar Qaddafi's secret training facility in Libya. Desperate to recover power, as I understand it, the Sierra Leonean government enlisted these exiled Liberians. Apparently, there weren't enough men to fight the rebels and recoup control of Liberia. This is when someone got the bright idea of going hut to hut and recruiting child soldiers.

"They took us at night. They took us at gunpoint," Mohamed said. His parents protested, but what could they do? The rebels needed their children "temporarily," so that everyone could return to Liberia and live in peace forever. Mohamed never saw his parents again. The rebels took him to a training base near Freetown. He lived at the base for a week and was moved to another. By day, Mohamed learned to salute, march, crawl, and handle heavy weapons. At night, he dreamt about his family living without food under a flimsy shelter. Soon, the rebels gave Mohamed something to help him forget. They taught the boys how to take grass and mix it with opium to make cigarettes. "They used to tell us if you don't do it, we will hurt you," Mohamed said. "So we did."

With just three weeks of training, Mohamed was put on the frontline. He fought for the LUDF for two years. In 1992, the rebels merged with other rebel groups to form one of the most powerful factions in all of West Africa: the United Liberation Movement of Liberia for Democracy, or ULIMO. When ULIMO split into rival factions ULIMO-J and ULIMO-K, Mohamed sided with ULIMO-K and worked closely with its leader, Alhaji Kromah. He was promoted to general. Two years later, Charles Taylor purchased Mohamed and three other generals for four thousand dollars apiece. "Diamond money," Mohamed said.

He joined the NPFL's Small Boys Unit. Mohamed fought with and for warlords and soldiers with strange, brutal nicknames they were expected to "live up to." General "Pepper and Salt" was rumored to eat the hearts of his victims. There was no mercy from "Black Jesus": If he appeared before you, you were dead. General "24 Hour" didn't waste time. He would burn, loot, and kill everything in a day. There was General "Blood," who cut his victims' throats.

The list went on. General "Kill Man, No Blood" knew where to cut so there was no blood. ("The Achilles tendon, for instance," Mohamed clarified.) Wherever you went, you could not protect yourself from "Mosquito" or his enemy, "Mosquito Spray." Mohamed told me about a woman named Alice whose nickname was "No Mistake." You slip up? "She didn't think twice. She'd kill you on the spot."

Child soldiers had nicknames, too. Those who were "small, but did big, big things," according to Mohamed. "Frisky Rebel" was a nine-year-old NPFL fighter who caused a lot of damage. "TuPac" was only seven years old but rough like the rap singer. Mohamed chose TuPac to be his bodyguard. "I never gave the little guys weapons, just ammunition," he said. As a child soldier, Mohamed had worn a mask and sunglasses and smeared bleach on his face to camouflage his features. When he joined the NPFL, Mohamed instructed the boys under his control to do the same. "That way," he said, "nobody knows if you are John or Paul."

Mohamed described the operations he had been a part of: prominent towns and villages the rebel groups he fought for had attacked, "killing, burning, raping, and looting." Mohamed said he had carried out a bank heist for Charles Taylor in Foya town. He had led a group of soldiers who ambushed the town at night, broke into the bank, and made off with safes of money. Hovering helicopters flew the spoils to Taylor's presidential mansion. Mohamed said he had led charges and killed many people for Taylor. "It wasn't difficult." Mohamed shrugged.

"He made us feel powerful." According to Mohamed, Taylor exhorted his men to battle by bragging about the powerful people who were behind him: the White House, the FBI, the CIA, the KGB, Jimmy Carter, and Jesse Jackson. "You don't say no to a man like that," Mohamed said. "We were willing to stand up."

Taylor instilled a powerful fear of betrayal in his soldiers, and Mohamed witnessed the consequences of treachery first-hand. When Taylor won the presidency, he was told that one of his commanders, a Sierra Leonean rebel soldier, had conspired against him. Taylor sent an order to remove the commander and his forces from the battlefield. Oblivious, the commander left the frontline with his wife, mother, and young children. He was invited to have a meal with one of Taylor's generals and Liberia's then vice-president. After the meal, the general ordered the Sierra Leonean commander and his men to march into the forest. There, the commander and his men were tied to trees. Taylor's soldiers executed the commander, disemboweled him, and dumped his entrails into a bucket. The grisly remains were messengered back to Taylor, so he could see them with his own eyes and "stay in power for a long time."

Seven hundred men loyal to that commander were executed that same day: a blood sacrifice to teach Taylor's men a lesson. "Taylor didn't trust anyone." Mohamed shook his head. "It was wicked, but I was terrified and stayed quiet."

"Were you ever hurt?" I asked Mohamed. He told me he was shot once in the leg, but not badly. And that he lost the tip of his finger to a rocket-propelled grenade. "That's it?" I said. "That's it." He nodded. I asked him how it was possible he hadn't sustained any more injuries. "I survived, Auntie Agnes." Mohamed smiled mysteriously. "I just did."

Mohamed added that there was this native medicine, juju: "When you use it, no bullet hit you." He had joined secret societies that encouraged soldiers to cut their arms with razor blades and abstain from having sex. The leaders of these secret societies swore the measures would keep the soldiers alive. Mohamed showed me the razor scars on his arm as proof. "They said you could be hit by a bullet fourteen times and not die." Mohamed counted off the notches. "So I was always counting."

What shocked me most was the way Mohamed had maneuvered from one fighting unit to another. Warlords had boys they trusted, "right-hand men," if you will, and I guessed that Mohamed had functioned as the right-hand man for several powerful warlords. Once I asked Mohamed if he was a spy, but he shook his head no and replied that he was a "strategist," who knew what he wanted: "I'm intelligent. I didn't make mistakes. That was my defense."

The eeriest thing about Mohamed was how exact he was. He told me how he was recruited, escaped, and how he had killed the same way each time. Up to this day, I ask Mohamed about the war and he tells me the same stories, never adding or subtracting a detail. Sometimes I would stop and ask him, are you sure? And he would sigh and say, "Yes, I'm sure. I was *there*." I believe Mohamed has a photographic memory. He knew so many details about the war and was friends with dangerous people. I took his story to the TRC.

"I have a story you need to hear," I told Jerome. "Listen to this story."

Jerome was thunderstruck. He encouraged me to bring Mohamed in to give a statement. I said I'd try. I was having a difficult time convincing ex-combatants to give their testimonies, but agreed that Mohamed's was important and might clear up several mysteries the TRC was trying to solve.

Mohamed was the first perpetrator to give his testimony to the TRC. He spoke at the inauguration of the TRC's statement-taking process. The TRC had decided to showcase two Liberians' statements as an example of how the process worked, one from a victim, the other from a perpetrator. Mohamed gave the full details of the crimes he had committed and named rebel recruiters and commanders who had ordered executions during the war. Then the victim gave his perspective: a deeply moving account of what it was like to be terrorized all those years. Afterward, Mohamed apologized to the victim and embraced him in front of media flashbulbs. Some people in the audience clapped. Others cried. Still others shook their heads angrily in the back of the room. There were mixed feelings about who this young man was, why he was being given a microphone, and whether it was genuine or all for show. I walked around, getting opinions from these Liberians and other audience members who came from neighboring African countries.

Many people questioned the TRC process after Mohamed's appearance, and Jerome and the other Commissioners spent a good deal of time clarifying the mission in the weeks that followed. Eventually, Mohamed appeared at the TRC public hearings, confirming his earlier narrative under oath, and provided additional details. It took two whole days to record his story. When he was finished, Mohamed signed a document validating that everything he had told the TRC was true.

Jerome and I agreed that I shouldn't air Mohamed's story on *Straight from the Heart*. It was too sensitive. Instead, with Jerome's consent, I started taking Mohamed around with me. We drove to different places Mohamed had told me about and he would say, "Oh this happened here. That happened there. This is where Charles Taylor stood. This is who he killed."

Mohamed showed me all the houses where he had lived during the war. He boasted about the money and rich things he had owned. It was obvious Mohamed had lived the high life, and that his status still meant a lot to him. At the end of the day, I would drive him home to the ghetto where he slept on a bare floor. Always a different address. When I asked Mohamed why he moved around so much, he told me people were out to get him. "Oh . . . who?" I asked. And, oh, Auntie Agnes, gunmen had broken into the first house, he said. He had been targeted since he spoke at the TRC event. Some men told him to keep his mouth shut about the war, "or else." So he had to find another place. But the same thing happened again. All the warlords were hunting him now. One time, a gunman burst through his window and Mohamed had to escape through the ceiling.

"You are a cat with nine lives." I shook my head. I wondered where Mohamed got his money and fancy clothes. I wondered how he took care of himself, and whether these stories were real. I wondered how Mohamed had not been captured.

"It's hard to get me." He smiled. "I always escape."

In time, I came to feel uncomfortable around Mohamed. He made me feel that I was the reason he was being hunted, and that I owed him something because of it.

"Are you afraid, Mohamed?" I asked. "Regretting what you have told me?"

But Mohamed just smiled cryptically, or, when we were driving, he would lean over and say, "Don't worry, I am with you." And I would look at this boy and remember all the terrible things he had told me and think, how is *that* supposed to make me feel better?

One day, a powerful warlord was being flown to The Hague to testify against Charles Taylor. Mohamed was restless and kept repeating that he needed to see this warlord before he left. "That warlord is a dangerous person," I said. Mohamed laughed loudly. "Why are you with me, then?" he crowed. "Don't you know that I am a dangerous person too?"

I tell you, chills went down my spine.

Over time, I began to fear Mohamed. What was he looking for? Why had he come to the center? Not for friendship, surely. With his high-and-mighty ways, he didn't get along with the other boys. Not for meetings or meals, either. Mohamed was rail-thin and hardly ever ate. I began to wonder if he wasn't manipulating me. I had been drawn in by his charm, his information, and his cool and easy manner. Now I wondered if I had become Mohamed's tool, or even Mohamed's target.

He is too intelligent for my comfort, I decided. Mohamed spoke of battles without a trace of remorse. So different from the other boys, who described even the smallest detail with the greatest difficulty. Mohamed gave me information but talked far beyond it, telling me stories that went in and out of my head, folding over on themselves like a maze. And he was shorter than most of my boys, which somehow made the tales of his exploits even more sinister. That, and I did not like how he treated them. Mohamed interrupted the members of Straight from the Heart Center when they spoke, and he behaved as if he was better than them. Anytime I would be talking to someone, Mohamed would interject and announce that he had something to say. I felt the need to rein him in, but how? I didn't want to lose him. His stories were helping the TRC.

Then one day, Mohamed told me about a mass grave where Charles Taylor had buried many bodies. Did I want to see it? I hesitated. Hold on, I said, and telephoned Jerome. Jerome confirmed that there was a mass grave in the place Mohamed said. So I went to Mohamed and nodded, let's go there. We drove to this remote place deep in the woods. Mohamed led the way, directing me to turn left at this bush, and right at that tree. He read the bushes as if they were road signs.

When we arrived, I wondered if Mohamed had made an error. There was nothing to distinguish the place from the rest of the forest. Then he pointed to a large, blank patch of grass. "There," he said. "That's where the bodies are." We got out of the car. I'd brought my camera with me and started taking pictures. It was quiet in the woods.

Not a hunter or a village person in sight. No birds chirping. No animals rustling in the undergrowth. All you could hear was the sound of my clicking camera and Mohamed's footsteps.

I experienced a strange sensation standing in that place of death. I was walking around the perimeter of the grave, and Mohamed was behind me. I heard his light footsteps, his low, off-putting laugh. I couldn't see him, just heard his voice curling into my ear, describing the horrors that had occurred there. As Mohamed quickened his pace, I started sweating. Suddenly I wished I had brought someone else along. I didn't think Mohamed intended me any harm, but I was scared. He had cozied up to many people, many of whom were no longer alive, and now Mohamed had cozied up to me. I panicked.

Mohamed noticed. "You are sweating . . ." he murmured.

"Let's go," I said.

Mohamed shrugged. "My eyes are behind you."

We got in the car and left the woods. When we got to the main road, I breathed a sigh of relief. I followed the signs for Monrovia and stayed so close to the driver in front of me, our cars were practically touching. Mohamed made small talk, but I didn't feel like chatting. I decided I'd gotten all I needed from him.

The feeling I'd had at the mass grave didn't pass. Mohamed knew where I lived and was coming to my house every day. He would wait in the bush where he could see me coming and going. When I left for work or came home, Mohamed would appear as if he were "just passing through" and ask for money. He denied that he had been spying on me.

"Then how do you know when I am coming home?" I challenged. "And what if I hadn't? Would you have waited?"

Mohamed started playing games with my head. He told me he had taken a young girl as a wife during the war. Mohamed had taken one look at her lovely, terrified, fourteen-year-old face and rescued her before NPFL rebels razed her village. "It was love at first sight." He smiled. And I nodded uncomfortably, because I did not see much to smile about.

Now the girl was pregnant. Mohamed wanted her to have the baby in a hospital, but he couldn't afford the bill. Could I help? I gave him some money. A few days later, Mohamed returned. His wife needed money to be discharged. Then it was clothes and baby food. It went on like this for some time. His wife needed this, she needed that. I was doing my best to help Mohamed's family, but every time I asked to meet his wife and baby, he had a convenient story as to why it was impossible. "My wife is tired," he would say. Or, "She has just left for Guinea." Or, "She is sick." I wonder if she existed at all.

I don't know why Mohamed opened up to me. One day, I asked him. "I trust only you." He shrugged. "Nobody else." Perhaps it was because I was not afraid of him, initially. Or maybe I reminded Mohamed of his mother. I think this was true of many of the boys at Straight from the Heart center. In some ways, I felt I was making up for being such a poor mother to my own children by being one to them. I visited Reginald, Diamond, and Ogechi as often as I could. The nature of my work, Jeff, my mother, and I all agreed, was not exactly conducive to raising them.

Only Mohamed was different from the other boys. It was difficult to feel like a mother to him. He was a fancy son among poor ones, and with his cocky ways, he soon made enemies. He would befriend a boy and then turn on him. Then one day, Mohamed turned on me.

It happened over a cell phone. Mohamed's stories were vital, and Jerome and I agreed we should be able to get in touch with Mohamed at any time. I suggested we buy him a phone, so that he could contact perpetrators who were giving their testimonies and encourage others to share their stories. Mohamed was also receiving death threats, and we saw the cell phone as a necessary security measure.

Jerome gave me a hundred dollars to buy Mohamed a cell phone. No sooner had I done so than Mohamed started bragging that the TRC paid him for his stories. This was a lie and patently against the TRC's mandate. When that story didn't take, Mohamed said the TRC had given him money, but that I had kept it. There was an outcry among my boys, and I was angry with Mohamed.

Thank God I kept the receipts. I brought them to Mohamed. He was annoyed, but it calmed the boys down. Then I went to Jerome.

"Now do you see why I told you to be careful?" Jerome sighed, relieved but highly exasperated.

It caused problems in my work. People started accusing me of buying stories to implicate people. Kojo and Patrick said I should be more cautious. UNMIL's reputation was at stake, not to mention my own. It didn't seem fair, but what could I do? I was frustrated and embarrassed.

How do I explain Mohamed? I believe that he cared for me, but he cared more about himself in the end. Mohamed used me to get what he wanted. He knew I wanted stories, and when it came to those, he never ran out. Eventually, I forgave him. We mended bridges. These days, I see Mohamed from time to time, when he wants to be found. He doesn't work, just does small things to make money, including some that make me squirm. Selling pints of blood to the local hospital, for instance.

I have dealt with a lot of perpetrators, and when they tell me their stories, I see the remorse in their eyes. Not Mohamed, though. He was different from the beginning. He didn't seem to feel guilty. He told me all these things I have told you with a straight face. Mohamed has nightmares (he calls them "funny dreams"), but that's it. He must be traumatized, but I do not see it.

When I ask Mohamed how he copes, he just shrugs or says something useless like, "Because I am a man."

Everybody has a way of coping, but I want to know Mohamed's. I want to learn his technique, so I can help the boys who lost their minds in the war and can no longer function. Otherwise, how will we get on? So there it is. I believe Mohamed is a person who can help other child soldiers. This, more than all of the tales he shared with me, is the reason I keep him close. When I need him, I know he will appear.

19

I WAS WATCHING a neighbor's baby when a woman named Betty said she would go for water so we could cook. While she was gone, I tried to build a fire in the hallway. Suddenly, my arm was hit. I saw smoke all around. I saw particles sticking out of my legs. I was leaking on one side!

I ran to the first person I saw, but he drove me away. "Go back! I can't do anything for you!" So I ran crying with my neighbor's baby. Finally, somebody took me to the hospital. There were iron particles in my head, but they stashed me on the floor while the doctor made his rounds. I wasn't even breathing. At last I sneezed. That's how they knew I was alive.

When I opened my eyes, they had sewn up my mouth. They had taken the iron particles out of my body. Then a man came and said I had lost my right arm and one of my kidneys. They were looking for my family, but I had nobody to sign for the procedure, just myself. So a nurse picked up my remaining hand, put my fingers in the ink, and I signed. Then they did the operation. Up to this day, I still have particles in my hand and some in my stomach. Two places here and there. The particles are still there.

—Mercy

SOMETIMES I get overwhelmed. The life I have chosen is too much. I start getting headaches, digestive problems. My body shuts down. Back then, not long after the incident with Mohamed, I started to feel quite ill. I went to see Dr. Harris for my annual physical exam. He fastened a Velcro cuff around my arm, turned the knob, listened to my pulse, and forbade me from going back to work.

"Your pulse is through the roof!" he declared.

I was admitted to Monrovia Catholic Hospital for high blood pressure and high cholesterol. They put me in a light green room not far from the one where I was born. Kojo gave me three hundred dollars to cover my expenses and told me not to worry, Patience would host the show that week. He added that if he saw me in the office he would kill me.

"Understood," I said.

I packed a small bag, just some clothes and my radio, and smiled wistfully as Patience explained my absence to listeners:

"Agnes is not here for reasons beyond her control."

I didn't tell my boys I was in the hospital. I didn't want them to worry. When I failed to show up at the center that Sunday for our meeting, they were concerned. Ebenezer tried to call me, but I had turned off my cell phone. So then he and about fifty other boys decided to find me.

Kojo lived in a house not far from Straight from the Heart Center. He often complained about the racket we made. I would try and quiet the boys down, but it rarely worked. That particular Sunday, the boys surrounded Kojo's house and started banging on his door and shouting at the top of their lungs: "We know you are in there, Mr. Mensah! Open the door!"

Kojo, interrupted on his single day of rest, rushed outside scowling and covering his ears, trying to quiet them down. "Why are you people shouting?" he cried. "Don't you know your mother is sick in the hospital?"

And oh, they were surprised! Our mommy in the hospital? My boys couldn't believe it. They wanted to visit me straightaway. Ebenezer and the others started talking about how they would hitch a ride there. UNMIL has strict rules about who can ride in UN vehicles. But Kojo must have been moved, because despite the rules, he said he would take them personally. He piled several boys into his car. The rest walked. The group in Kojo's vehicle arrived just before visiting hours ended. Their sandals squeaking on the hospital floor, the boys raced upstairs to the front desk, and when they couldn't find me, started going room to room. They peeked into patients' rooms shouting, "Mommy! Mommy! Your boys are here! Where are you?"

The hospital staff didn't know what to do. A woman who cleaned the floors and lived near the ghetto recognized the boys as ex-combatants. She told the nurses and doctor on call that the hospital might be under attack.

"Where is our mommy?" my boys demanded. "Where is Sister Agnes?"

Terrified, one of the nurses pointed down the hallway toward my room. "She is in there! She is inside that one!"

There was a sign on my door that said DO NOT DISTURB. The boys didn't see it, or didn't care. They burst into my room like fireworks. I was drifting in and out of sleep when the door opened and a dozen beaming faces flooded the door. I was taking heavy drugs to lower my blood pressure, and when I saw Ebenezer's and Fofee's faces, I thought they were an apparition caused by the medication I was taking.

"Old Ma!" they rushed in, shouting. "You're sick? What's the matter? You didn't tell us, oh! Why?"

The boys came to the head of my bed. More boys crammed in around the sides. Some sat on the bed or hung over the railing. Stunned, I moved my legs so more could squeeze in.

"There's room on the floor, oh!" somebody shouted.

Then the second group arrived. Boys were pouring in from all directions. More stood in the hallway, craning their necks to see inside. They smiled and waved. They leaned against the door, inspecting the metal clipboard that was hanging there. I was dazed. I didn't know how this thing had happened. Then, who should I see standing among them, smiling devilishly and smoking a cigarette in violation of the hospital rules, but Kojo. He flashed a huge grin. Everybody was talking at once.

"Oh, Ma, we're sorry we wore you out!" "Why didn't you tell us you were here?" "We're sorry for fighting and making noise!" they shouted. They were like children apologizing for their misbehavior. I laughed and assured them it wasn't their fault, I just needed a rest.

A nurse came in to check on me. She was holding a tray and looked extremely uncomfortable as she handed it to me.

"Who are these people?" she whimpered.

The boys didn't wait for me to answer. "Oh! That's our Ma! That's our Ma! That's Old Ma, yeah!" They slapped their knees and laughed.

"These are my kids." I beamed.

Rumors began circulating around the hospital. Those are the boys who live in the ghetto—the former fighters! The wicked ones! But our patient says they are *safe*! The boys stayed long past visiting hours and promised to return the next day.

My boys visited me every day I was in the hospital. They arrived individually, in pairs, and in groups of three. Edwin and Jefferson. Napoleon and Moses. David, Honest, and Varlee. Jimmy and Dwe. Mohamed came every day. Ebenezer came every morning and afternoon.

"Can't you come together?" I begged. I wasn't sleeping. My room was packed at all hours of the day and night. "Maybe you really do want to kill me!" I joked. Gravely serious, they replied that they loved me, and that I was not to work again.

"Oh, and how will that work?" I teased.

The boys brought me little gifts: orange juice and bananas, peanuts and small candies, fried plantains. They held them out wrapped in cones of newspaper, so proud and pleased at the smile it brought to my face. I don't know where they got the money, and I didn't dare tell them most of the treats weren't on my diet. I ate most of the fruit. When the nurse brought my tray in, I gave the boys money to go buy food for themselves. Then I distributed the candy among the nurses and hospital cleaners.

On Monday, Dr. Harris came to check on me.

"You had visitors," he said as he consulted his clipboard. "I said no visitors!"

I sighed.

"You need rest." He frowned. "You must take a break from these people. These people are difficult to work with!"

"Sometimes," I admitted. "But this is the work I do."

I stayed in the hospital for two more days. I got no rest and barely adhered to the nutrition regimen. Nevertheless, when Dr. Harris discharged me, he said that I showed remarkable improvement. He couldn't explain it. Maybe for some people, rebels really were the cure.

Ebenezer continued to visit me at home. He reported that things were under control at the center. Everyone was eating. Boys were going to school. They were trying to keep the noise down for Mr. Mensah. I pictured the doctors and nurses at the hospital making their peaceful rounds. It must seem very quiet without them. Other people's families visited, but they didn't bring one hundred sons! When my father called to ask how I was feeling, I told him about the boys' visits and he was amused. No, he agreed, the hospital had probably never experienced anything quite like it.

When I finally returned to the center, I thanked the boys for coming to visit. They had really looked out for me. I told them I felt proud and grateful to have them in my life. These boys, who had sent so many Liberians to their deaths . . . inflicted wounds, physical and emotional, that no hospital could cure . . . they had cared for me.

"You boys have really changed," I said, looking from one to the next. "You will be running this center yourself soon."

They shook their heads. They didn't believe me. But I knew it was true and smiled. My boys, who made up in kindness what they lacked in decorum, were making progress.

20

WELL, I'M JOSHUA BLAHYI. I'm the one that is referred to as "General Butt Naked." By the grace of God, I went to the TRC, inspired by my faith in 1996. I thought there were a lot of hidden things in the Liberian war that needed to come to light.

With the hope that I would expose those things so that other young Liberians would not be victims, I started going around speaking the truth. I went from church to church, giving the testimony. Moreover, my faith, Christianity, that I got converted to, told me if I spoke the truth, the truth would set me free.

When the TRC came, I saw it as an opportunity to free my spirit. I was not actually thinking about amnesty, because I thought it would be impossible. I wanted to free my spirit and free my conscience. But then, things started becoming political. Witch-hunting, people threatening us. So we started to withdraw.

Then I came across Agnes. She was a counselor to the perpetrators. She started coming around. She broke into me very strangely. I said, "This woman know me?" I always thought everybody would be afraid of me because of my past. When I met Agnes, I wondered if this woman was really a Liberian, or she really knew what she was doing? But she was very serious.

"**D**ARKNESS CANNOT put out darkness," I used to tell my boys. "Only light can do that." The idea that one rebel army was glorious or justified in doing what it did must be wiped from the slate. No side was glorious. Not when so many Liberian men, women, and children lie under the earth or walk upon it with crutches.

For many of my boys it took a long time for these lessons to sink in. In the same way that some Liberian victims did not want to forgive perpetrators or be reconciled, many of my boys were unwilling to repent because doing so would destroy all they had stood for. It isn't easy to tell someone, "You have been used. You fought a war of lies—for nothing!" You can't. Not all at once. You have to break down a belief system in stages, while keeping a person's hope intact. Deliver the shocking truth, but prevent them from spiraling into an even darker place. Find a way to say, "You killed, but this is not the end of you."

Then one day, it occurred to me. Warlords. The men who forced these boys into battle. The leaders who created cults of children and committed unimaginable crimes in the name of democracy and peace. Maybe bringing them on *Straight from the Heart* would show my boys and other Liberians what they really were: men who stole girls' and boys' childhoods for power and money.

But Agnes, you are probably thinking, weren't these warlords in jail? Shut away somewhere? You will be surprised when I tell you that many of these men were and are still walking free. Warlords are powerful. Liberia's justice system is practically nonexistent. To many Liberians, they are still redeemers, freedom fighters, and celebrities who saved Liberia from Samuel Doe and Charles Taylor. When the war ended, political control wasn't wrested away from them but *given* to them to prevent a mutiny. Sitting in Liberia's House of Representatives today are Charles Taylor's ex-wife (who is not a warlord but was married to one), Jewel Howard Taylor, and Prince Johnson, Charles Taylor's notorious field commander. Is this any way to run a country? People call it "the price of peace," but I don't know. I realize there is no such thing as a clean slate in a country like Liberia, but I worry we are setting ourselves up for future calamities.

In time, several warlords would testify before the TRC. They hadn't at the time of my program, and it started to bother me. I wanted to hear them talk and try to explain their actions. So I decided to do what Liberia wasn't and bring them into the conversation. I didn't know if it would work.

I went to Kojo. He was skeptical. "Just because no one has tried to talk to warlords on the radio doesn't make it wrong," I said, which really amused him. Is this the same Agnes I practically had to push out the door not long ago? I reminded him about the radio program I'd helped with in Nigeria and how it had changed people's minds. If we aired warlords' stories, people might see them for what they really were: politicians, convicts, cowards. People might even see child soldiers, their fighters, in a new light. It could be a breakthrough. Maybe people would finally understand the diabolical influences my boys had acted under. They had committed senseless violence, because they were young, drugged, traumatized, and brainwashed into believing killing was the right thing to do.

"And how do you propose to do this?" Kojo was incredulous.

That night, I went home and drew up a list of warlords: names Mohamed and the others had told me about. Then I created lineups, mixing and matching enemies from different factions. I got goose bumps thinking what it would mean if we could actually do this: bring warlords who had fought on the battlefield into UNMIL Radio for face-to-face talks.

I brought my list to Kojo. He whistled and made a low, rumbling sound in his throat, which indicated that he was one-half impressed and one-half skeptical. I held my breath. He took a pen and drew a thick red line through the name at the top of the list and handed it back to me.

"Prince Johnson?" I frowned, looking at the deleted name. "Why?" Kojo shook his head.

"But he is a public figure!" I protested.

"The UN has placed an embargo on any radio interviews with that man," Kojo announced. "End of discussion."

Senator Prince Johnson was undoubtedly a cruel man. In a video you can still buy in some Liberian stalls, he takes a sip of beer while one of his soldiers severs former President Samuel Doe's ear. Some people say Prince Johnson forced Doe to eat his severed ear before killing him. During the war, he led the rebel group, the Independent National Patriotic Front of Liberia. In time, the TRC report would name him as one of the most notorious perpetrators and recommend that he be prosecuted for war crimes. Was UNMIL worried Prince Johnson would hijack media airtime and use it for his own ends? I wondered. Everyone else was fair game, Kojo said. I skipped to number two on my list: an interview with Roland Duo and Kabineh Janneh.

As far as warlord chemistry went, you couldn't do better. Both came from Nimba County, but that was about all they had in common. Roland and Kabineh were fierce adversaries during the war. As director of Charles Taylor's Small Boys Unit, Roland had managed thousands of boys and girls whom Taylor kidnapped and turned into soldiers and concubines. Now Roland was launching his political career and pursuing a university degree.

Councilor Kabineh was a former spokesperson and strategist for LURD, one of the many rebel groups that originated during "World War II" to oust Charles Taylor. Just like the NPFL, LURD committed widespread atrocities and conscripted many child soldiers. Today, Kabineh is a Supreme Court justice.

"And what do you propose to ask these men, Umunna?" Kojo said. It was a serious thing I was proposing, and Kojo needed a good reason to convince his UN bosses to get on board.

"I will ask them about the war," I said. "Did it bring prosperity or happiness? Create a society we can all be proud of?" Most importantly, I told Kojo, I wanted to ask the warlords why they did terrible things to children, and what they were going to do for these traumatized young people now.

Kojo chewed on it for a moment. "Okay," he said. "Go and do it."

I smiled and thanked Kojo, a man whom I had convinced to let me interview warlords on the air, but who once had to force me even to talk to child soldiers. Once again, I was off to hear the other side of the war.

First I had to locate Roland's and Kabineh's telephone numbers. Finding Roland's was easy enough; Kabineh's was a bit more challenging. I was thrilled when both men accepted my invitation. This is probably because I didn't tell them about each other, having decided a surprise was best.

"Roland, why don't you come at two thirty," I suggested. "Kabineh, I will see you at two forty-five." I scribbled it down in my planner.

Kojo and I decided we would keep them in separate rooms until showtime. He would help ensure neither saw the other until the last possible second. Colleagues would act as a "buffer zone." In the meantime, I asked a child soldier named Armstrong to record his story for the program. Armstrong had fought for the NPFL under Roland Duo. I intended to turn the microphone on Roland after Armstrong's story and ask him what he had to say.

On the day of the program, I waited by the telephone. Warlords are busy men with big egos, and I was sure one of them was going to cancel. When neither did, I started sweating. I burst into Kojo's office several times: "Is it going to work? Is it going to work?" "Umunna, it will work!" he shouted. Just like the first day I hosted *Straight from the Heart* alone, I kept checking my notes and the clock on the wall. I had been so busy preparing to book these guys, I hadn't done that much thinking about the actual program. How *do* you talk to a warlord?

A few minutes before two thirty, Roland pulled up to UNMIL Radio in a small car. From my research, I knew that Roland, one of Taylor's top men, had lived the high life. But that day, he walked into the studio wearing casual clothes and without any fanfare. *He looks just like one of my boys*, I thought.

Not long after that, Kabineh arrived in a chauffeured Jeep. He created quite a stir entering UNMIL Radio in a dapper business suit and flashy sunglasses. I'll admit I was less thrilled to see Kabineh. Unlike Roland, he was a grown man when he fought the war, a lawyer who knew his left from his right. Why had he done these things to children? Struggling to maintain my neutrality, I took Kabineh into the studio and we chitchatted briefly. Like Roland, he was still under the impression he would be interviewed alone.

About one minute before the show began, Kojo brought Roland into the studio. Kabineh had no idea what was going on. Neither did Roland. Both men stared at each other, stupefied.

"Roland, meet Kabineh," I introduced them, trying to conceal the mischief in my voice. "Kabineh, I think you know Roland."

Calmly, I explained that this would be a double interview. I had designed it this way to better inform the Liberian people. And oh, you should have seen the looks on those warlords' faces when they realized they were going on the air together!

You cannot shake hands with a clenched fist, and those men did not shake hands that day. Kabineh avoided eye contact when Roland sat down. Roland looked at the ceiling, pulled out his cell phone, and started punching numbers into it as my theme song started to play. During my opening monologue, Roland and Kabineh straightened their collars. When I played Armstrong's story, they loosened their collars and shifted uncomfortably in their seats:

Anyway, I'm Armstrong. And you know the war brought so many things. They killed my father, and that's the reason why I joined. My mother told me, "They killed your father in the cocoa bush! What should we do?" She showed me the area, right by where he used to draw water and drink after working in the hot sun. Now he was lying on that field. His skin was already rotting. They had tied him, beat him. Beat him until he died. I told my Ma, "I cannot see my father rotting like this!" We packed up his bones and dug a hole and prayed over the grave.

After that, I sat down and did some thinking. I still saw my father on that field, even though he was lying in the ground. The people have a recruitment center in Bong County. So I said, "Well, since they killed my father, I will join and fight." My grandfather say, "Do not join. Try to say in school!" I say, "Yes, I am in the ninth grade. But I must fight to see the end of this war."

I started fighting. I took it step by step. The people assigned me my own unit. I tried to recruit boys and put them together, fighting place to place.

And one thing I want the Liberian people to know: We all know what happened. It is not something that people say, "Oh, I took arms, I never do that." The bullet does not pick and choose.

Now we youth, we are seeing one another. There are no jobs and most of our friends are on the street taking people's food, stealing people's things. All the things that are not good at all.

I think we should look up to God. Let's try to do something
that will help ourselves.

I think everybody who fought the particular war should try
and reconcile. You should feel happy to see somebody saying,
"This is what I did to him, what I did to her." But we should not
point fingers and say, "This one go to court, try and pick out the
people among us!" No. The people that were the big-big people
among us, they themselves know who supported it. You say,
"I'm carrying Armstrong to court"? You think it's fair to take
me to court because I recruited boys to put on the front line,
and I was supported by you? I would like to call on *you*.

So instead, let's try to forgive one another. Be together as
brother and sister. You can be a white man, be a black man, be
a blue man, be a yellow man. We are the same people. Different
color, one people. We all did bad in the war. We should forgive.
That what makes you a man.

When the story was finished, I turned to Roland and Kabineh.
Armstrong's story had many elements to it—poverty, lack of education,
revenge, reconciliation. His mind was clearly cluttered about what he
should do and how he should feel. Still, Armstrong was working hard
to make sense of the war and his life, and it was time for the warlords,
who had commanded fighters like him, to do the same.

"You both have heard the story," I said. "What do you want to say
to Armstrong?"

Kabineh and Roland were silent. At last, Kabineh spoke. He un-
derscored the need, "the desperate need," for Liberians from all walks of
life to sit down and reflect on our history as a way of moving forward.
Kabineh said he believed that Liberia could make tremendous progress in the future, so long as Liberians came together and reconciled.

"Okay," I said. Typical words from a politician, I thought. "Roland," I said. "You have heard the story. What do you want to say to Armstrong?"

Roland sat up in his seat and nodded. "We listened to our brother. He spoke very well. And as I always say, there is no good war or bad peace." It sounded like a line he had delivered many times. Then Roland advised Liberians to put things behind them and reconcile. Kabineh agreed and seemed pleased by Roland's words. "Reconciliation is not a desirable thing in Liberia, it is a *must*," Kabineh emphasized.

I felt like yawning. *How can you guys be saying these things? You caused this war! Don't you feel any responsibility?* There was no emotion, no impact. Neither one convinced me he believed the words coming out of his mouth. They spoke as if they were in separate rooms, living in separate Liberias.

When the break came, I played a song that highlighted the themes of that particular program . . . or at least, my intentions for it. It was called "Wake Up Everybody," and was about teaching children and making the world a better place. I motioned to Kojo through the glass . . . "Boss, we are not getting anywhere!" . . . and he signaled his agreement. Let's face it, I said to myself, these guys are pros. They hadn't risen through the rebel ranks and commanded entire battalions for nothing. I was worried the show would be a disaster. A waste of my listeners' time, Armstrong's, and mine. Then I saw the studio technician waving, indicating we had a call.

I took the call.

"Hello caller," I said. "You are on the line. Welcome to *Straight from the Heart* on UNMIL Radio."

My heart was beating fast as the young man introduced himself and proceeded to rake Roland and Kabineh over the coals. He accused them of destroying the youth in our country. He called the demobilization process a "blunder." He said Kabineh and Roland were in positions of authority and had a responsibility to ensure the child soldiers harassing people in the streets disarmed. The caller attacked Kabineh and Roland for their corrupt ways. He said they were solely focused on amassing funds for their personal pleasure. "You don't need the money!" the caller said. The child soldiers and humanitarian agencies that were trying to help them needed the money!

"Kabineh Janneh has not been harassed. We are the ones that have been harassed," the caller said with great emotion in his voice, talking about child soldiers. "They harm you for your cell phone. It's all because Janneh and Roland Duo were using them!"

It was really something. Kabineh and Roland didn't know what to make of it. They tried to defend themselves, talk the caller down, and embellish their roles in the disarmament process. They said it was complicated. "We were not in a money-making process," Roland protested, visibly uncomfortable. Kabineh agreed that the charge was unfounded. As for the caller, he stood his ground. Clearly, he was not impressed by what they were saying.

And suddenly, it was a curious thing. Roland and Kabineh weren't talking to me anymore. They weren't talking to the caller. They were no longer behaving as if the other warlord wasn't in the room. Kabineh and Roland were talking to *each other*, praising the other's perspective, and saying it was high time Liberians "give reconciliation a pat on the back."

Eventually, Kabineh and Roland started talking about the ways warlords like them could help the peace-building process. I don't know if it was for show or what, but it *seemed* genuine, and I'll tell you this—it wasn't happening anywhere else! I think Roland and Kabineh felt the interview had gone well, but I believed we had exposed them for what they were: weak and unconvincing men who didn't have all the answers and should no longer be leading Liberia. Privately, I hoped my listeners would compare what these warlords were saying to what my boys were trying to do—move forward and do something for the communities they had destroyed.

When we were just about out of time, I turned to Roland and Kabineh and asked if they had any last words. "You guys have been fighting all these years," I said. "What are you going to do for Liberia now?" And I remember they said they would do something for Nimba County and the child soldiers who fought. With that, I delivered my final monologue:

> On an individual basis, I think we in Liberia understand the power and purpose of forgiveness pretty well. The only thing that may be harder than forgiving a transgressor is being that transgressor, and accepting the extended hand of forgiveness. In order to acknowledge that you are being forgiven, you have to admit to and acknowledge what you have done is something that *requires* forgiveness.
>
> You have to swallow your pride.

When the technician gave me the all clear, Kojo burst into the studio. Everyone was talking loudly and shaking hands: Roland, Kabineh, Armstrong (who was in the studio), and Kojo. Roland and Kabineh said they were free for follow-up interviews anytime. Kabineh invited me to a meeting he was chairing in Nimba County. Then Kabineh offered to drive Roland home so they could discuss the peace process. My colleagues were shaking their heads. *What just happened? Did that just happen here?*

I had more warlords on my program after that. Kojo, Patrick, and I made sure every rebel faction was represented. Many came with bodyguards. Some like Kabineh showed up in fancy vehicles and fine suits, which always amused me, because on the radio nobody can see what you are wearing. But I think that was really my message during those shows: Peace isn't about spending money to get your voice heard.

One of the more memorable interviews I conducted was with Sekou Damate Conneh, Jr. Like Kabineh, Conneh was a leader of the rebel faction LURD. To this day, Conneh, who supervised some of the bloodiest battles LURD waged, takes credit for removing Charles Taylor from power. After the war, he ran for the presidency but he barely collected any votes.

When Conneh came on my program, he called himself a "victim." I asked him to listen to an interview from a child soldier and then introduced him to a woman LURD had terrorized. She was sitting in the studio and had been listening to Conneh's speech. When he called himself a victim, her eyes bulged.

"What are you talking about?" she gasped. "Your guns came inside my house and killed my people! You are not the victim! We are the victims!"

I tell you that great warlord was silent.

I received mixed reactions from my listeners for interviewing warlords. Some people felt the experience was valuable. Others questioned my intentions. It was just like when I started interviewing child soldiers: *Why are you giving these people a platform? Who do you think you are? You call yourself a Liberian?* People expressed outrage at the warlords who continued to defend their actions. They accused them of stealing the peace process to promote their political careers.

Then I started inviting warlords to speak to my boys at Straight from the Heart Center.

Why did I do this? Well, many of my boys still looked up to these warlords. Now that I had access, I wanted to disabuse them of their hero worship. Warlords are not heroes. They are men who went to good schools, amassed great power, waged gory battles, and used children to do the worst of their bidding. Finally some had been exposed,

and I wanted my boys to meet these warlords, their former commanders, and compare what had happened in their lives. "These guys made
you fight," I said. "They accumulated great wealth at your expense, and
they are doing *nothing* to help you now."

The second reason was more inspirational. With education and
effort, I wanted to show my boys that, just like these warlords, they too
could make something of their lives. Don't get me wrong. I wasn't saying, "Go out and be like these men!" Just that here were people who
fought the war and fighting the war is not the end of life. Life is a journey, and my boys had more of it. It was a complex message, but Liberia
is a complicated place.

I would call my experiment "somewhat successful." I had high
hopes for Sekou Damate Conneh, Jr. Unfortunately, he spent most of
his speech grandstanding. He spoke to my boys as if they were voters
wondering whom to cast a ballot for instead of traumatized youth with
barely enough to eat, living in the ghetto, and trying to scratch by. After
his speech, Conneh asked Ebenezer to help him run his presidential
campaign. Ebenezer was thrilled until Conneh's party asked him for
money. Ebenezer didn't have any money, so Conneh's party was no
longer interested. Nevertheless, Ebenezer thanked me for inviting that
warlord to come and talk. "When he spoke," Ebenezer said, "I felt the
war was finally through."

Edwin Snowe had been Charles Taylor's personal driver and married Taylor's daughter. Unsurprisingly, he became a prominent member of Taylor's government. After the war, Snowe was elected speaker
of the House amid allegations he had used embezzled funds to buy
votes. Snowe agreed to speak to my boys at our Sunday meeting.

Snowe came from church, and he was wearing a sharp suit when he
arrived. He took one look at my boys in their hand-me-down clothes
and said he would be right back. Snowe returned in a T-shirt to speak
to them. In his speech, he urged my boys to hang in there and hang on.

He encouraged them to help push Liberia's peace forward. Snowe said he had come from nothing, and they, too, could rise up. "Just because you fought the war, you are not nothing," Snowe said, and my boys cheered.

Eventually, I met Prince Johnson, the fearsome warlord Kojo had crossed off my list. I went to talk to him about post-war justice, and he told me to follow him to Nimba County, where he would share his perspective. I didn't dare follow him. I feared I might not come back! Instead, I agreed to meet Prince Johnson at a hotel on Twenty-fourth Street. Everyone was staring at me as I entered that hotel. I left the door to the room open and didn't get much information, but I encouraged Prince to visit the TRC. The next time I saw him was at TRC headquarters. Prince Johnson said he had an urgent meeting but promised to share his story soon.

He never did. But later, during his public hearing, Prince started talking about a woman who had advised him to go to the TRC and come clean about his actions. Prince blamed the TRC and said its investigations would send our country right back into war. Newspapers started calling me, asking if I was the woman who had convinced Prince Johnson to testify, but Patrick didn't want me answering any calls from the press.

Finally, there was Joshua Blahyi, alias "General Butt Naked." Like Mohamed, that warlord's story was on another level.

When he was just eleven years old, Joshua claimed to have received a phone call from the devil. Tribal elders in his village inducted him into a secret priesthood. In time, Joshua became the spiritual adviser to President Doe. According to Joshua, Doe made critical decisions about the country based on visions Joshua had received. If Joshua said, "That man is a traitor!" Doe would have the man killed. When Prince Johnson's men murdered Doe, Joshua fled and formed a small army of his own. He became famous for leading young fighters into battle wearing nothing but an AK-47 and lace-up boots. Joshua and his "Butt Naked Battalion" would later take responsibility for the deaths of twenty thousand people. Joshua confessed to other things, too: ritual sacrifice and cannibalism.

Now Joshua is a born-again Christian. He preaches the Word of God on street corners and leads prayer revivals. He credits a vision of Jesus on the battlefield for his dramatic conversion. I met Joshua when the TRC was taking statements. After his public hearing, Jerome told me to go and speak with him. Joshua told me his story calmly enough. But when I asked Joshua what he would do if someone did to his family what he had done to other people's families, he burst out crying.

"They are serious crimes . . ." I said.

"I don't even know why you are speaking to me!" Joshua wept. "But whether I am placed in prison or hanged, I will speak the truth and ask for forgiveness."

You may wonder why I decided to trust this man. And I will admit I sometimes get a strange feeling around him. I walk down the street with Joshua and envision the cold-blooded murders he committed. We sit down to eat, and I shiver wondering what grisly things he consumed during the war. Still, this is the work that I do. I wanted to hear his story. And if there is one thing I am confident of, it's that Joshua has changed.

How do I know? I saw repentance in his eyes the day of his public hearing. He seemed genuinely sorry and tormented by his actions. That, and I felt he had a unique opportunity to help boys like mine, boys whose lives had been destroyed during the war. And so I started going around with him.

When my father found out I was working with Joshua Blahyi, he sat me down for a talk. "Why are you concerned?" I asked. "I am concerned when there is a reason for concern," my father said. "That man Butt Naked threatened to kill me many times during the war!"

I hadn't known this. My father said it was true. Back in 1996, Joshua (Butt Naked then) had commandeered UN trucks and seized the WHO's walkie-talkies. He knew the UN frequencies and used them to interrupt conversations and issue death threats. Butt Naked had a long list of enemies, my father said. He would single out agency heads for all kinds of "infractions." My father said he tried to keep a sense of humor about things, but it was challenging. Butt Naked was to him a crazy, determined man.

"I don't want you working with him, Agnes." He put his foot down.

I felt conflicted. I suppose every child, however grown-up, feels this way at some point. No matter how old you are, your work pulls you one way, and your love and loyalty another. I kept working with Joshua, but I didn't tell my father. Then one day, I decided it was time to reintroduce them. When I told my father Joshua was coming over for dinner, he nearly fell off his chair.

"Joshua is a changed man," I said. "He is my brother." Then I asked my father a question I had asked many Liberians at that point. "How would you feel about me if I had become a child soldier, or a warlord like him?"

This was difficult for my father, but it is something all of us must think about. *What if this ex-combatant was my child? What would I do? Take him back? Turn her away?* Because this is exactly what is happening in Liberia. People are being forced to ask themselves these hard, soul-searching questions. The most vulnerable are taken by the most wicked, and when everything's done nobody will touch them. But what if it was your child? Would you feel the same way?

I told my father Joshua was helping me connect former fighters to their victims, so that they might seek forgiveness. In return, I was advising Joshua on the rehabilitation center he was building. "The days of General 'Butt Naked' are over," I said. "He is helping child soldiers. It is really something." My father shook his head and looked at me as if I had been the one racing around a battlefield with no clothes on. Joshua could come to dinner, he said. But only if I promised to get my head checked.

For as long as I live, I will never forget the bewildered look on my father's face, or Joshua's, when my father met him at the door and confronted him about their "previous encounters." Joshua apologized for the death threats. "It was a different time," he said. "Yes," my father agreed. "That is certainly true." Joshua was gentlemanly and contrite. My father went from shocked to confused to genuinely charmed. I sat there silently as Joshua and my father discussed God, politics, and the war.

"I like the man." My father smiled when Joshua left.

Now my father respects him from the ground up. He even invited Joshua to stop by his office to chat. Joshua owns a farm outside Monrovia where former child soldiers come for detoxification and rehabilitation. They farm, read the Bible, sing hymns, and prepare to return to their villages for cleansing ceremonies. Joshua says his own experiences and brutal past allow him to communicate with ex-combatants in a way people who didn't fight the war can't understand. I believe him. He is dealing with some very traumatized youth. Joshua says he can reach the most violent boys—boys who, like him, believe that they are beyond redemption.

Some Liberians call Joshua a hero. Other people say he is a wolf in sheep's clothing. "Butt Naked is still fighting! He is the same bad person! Butt Naked played the God card during the war, and Joshua Blahyi is playing the God card now!" Even a couple of years later, it is difficult for some people to grasp that the war is actually over. Besides, should a man who confessed to eating children's hearts really be working with children? they ask. And, you know, in another time and place—in another country—I would agree with them. But here is the thing: Beyond a few admirable humanitarian organizations, so few people are helping these kids, and they need all the help they can get. If Joshua doesn't do it, who will?

Recently, I visited Joshua's farm and spoke to some of his fighters. "They were very hard when they arrived," Joshua said, "but they have changed."

I asked Joshua what made him so successful.

"God's grace." He gestured to the sky. "They know the diamond is with me." I took this to mean God's power.

Joshua has a wife and three small children. On the day I visited, they were standing off to the side as Joshua's boys praised God, clapped their hands, stamped their feet, and sang hymns. At one point, Joshua's tiny daughter came over and sat on his knee. She has big, moon-shaped eyes like him and is very sweet and shy. She stared at the dangerous boys her father works with while her brother hid behind a post. Joshua stared back at them, his children. And the way he stared, I could tell they meant so much to him. Considering all the horrific things he had done to other children, Joshua felt he didn't deserve them.

Joshua's wife is a beautiful woman with a swanlike neck and a long ponytail that trails down her back, who comes from Joshua's village. They were married in 1998 between the wars. I was curious to know what it was like to be married to a man like Joshua, knowing all that he had done as "Butt Naked." I asked her.

"The past did not affect my choice," she said.

Say what you will. Love is powerful. It can do so many things. Do I believe her? I don't know. Do I believe that Joshua has transformed himself into a man of religiosity? If I believe in my boys, I must. I must trust that people can change, and that a person's childhood does not determine who he is as an adult.

As for the warlords sitting in the House of Representatives today . . . well, I say we must keep an eye on them. There are warlords I trust and those I don't. Messy company and clean slates. This is the story of Liberia. Over time, I have come to believe that there is a killer and a saint in all of us. But, like Joshua's wife, I choose to focus on the future and the *potential* in people. I work with Joshua because of what he is doing for child soldiers, and what he has done to save himself. Like Mohamed, Joshua may be one of the few people who can get through to them.

21

SHE TOLD ME, "Ernestine, we have to cut your hand, because if we don't cut your hand, you will not make it." I said just carry me to my husband. They took me to my husband, and he started crying. He said, "My wife was the breadwinner for the home. If you take away her hand, how will we survive?" He cried, oh he cried! He said, "Let it not be today! Let it just be tomorrow. I am not feeling good about the way things are going today!"

PERHAPS IT WAS inevitable that all we had worked for would tumble down. Straight from the Heart was a place that provided food and family, but not what many boys craved: quick money, drugs, and an outlet for their anger. The things that lure people to violence make it hard for them to quit. When you cannot see the opposite shore, it is easy to stop swimming. In spite of my best efforts, sometimes the food ran out. The Sunday meetings didn't happen. Boys lost their jobs, other boys couldn't get jobs. They started fighting and reorganizing into the factions they had fought for during the war. It was a terrible time. I felt helpless, paralyzed. Suddenly, Straight from the Heart Center was spiraling away from me, and I didn't know how to stop it.

It started with the cook. Some of the boys accused her of stealing food from the kitchen. "She gives it to her boyfriend!" they growled. Even Ebenezer joined the fray.

"You must fire her, Sister."

"Over my dead body," I said. "Who else do you think will cook for you? Should we just send everyone to your house for dinner, Ebenezer?"

That quieted them down.

Only then the boys started picking on Ebenezer. They accused him of stealing money. One of the big warlords had visited the center and given Ebenezer cash to buy things. "Ebenezer pocketed it!" they cried. "He stole the money! Ate the money!" Others blamed Ebenezer for *not* taking the money. They claimed he hadn't taken it "on philosophical grounds." Even Ebenezer's close friends betrayed him. They said he didn't deserve to be chairman, or that I was giving Ebenezer money on the sly because of his "special status."

It really hurt Ebenezer. "If Sister Agnes is really giving me cash, would I be so thin? Wearing these old clothes?" he begged. His voice was shaking. He had done so much for them, but they didn't see it. They saw only their own needs.

I tried talking to them, saying that I trusted Ebenezer. I had given him money to build a center, and he had done it. I asked him to set up a feeding program, and he had done that, too. If I sent Ebenezer on an errand, he kept the receipts. "They are back at my office if you boys don't believe me," I said. "Ebenezer is a thief? Bring me proof!" They had none, of course. "You see?" I said. "Ebenezer fears God too much to steal or lie."

Still, they grumbled. "What are you going to do?" I asked Ebenezer. "These are the boys you trusted. You see how they treat you when the chips are down?"

Ebenezer came through in the end. He brought the warlord's money to our meeting that Sunday. In front of all the boys, he explained that he had been keeping it until we decided what to do with the money as a group.

"If it means so much to you people to hold it," he said, looking from face to face, "then someone else should hold it." I was proud of Ebenezer. It was a big moment for him. But the boys were unbending.

Down with the chairman!

He is bluffing!

He no good, oh!

They wanted power and control. They would recognize Ebenezer's authority only as long as their own was increasing. "We can't all be captains," I tried to say. "Some of us must be crew." Or, "See the fingers of the hand. They work together but are not equal, as we are not equal." But no, these boys were used to excitement from violence. They were tired of waiting for their lives to improve. They had no patience for the slow, uncertain paths of school or work. When change doesn't happen quickly enough, the wrong kind of memories and impulses start to set in. Try as I might, my messages were no longer getting through to them.

"I'm doing my best," I pleaded with them. "Money is tight."

I'd run through my savings. Every paycheck was gone. Our benefactors were exhausted. Kojo and Patrick had bills of their own to pay. Most of the boys had never gotten an education. Without one, it's difficult to envision a different life, or a future. They grew angry with the people who wouldn't hire them or give them a chance, as if they were entitled to these things. Tensions mounted. Temperatures rose. I was worried they would start doing drugs again and stealing. Then they started stealing from me.

It was one of the saddest moments of my life. I had taken a group of boys to the TRC to give their statements. I left my purse on a table when I took the boys into the recording room. When I dropped them back at the center, saying how proud of them I was and what a big thing they had accomplished, I reached into my purse to give them money for food but it was gone.

"Why did you take the money," I said, "when it is going to you anyway?"

They denied it. They wouldn't meet my eyes. I drove off feeling like I had been knifed in the back. I had trusted them, taken a chance on them. I was trying to get other Liberians to do the same. And here they were doing the wicked things the Liberian people accused them of. *To someone who cared for them!* It is difficult to believe in someone when they start to take advantage of you. The warm space in your heart feels like it's been cut up on the inside.

Back at the center, things were deteriorating. The boys started arguing over old, perceived injuries from the war. They traded threats and insults. You could almost see the battle lines drawn in and around the table and chairs: NPFL, ULIMO-J, ULIMO-K, LURD, MODEL. One day, I noticed that one of the boys was missing. "What happened to Bombo?" I asked. And, "Oh, that boy had to leave, Ma. He had to leave . . ." they said. It was disturbing . . . the way they said it. I felt like checking under the table and chairs just to make sure there wasn't a body. Was I losing my mind? When Bombo didn't return, again I asked them where he had gone. They made balls with their fists and punched their hands, and I stopped asking.

Then they started abusing the cook. Again, the same allegations: "She's a thief! She steals food and gives it to her boyfriend!" I grew worried and wondered if I should send her away, or hire a male cook. To this day, I wish I had followed through on that instinct. When Ebenezer called and said I should come quickly, something had happened, my body went cold. I drove from UNMIL Radio at breakneck speed. When I arrived at the center, Ebenezer stepped forward.

"It's the cook," he said.

"What about the cook?" I demanded. "Where is she?"

"Somebody threw a punch . . ." Ebenezer said, shuffling his feet, "at that lady."

I felt my knees give way.

"What?" I placed my hands to my face. "Where is she? Ebenezer, please tell me you are joking!" I cried hysterically.

Ebenezer was silent.

"Oh my God . . ." I said, looking from boy to boy. "Who has done this? Who?!" I demanded. No one spoke. Guilt was etched on every face. I didn't want to know who had done it, but I had to find out.

When the boy stepped forward, I shook my head but I wasn't surprised. He was a tall, sickly looking boy. He had never told me his story, but I knew he came from Nimba County. According to the others, he had fought for the NPFL Small Boys Unit and done some very depraved things. "You. What were you thinking?" I shook my head. The boy didn't answer. "Don't you see what you are doing?" I said. "Being the wicked boys everyone says you people are?"

I suspended the boy from the center. Then I went and apologized to the cook, who was clearly upset. "You have helped us so much, and I understand if you don't come back," I said. Later, the boy wrote her an apology letter. But things were never the same.

I was seeing a whole new side of them. Or rather, I was seeing the old side of them, the side behind the stories. It frightened me. I was afraid to be around them, afraid to leave them. I had a terrible premonition that something worse was coming, something we would not be able to recover from. Could all we had worked for end with the blast of a gun?

I didn't know. Growing up, boys I knew traded threats and small punches. Occasionally, disagreements came to blows, but things never went very far. A boy might say, "I'm going to kill you!" He didn't actually mean it. He didn't actually *do* it. But these boys? They *had* done it. They had tortured and killed. As bad as something is, once you've done it, you know you have the power to do it again. Once you've crossed a line, it makes it easy to cross it a second time.

Then one day it happened. I drove to the center. I was locking the driver's side door, when I heard the shouting. *Oh God no,* I thought. *What is happening now?* I sprinted inside. I saw the mob. Some of the boys had backed Ebenezer into a corner. They were shouting, stabbing their fingers into his shoulders, and bullying him. One boy had his hands around Ebenezer's neck, choking him. Ebenezer's eyes were wide with fright.

I charged toward them. "Stop it!" I screamed, waving my hands. "Stop it! Stop it! Stop it! What are you doing?" Everyone was yelling at once. Nobody heard me. I tried picking individual boys away from the fray.

"You!" I shouted, grabbing one of the boys by his shirt collar. "What are you doing? You are no different than him!" I said, jabbing my finger in another boy's face. I tried to pull off another one. "You!" I shouted. "What about you? The war is over! What good are these factions? They don't *exist* outside this center!" I turned to another one. "You need a faction?" I snapped. "Liberia is the only faction that counts!"

I started saying things I didn't mean. *You good for nothings! You stupid boys!* I lashed out at them because I was frightened. It saddened me that we'd fallen to this low place. "We should be talking and doing things to *improve* ourselves," I wailed. "Not tearing each other apart. If you want someone to disrespect you, you fight about it," I shouted. "If you want them to respect you, you talk about it." Liberia had wronged them, but wronging Liberia was not the answer. An eye for an eye only ends up making the whole world blind. Why was that so difficult for them to understand?

"Why is it so difficult for me to organize you?" I said. "Is it because I do not use a gun? Or drugs?" But they weren't listening. I wasn't getting anywhere. I was losing them. And in that moment, I realized I had to do something drastic. With a deep breath, I took off my bracelet and rolled up my shirtsleeves. I placed my bracelet on a table. I made a ball with my fist, raced right into the middle of the mob, and yelled: "Fight me!"

I had no idea what I was doing, only that my fists were trembling wildly. Then I took off my shoes and socks and tossed them aside. I swayed back and forth as I'd seen actors do in the movies, hoping I looked somewhat convincing.

"Once and for all," I said, the fury rising in my throat, "leave Ebenezer alone." The boys looked at me as if I had lost my mind or started speaking in tongues. "Or, if you boys want to fight," I continued calmly, "fine. Start with me."

The boys were taken aback. They stared at me in disbelief. Their jaws were really on the floor. One of them laughed. Most just stood there. They hadn't expected this and clearly didn't know how to process what was happening. I felt depressed. I felt as though I had crossed a line I had been working hard to pull them away from. They looked at me as if I finally understood.

Are you serious, Mommy?

What are you saying?!

Don't be crazy!

We don't want to fight you. . . .

Their faces softened. They looked sheepish. They were civil again, children again, but I didn't trust them anymore. "I'm not leaving until you promise to leave Ebenezer alone," I repeated. And, "Okay, okay, okay, Mommy . . ." They gave me their word. "Good," I said. "This thing is finished then." And afterward, I think I said something like, "Now I'm going home, and when I come back, I expect it to stay that way." And again, "Okay, okay, okay, Mommy . . ." So now they knew me and were afraid of me, which was a good thing, but I felt like a hypocrite. By threatening violence, I had become the very thing I had tried to steer them away from.

This "ceasefire" lasted about a week. The boys started bumping heads again. They argued over the same things, new things, pointless things. Every time I visited, there were new gripes and accusations. Finally, they accused me of keeping money the UNMIL had given them, which really hurt my feelings. That next Sunday after our meeting, I cleared my throat and said I had an announcement to make.

"You boys are better than this . . ." I began.

With deeply disappointed eyes, I told them I was leaving. The center was falling apart, our experiment had failed. I thought they were young men who wanted to move on with their lives but had learned they were fighters who didn't care about their futures, or other people's feelings. I said the fights had drained me. I had a lot of energy, but I wanted to put it into good places and people who cared. I had trusted them and they had fooled me, but they would not fool me anymore. I was throwing in the towel, it was over, my mind was made up, and there was nothing they could do about it.

"I'm sorry I have failed you," I said, with sorrow in my voice. I shook my head, shrugged, and said good-bye. I did not tell them it was only temporary. The boys protested, but it was too late.

No no no!

Mommy, we weren't serious!

Mommy, we're sorry!

I was out the door.

22

THIS WARLORD HAD two wives and called me his "spare tire."
He used to have three wives, but he killed one and put her head on
his car. I was his slave and his donkey. When he needed blood for a
sacrifice, he would kill children like me.

One day, the warlord called me over and say he sorry for killing
my mother. I cried and asked him, why? And he said he wanted me to
be his wife. Life was terrible as his wife. His other wives circum-
cised me. Beating was my daily breakfast. That warlord beat me like
an animal morning, noon, and night. He used to put a gun on my head
and called me "his table." He would set his gun on my head and shoot,
so I would not be afraid of the sound.

We suffered so much in that warlord's hands. I cried and cried,
but who was there to help? I used to wake up early in the morning to
sweep his yard with a broom. When I got outside, the warlord would
come to try and put his penis in my vagina. If I tried to protest, he
would say, "If you make any sound, I will kill you!" And I would
look at him and cry in my heart.

One day, we were riding in a car. He told me to get out of the car.
He pushed me inside a house. That warlord took his knife and cut off
my clothes and raped me. Since that day, I have never been myself.

Finally, I heard that warlord was planning my death. I decided to
run away with another girl. We escaped through a window. When
we got to Ganta, we lived in a house with other girls. But after a few

weeks, the girls started behaving funny. They used to sleep out every night with men and said everybody should do the same. They said, "If your friend will not get three to four boyfriends to help us, she should not use the items in the house." And I said, "If this is so, let us go because this kind of life is not good for us."

Recently, my pastor encouraged me to go to the TRC. I was ashamed that people would laugh at me. Some people say that I am mad. That my experience in the war made me crazy. Some people blame me for what happened. They say I enjoyed being hurt, because I never killed the man who killed my mother. But I feel that God would not forgive me if I did that. I am not the giver of life, so why should I take it?

I need happiness in my life. If someone want to give me gold or silver, I don't need any. I simply pray the sun will shine on my family again, and the rain will stop.

—Finda

I LEFT THE CENTER and didn't return the next day. Or the next. Or even the following one. I ignored the boys' calls, even Ebenezer's. A week passed. Oh, they were upset! Where was the food? When was I returning? My phone was ringing up and down.

"Old Ma, hey!" they said on my answering machine.

"Ma, come back! We na' mean it . . ."

"Sister Agnes, please come back. Your children need you," Ebenezer beseeched me.

"You guys are disturbing me," I replied when I finally picked up the phone. "You make up your minds how you feel about things and we will talk."

"But Sister—"

"Ebenezer, don't worry," I said conspiratorially. "Between us, this is just a temporary measure."

Punishing someone is never easy, and Ebenezer had always been my ally. He was not the problem, but he was one of over two hundred former child soldiers who needed to understand that the past few weeks of misbehavior were unacceptable. I knew the boys would be all right. Kojo was giving them money for food, and I would return in short order. My plan was to leave them to their condition for a while and let them mull it over.

But oh, what to do with the time? These boys were my life, my work, my friends, and my family. The clock ticked *very* slowly the first day I was away from them. Initially, I just worked longer hours at UNMIL Radio. Kojo, ordinarily impressed by obsessive dedication, sensed that something was wrong and asked me to explain. "Shouldn't you be holding a meeting at the center?" He consulted his watch. I explained to Kojo that I was punishing the boys, but only momentarily. He said okay, but you know you have started something. He was worried the center would fold. I assured him Straight from the Heart would not fold. I just needed to teach the boys a lesson. Kojo frowned. "Don't worry," I told him. "The real reason the center won't close is because I miss them too much."

I wanted to use my time well and started investigating my options. I had heard about another center for ex-combatants, girls, and decided to pay a visit. This center was located at the old Government Services building where Charles Taylor used to work. He was employed there until Doe accused him of embezzling money and he fled to America. Now the Government Services building looked like any other building in Monrovia: burned and bombed. "Girls took it over," people told me. "Hard girls from the war." People said there were amputees living there, too.

I visited the Government Services building on a weekday. Even in broad daylight, its fortress-like exterior swallowed the sun and cast a gloomy shadow over everything. The walls were soot-colored. The windows were no longer windows but dark holes fringed by menacing jaws of broken glass. I pictured Liberian bureaucrats hurrying in and out the front door before the war. Now only a gaping, black mouth remained.

When I entered the building, oh the noise. There were about a hundred girls sitting on a concrete floor, many of them with half-naked crying babies on their laps. Their voices and their babies' high-pitched squeals ricocheted off the walls, creating an earsplitting din. Some girls sat in tight clusters with their backs against the walls. They smoked and drank. They laughed loudly and talked over one other, so that no one heard anything. They were skinny as poles and wore clothing that looked like it had never been washed and had been forcibly ripped from their bodies many times. Some girls breastfed their babies from bony chests. Most looked to be about seventeen years old.

I approached a group of them. "Hello," I said. "How are you?" I suppose I felt confident after these many months with my boys and believed they would respond to me in a similar fashion. I introduced myself as Agnes. The girls ignored me. My voice might have been a gust of wind. Somewhat disconcerted, I tried another group. "How are things?" I said but received the same reaction. The girls in the third group eyed me as if I was a hostile intruder, or a fool looking for a fight. One girl made a motion like she was going to get up and take a swing, and I backed away hastily, wondering what was wrong with them. Even my boys weren't this aggressive.

I was about to give up. Then, from out of nowhere, a girl in the first group I had been talking to stood up and extended her arms as if parting a curtain. She started walking toward me. She was about five feet five inches tall, with a broad, luminous face and enormous, sad eyes. She had a thick pile of braids mashed on top of her head like a crown. Her skin glowed in the dim light of the building. She jutted her hips as she approached.

Tossing back her head, she raised her arms in a victory pose and announced: "I'm a rebel! I fought the war! I won't hide!"

Then she burst into laughter and started dancing with her eyes closed.

It was strange. I didn't know what to make of her. Then I noticed she was dancing wildly and off-balance, and I recognized the signs of alcohol or drug abuse. Swishing her hips, the girl introduced herself as Rita. She said she knew everyone in the building. I wanted fighters? She could bring them. Give me five minutes, she said. And Rita did. She waltzed around the building, encouraging girls to "come talk about the war," and they listened. I soon learned Rita was a leader in this female rebel gang.

I sat down with the girls Rita brought me. I was nervous but thanked them for changing their minds. They shot me dark looks. Most held bottles of beer in their hands. They sipped from the bottles as they breastfed their babies. It was a depressing scene. Suddenly, I wished I was back at Straight from the Heart.

"Well," I said brightly, fending off my unease, "why don't I start?" I have learned that it helps other people open up when you show them you're willing to do it first. And you know, I felt confident I could find some common ground. I decided to talk to the girls not as fighters, but as young women.

"I had a baby when I was eighteen," I began. "I know how it feels . . . like your life is over."

As I explained my mistakes and misdirection, they began to put their bottles down and move in closer. When I spoke about my star-crossed love with Jeff, they shook their heads and hollered. When I described giving birth to my daughters, Diamond and Ogechi, a single mother and alone, they nodded and snapped their fingers like they knew where I was coming from. Soon they started telling me their stories.

"Did you fight?" I asked. "Oh yeah, we fought," they said. "For which faction?" I asked. And, "Oh, all factions. All factions. NPFL, LURD, ULIMO-J, ULIMO-K . . ." During the day, they fought; at night, they were soldiers' wives. One girl called Finda was kidnapped twice, repeatedly raped, and forced to become the wife of the rebel who had mutilated and murdered her mother. She described the horrific things the warlord had done to her, and I felt sick with grief.

While there is no way to compare the things that happened to the children of Liberia, as the girls spoke, I began to wonder if they had had it worse in the war. Their jobs weren't done when they left the battlefield. Once again, I was seeing another side of the Liberian war:

I was about the age of fourteen when Charles Taylor's supporters arrested me. I became their wife and cooked and worked for them. There in the bush, I witnessed a lot of terrible things. I saw people been tied on trees and shot. Some were beheaded. Others were flogged to death. I was afraid and terrified when these things were going on. I had no say, because I was just a housewife and did my job as a housewife. I did not fight, but I benefited from the fight in a sense—wearing looted clothes and eating food the soldiers looted.—Pendorah

They killed my own father in front of me. I could not stand it. That's how I came to join. I became a warrior. I was all the way in the bush. I'm not feeling good about what they do. We were just in that place there. I not kill no one. Yeah, we had a gun, carry it on our shoulders. But I not kill no one. A man get with me. The children he left with me. I have to hustle so we can eat. I have to hustle to get my daily bread. I have three little children. But I don't want no man to help me. I can support myself. Myself can help myself.—Comfort

I asked the girls what they were doing in this building. And oh, they were raising babies of rape and struggling to get by. Many were alcoholics. Some were sex workers. Others were on the verge of entering the sex trade. "What choice do we got?" they asked me. Many had sexually transmitted diseases, and I worried some might have AIDS. But the girls didn't know, because they had never been tested.

Then there was Rita, twenty-three years old and pregnant with her third child. After the girls had shared their stories, Rita turned to me. "I have no problem telling you my story," Rita said. "I remember what happened, just not the days."

Rita was the first of five children born to a poor farmer. She had been at a neighbor's house when the NPFL army attacked. Rita ran home but her family was gone. Twelve years old and terrified, she hid in her family's house and tried not to make noise, so as not to attract the NPFL soldiers' attention. She knew she could not hide forever.

One day, Rita was making bread. She had to use rice instead of wheat, because it was all that was left in the village. In Liberia, neighbors borrow freely whenever they need something, and Rita needed a sifter. She went to look for one in the empty house next door. Rita was cleaning the sifter when she heard a sharp knock. The caller didn't wait for an invitation. He barged right in and Rita jumped. He was a powerful NPFL general whom Rita recognized. Her knees started shaking. The general looked Rita up and down, and then ordered her to follow him outside. When Rita did, the general called over to one of his boy soldiers.

"Come here! I need a witness!" he barked.

The general stared at Rita.

"You were looting!" he bellowed when the boy soldier approached.

"What?" Rita said. She was struggling to put two and two together.

The general said he had seen Rita take a sifter from a neighbor's house, and it wasn't the first time. The general had seen Rita steal things before. With lustful eyes, he told Rita he had been watching her for a *long* time.

"Undress her!" he ordered his child soldier. "Let's see what else this thief has stolen!"

Rita started crying "No, no, no," asking the general why he had to do this, begging him not to. He ignored her. Wiping the sweat from his brow and gazing at Rita's body, he coolly explained that women had a "place" inside them, where they could hide things: babies, kitchen implements, weapons. He needed to check Rita's "place" to ensure she had nothing else hidden inside her.

"I have no weapons inside me!" Rita wept.

The child soldier undressed Rita. He started touching her. At that moment, another general approached and asked what was going on.

"What has this girl done?" he demanded. "Why do you charge her?"

The boy soldier stared at him. The first general accused Rita of being a spy. But the new general called off the investigation. He ordered the first general to leave Rita alone and helped Rita to her feet. She ran home crying, but days later, when another rebel group attacked and the NPFL retreated, Rita went with them. She had no idea what would happen, but she figured following the general who had saved her life was better than staying put and risking death.

"We walked for sixty-eight days," Rita said. "We slept in the bush. We chewed leaves. We drank alcohol and stream water to survive."

One of Charles Taylor's generals took a fancy to Rita. He hired her to be his bodyguard.

At this point, Rita's eyes got a faraway look. The bold young woman from before seemingly evaporated. "He taught me about life," Rita said quietly. She told me how she had lost her virginity to the general on the jungle floor. She described the terror, the pain, and the confusion when her period stopped and her stomach started swelling. Due to Rita's poor diet and living conditions, she delivered the baby prematurely and it died. Then the general abandoned Rita. He said she was "old enough to love but too small to be a mother." Other soldiers moved in. They started taking turns with Rita. "'Okay, we want you to be our wife to-day!' one soldier would say and rape me," Rita said. "Okay, now you are my wife!" another would announce and sleep with her.

At last, Rita teamed up with other girls who were tired of being sex slaves. By sticking together, they discovered they were more powerful than the boys and could fend off most rape attempts. When the NPFL reached Monrovia, Rita was picked up by humanitarian workers and taken to a demobilization center. "They tried to teach us how to take good care of ourselves," Rita said. But it didn't work. Rita was a hurt, angry child and an alcoholic. She was aggressive with the staff and kept demanding to "see the general who did this, so he can see how it feels!" Rita left the center and found the girls she had fought with. They started living in the Government Services building. For the most part, nobody bothered them. She got a boyfriend and found out she was pregnant. Rita didn't want to have the child, but if she had to, she hoped it was a girl.

"I hate men . . ." she said quietly. "I don't want to bring another one into this world."

Hearing Rita's story, I felt so guilty. I pictured myself as a twelve-year-old girl, going to school, playing outside, and sleeping in my warm bed at night while these things were happening to Rita. It was horrific. Unfair. "You poor child," I found myself saying over and over again. "I wish no one had ever hurt you. I wish no one had taken away from you what was not theirs to take."

I asked Rita if I could take her to the UN medical center. Rita said yes, and let's take some of the other girls, too. She helped me organize them. There was one girl who was unwilling. She had been Rita's commander during the war and now worked as a prostitute. "She is sick," Rita said. Eventually she encouraged the girl to come talk to me. "You want to go to hospital so that my mother can treat you?" she asked the girl, Benatta. "You have a good story. You should explain it to her!" Rita encouraged Benatta, but she was reluctant. I wanted Benatta to get checked, so I told her I didn't want her story. I just wanted to take her to the clinic. At last I convinced her. We went to the hospital and they treated Benatta. I encouraged her to get an HIV test, too, but she was afraid of the "stigma." The clinic gave her some medicine, and I said, "You must take it on the specific days and at the specific times." Benatta said she would.

After that, Benatta started coming by my house with Rita. I urged her to stop sleeping with men and to try and learn a trade: hair-braiding, tie-and-dye, or house-cleaning. In time, Benatta opened up to me. I was happy she was turning a corner, but later found out that she had stopped taking her medicine. I was worried she had AIDS. I tried to reason with Benatta, but she didn't seem to care. It was the same with some of the boys: Some were so far gone, they didn't care what happened to them.

Rita was different. She gave me hope. She possessed a strong will power and desire to rebuild her life. Still, she had problems. Like a broken record, I had to keep begging her to stop drinking alcohol.

We went to the TRC and UNMIL Radio and recorded Rita's story on *Straight from the Heart*. Because her story was powerful, Kojo ended up airing it several times. My boys heard it, too. They grew sullen. The phone calls started again. "When are you coming back?" "Have you abandoned us forever, Mommy?" they asked. They promised me they had changed.

At last, I knew it was time to return to the center. These girls needed help, but so did my boys. I had to figure out a way to keep assisting both of them. I promised Rita I would visit the girls as often as I could, and in the meantime I started pushing her to go to school. "Just think what a good example you can be to your kids . . ." I said. Rita confessed she was worried about being the oldest student in the class. So I told her about Nelson, a Straight from the Heart boy who attended elementary school with his children. "Forget your age," I said. "When you go to school after what you have gone through, you can really be something."

It took a long time to separate Rita from her bad habits. Sometimes I would visit the Government Services building and she would be cooking or happily playing with her kids. Other times, I found Rita cradling a bottle of alcohol and singing songs from the rebel gang. I tried to move her to a new home, away from the girls who kept Rita remembering and reinforcing, but these fighters like to stick together. When the future is uncertain, the past can provide a strange comfort. Even a past like Rita's.

After Rita gave birth to her third baby, she called me. She had another son, she said. It was all right, though. He was a smart boy. He would go far. "You must come and visit him, Mommy!" Rita said. She sounded clear-eyed and positive. When I went to see her, she told me she had started selling food in the ghetto and working as a hairstylist to feed her kids.

"But it isn't enough," Rita announced. "I want to be a businesswoman."

I helped Rita apply to school and take the entrance examination. She was accepted at the local high school. When I told her I would cover her tuition, she was so grateful it nearly broke my heart. Now Rita is learning to read, write, and do mathematics. At night in the ghetto, she helps her older son with his homework before completing her own. She is trying to move out of the ghetto. "I can't live here anymore," she said. "I can't concentrate on my studies, Mommy."

I told her I would help.

23

—◆—

I WAS A SOLDIER. Later I joined the rebels. During the war, my colleagues and I killed, maimed, raped, and looted. I killed so many men, women, and children. I looted various properties from defenseless people, ranging from cars, money, and household items. Most of the bad things I cannot even remember, because we were under the influence of drugs. I was among the first to be disarmed.

Today I am a changed person, a born again Christian. The Bible says when you have Jesus Christ in your life, you become a new creature. I have asked God's forgiveness and also asked Liberians that I have caused great pain and sorrow to. For we Liberians should pray for the nation and help rebuild it.

As I am writing to you, I have found a girl in my church to marry. My parents went to this girl's parents to do the formal introduction. When we got to her family's house, immediately her father caught sight of me. He was filled with anger and insulted my family, saying we were all rogues. He said I was the person who looted his car and properties during the war.

Her father said I cannot and will never marry his daughter. Auntie Agnes, this is the only woman I want as a wife. I love her and she loves me, too, but her parents will never forgive me. How will I carry on?

—Abdullai

O UR LIVES have a plan for us, even if we can't see it for a while. We search for our path, push, and pull away from our destinies, either because they are too big or too incomprehensible or scary or simply don't make sense. Back in August 1992 at Tubman- burg Junction, I would not have believed you had you told me I would be working with child soldiers as an adult. Then many years later, I was sitting with a boy who had been there that same afternoon as I. I said, are you sure? Fofee said yes, it was raining hard. He remembered the pregnant woman and the baby who died.

"That day at Tubmanburg Junction was one of the worst of my life, because I couldn't do anything," I told Fofee.

Fofee replied it was one of the worst of his life, too, because he had done so much.

On this particular day, Fofee looked upset. I tried to catch his eye, and from the look on his face I could tell that something was really, really wrong.

"Fofee," I said. "What's bothering you?"

He shrugged. "Nothing, Mommy."

"Did you get enough to eat?"

Fofee nodded.

"You want some more?"

Fofee shook his head.

I was about to give up, and then I remembered: Fofee had just re- turned from visiting his village. He had gone back to apologize for his actions during the war.

"Fofee," I tried again. "How did the meeting go?"

Fofee shrugged.

"Did you meet with your people?"

He nodded.

"Both tribes?"

Another nod.

"So, why the long face?"

Fofee has a different story from most boys at Straight from the Heart. Whereas many were abducted or left their homes to fight, Fofee was stationed at home. You can imagine how difficult it is to apologize to a stranger's family, but Fofee knew each one of his victims personally. At my urging, Fofee had returned to his village to try and make amends, but he had found his village divided in two: people from the Loma tribe one on side, the Mandingos on the other. Before the war, these tribes had lived in peace. During the war, they viewed each other with distrust and contempt. Their children fought for different factions. Fofee's mother came from the Loma tribe, but his father was a Mandingo. When Fofee went back to apologize for being a child soldier, both tribes rejected him.

"Get away from here! Go to your people!" The Lomas shooed him away.

"We don't want you, Loma boy!" the Mandingos cried.

Fofee didn't get to make his apology. And that wasn't all. Fofee needed to work to support his children and had no idea what to do.

When Fofee was demobilized, he had joined the Liberian police force. This was when Charles Taylor was president and nobody was really checking anything. When the war ended and UNMIL came in to clean house and restructure Liberian institutions, Fofee's name came up. People from his village wrote a strongly worded letter to the UNMIL official in charge of retraining the Liberian police. Apparently, that official listened. He fired Fofee. Fofee had two kids and no idea how to feed them.

"Do you know who wrote the letter, specifically?" I asked Fofee.

Fofee shook his head. People with political clout, I imagined. People who forgot the star student Fofee Fofana once was and remembered only the boy soldier he became. For so many Liberians, there is and will always be only one story: victim and perpetrator. From now on, Fofee will forever be: the Enemy.

"Fofee is not police material!" I could imagine the strongly worded letter saying. "Fofee is who the police are here to protect us from!"

It's hard. I understand why no one wants to trust a boy like Fofee. Giving Fofee a police uniform might seem very corrupt or unfair. I am sensitive to this, but I try to get people to see that maybe they don't know the whole story. Fofee feels terrible for what he has done. He has accepted his actions. His village had played a role in the war, and maybe Fofee's villagers aren't entirely blameless. Besides, I have told you about the warlords populating our government today. What is the difference between electing warlords to office and letting Fofee join the police force? I don't know if Fofee *should* be working for the police, I'm just saying we need to discuss these things. They are complicated things. Fofee was ready to apologize and take responsibility, but nobody would listen. He was a boy whose past had planted its feet firmly in front of his present. He looked dejected as a lost dog.

A thought entered my head:

"Fofee, if your village won't listen to your story, why don't you come on *Straight from the Heart* and tell the whole country?"

Fofee looked unsure.

"Maybe your village people will be listening," I said. "It is possible they might even forgive you. Then we can go to the TRC, and who knows? It could be a good thing." Fofee still looked perplexed. "Fofee," I said. "Forgiveness is difficult. It is never easy. It needs to be earned. We can't simply snap our fingers and, *poof*, the hurt or sadness disappears. We have to take *action*."

Fofee chewed it over. He reached into his back pocket. He brought out a plastic bag that contained his pink slip and photos from his days in the police force. Fofee showed them to me for the hundredth time that afternoon. If he went public, Fofee asked, carefully handling the documents, could he rejoin the police force? I said I wasn't sure. Going on the radio or testifying before the TRC wasn't a quick fix to all your problems. That wasn't how forgiveness worked.

"It may not be the solution," I said. "But I would encourage you to come on and tell your story."

So Fofee did. He came to UNMIL Radio and we recorded his story. I edited it and intended to play the recorded version, but on the day of my program, the tape jammed. Thank God Fofee was in the studio! He told his story live. He was really nervous. Fofee kept starting over, backtracking and providing lots of lead-up information and justifications. Finally, he settled into things. Here are the details of Fofee's story, including some he didn't include on the program, but which help to explain Fofee a little better.

"I was one of the students who was loved by everyone," Fofee said. "But when the war came, people looked at us as ugly even if we did good."

Fofee told the *Straight from the Heart* listeners that he had joined the war when NPFL rebels beheaded his grandfather and cut down his family's cocoa bush. When the rebel faction ULIMO-K arrived protesting the casualties, Fofee's parents encouraged him to enlist. Fofee said he didn't want to, but his parents pushed. Like many people, Fofee's parents thought the war would be a one- or two-day affair. "None of us knew this thing would be very bad in the end." Fofee shrugged.

Like Ebenezer, Fofee was an educated boy who had put himself through school. ULIMO-K needed boys who could read and write, and they offered Fofee a job as a recording secretary. Fofee declined. The rebels returned with a counter-offer. They threatened to harm

Fofee's family if he didn't join. Immediately, he was given a pen and paper and set to work.

Fofee told Liberian listeners he had "served at the table," recording ULIMO-K's daily activities. He kept track of enemy soldiers ULIMO-K had captured and functioned as an occasional spokesperson for the rebels. Fofee was not a policymaker, nor did he have the authority to execute anyone. He was a bureaucrat whose job was to protect civilians. Or, at least that's what the rebels told him. Soon, Fofee was given more responsibility. He kept track of civilians' loyalty: who was trustworthy vs. who wasn't.

"I thought I was a hero," Fofee said.

Once a popular boy in his village, Fofee became a local pariah.

I asked Fofee difficult questions during the program: "Why should people forgive you? You cooperated with a group that did the most horrendous things. You say you are calling on all Liberians to forgive the past and forge ahead for a better nation. Isn't that easy for you to *say*? What are you prepared to *do*?" I asked Fofee whether he had ever considered standing up to his superiors. No, Fofee said. You didn't do that. You couldn't do anything to stop it. If you tried, you would be classified as an enemy of the movement and killed. Not that this exonerated him, Fofee added. Anybody who took part in the war did something wrong. He was an older fighter, too: "Old enough to know better."

When it was time for the phone-in portion of my program, I wondered if anyone from Fofee's village would call. We had advertised Fofee's story in the hopes someone would, but I didn't expect it, just secretly hoped for it, you know? When you care about somebody, you hope that things will improve for them. Well, when the studio technician signaled I had a caller, I picked up the phone anxiously and glanced at Fofee. When the caller identified himself as a person from Fofee's village, both of us jumped. Finally, when the caller said he was calling in to corroborate each and every detail of Fofee's confession, I breathed a sigh of relief.

Fofee was sitting in the studio and recognized the caller. He sat there with a pained but appreciative look on his face. At a certain point, Fofee started talking over the caller. He was eager to agree with everything the caller said he had done. My heart brimmed over, listening to his confession and seeing the transformative effect it had on Fofee. There is nothing like admitting to one's darkest deeds and releasing all that pent-up shame and emotion.

I had invited a guest onto the program who knew about forgiveness and traditional healing methods. His position was that Fofee's tribes should take him back. Other people from Fofee's village were apparently listening to the program, too. Afterwards, to my great joy, Fofee's village decided to forgive him and Fofee went home. His tribes welcomed him with open arms and performed a ritual cleansing ceremony.

Solutions are often compromises. In the end, I think Fofee misunderstood what reconciliation meant, and what it would do. After the interview, he tried to rejoin the Liberian police force. Again, they refused him. Fofee was distraught. I sat down with him. "It will take time, but you must try to hang in there, Fofee," I said. I told him once he had reconciled with himself and asked forgiveness from his people, good things would happen. Soon, Fofee landed a job as a bouncer at a Monrovia nightclub. It wasn't the police force, but at least he was making a paycheck.

This might not seem that incredible to you, but Fofee is one of Straight from the Heart's biggest success stories. He was a haunted but determined former fighter who faced his past in the most public way possible to make peace with himself and his victims.

I often think back to that day at Tubmanburg Junction. Back in 1992, all I could do was sit in the backseat of Dr. Tshabalala's Jeep frozen with fear and look at the child soldiers. Times have changed. Boys like Fofee are now my children. Boys like him are moving on from their traumatized childhoods and becoming upstanding young men. It took time for Fofee and me to get here, but we are not at Tubmanburg Junction any longer.

24

UP UNTIL NOW I can still feel pain from the area, because during the time of the war, unfortunately there was no hospital in the bush. Instead, the people started to give us some country medicine and things. But still some bullet was left in my body, so up until now, I can still feel pain where the bullet entered in me. I still have the belief, in fact, that a bullet is still in me. Because anytime when I do hard work, I still feel pain in that area.

When the war was over, I managed to come in to town. My mother was living in Monrovia. When my mother saw me, she started crying. And I said, "Old Ma, don't even cry, because the thing that happened to us in the interior was not easy. Thank God I ran away." She took me to the barber shop, people cut my hair. She cooked for me. She gave me a lodging area, and up until today, I'm still with her. So in Liberia now, we the youth have to come together and rebuild this country.

—Willis

THE BREAK-UP of an important relationship, the death of a family member or a friend, a serious health problem, or being victimized by a violent act . . . all can leave us with painful feelings and cause us to wonder: "What can I depend on? What stays the same?"

Change is central to life. And lack of change is not good for us. However, people differ in how they feel about the coming changes. For those who are open to it, change is welcome. Others find it frightening. Most of us are somewhere in between.

In March 2007, my contract with *Straight from the Heart* ended. I wasn't out of a job, having started to host a radio program for the TRC called *Talking Truth*. Our aim was to inform and update Liberians about the TRC process. I also worked for another radio program run by an NGO called *Search for Common Ground*. Before all this happened, I met a historian famous for her work in transitional justice. Her name is Priscilla Hayner. She came on *Straight from the Heart* and liked what I did, and afterward she advised me to apply for a two-week fellowship in oral history, human rights, and transitional justice through Columbia University's Oral History program. I followed Priscilla Hayner's advice. I was the only female journalist to apply and the only applicant from Africa. When the acceptance letter arrived, I composed a brief response to convey how I felt: "Yes, this is Agnes. Thank you! I will be coming!!"

I took a non-paid leave of absence from work and made sure my boys were taken care of. When my father hugged me, I cried. He frequently made overseas business trips, but this was the first time I had been invited someplace based on my achievements. "This is what you always wanted me to do, and I will not let you down," I said. It was a proud moment for both of us.

I flew from Monrovia to Brussels, Belgium, and then boarded a large plane that took me across the Atlantic Ocean and dropped me in New York. It was a long trip, but I couldn't sleep. I was too excited about where I was headed and what I would learn there. All of my opinions about America came from my father and the movies—pirated films sold in the market between the dried fish and the plantains. Would America be like that? Lots of fancy people who always knew the right thing to wear and say? I imagined America to be a place where everybody was beautiful and intelligent.

I was groggy when we landed. Still, I kept my eyes open, because I didn't want to miss a thing. As the plane neared the gate, I gazed out the small, oval window. Large jets were parked at different terminals. Smaller planes from countries I had never heard of taxied down runways. Not a tree in sight. So different from Robertsfield, with its lone landing strip surrounded by jungle and populated with United Nations relief planes. For a moment I grew anxious. I wondered if everything in America would look like this—big and shiny. Would I seem as small and backward to the American people as Robertsfield airport suddenly felt to me?

The plane door opened. The flight attendants begged us to stay in our seats. Just like in Liberia, nobody paid any attention. I followed the other passengers to Customs Control. There, I waited in a long line with other people from foreign countries. You could spot us immediately: We wore colorful clothing and toted three times as many bags as the Americans.

At last, I collected my suitcase and walked outside into the bright sunlight. I had an address for Columbia University and asked the woman at the information booth to help me. The lady said I should buy a ticket for the bus. It cost money? "Oh yeah, everything costs money in America!" She howled a deep belly laugh. She sold me a ticket, and I had to wait forty-five minutes because the last bus had just left. To pass the time, I tried talking to her, but neither of us understood each other. We were both speaking English, but she was from Jamaica and had a thick accent.

I rode the bus all the way from JFK Airport to Columbia University. There was a lot to see along the way: yellow taxis carrying just one or two passengers, buildings so high they scraped their heads against the clouds. "Can you believe this?" I wanted to ask the person sitting next to me, but nobody else seemed impressed. They must be used to it, I thought. I wondered what it must feel like to be used to these things. To come from a home so peaceful and stable you weren't always wondering if it would be there when you got back.

As the journey wore on, I started comparing Liberia to America and wondering why Liberia looked the way it did. Many Liberians who were in office had gone to school in America. They came back with fancy degrees and letters after their names. The government put them in charge of things. They designed buildings and roads, but not like the ones I was seeing in America. American roads were smooth. Liberia's roads are bumpy. Our buildings crumble like bread. I had only seen one traffic light that worked in Monrovia, and not even all the time. So it got me thinking, why is America planned so well and Liberia so poorly? I definitely intended to apply all I learned in America when I got back home.

The bus driver dropped me off on the corner of Amsterdam and 116th Street, but the piece of paper I was holding said "Broadway." "Broadway is there!" he yelled. "Remove your suitcase!" I hurried off the bus and rolled my small suitcase down the street in the direction he had pointed. I'd packed a bag of African clothes that I intended to wear every day. In the end, I wore them once. The cold knocked the Liberian right out of me. When I reached Columbia University, a boy who worked there tried to help me. He said okay, you are here. Go right and turn left and then right and left and right again. My head was spinning. So the boy drew me a map on a napkin. Miraculously, I found the place. I was late, but the professor and other students welcomed me warmly. "Hey!" they said. "We were worried about you! We thought something had happened!" And I smiled and said no, everything was fine. And yes, I'd like some breakfast.

I learned many things during that two-week course. The other students and I shared similar interests, if not backgrounds, and I hoped to keep in touch with them for a long time. At the end of the course came the biggest surprise of all. I submitted an application for a nine-month program at the International Trauma Studies Program at New York University and was awarded a full scholarship! The professor who ran the program was famous for his work with traumatized populations. He helped Liberian refugees who lived on Staten Island. Did you know that Staten Island is home to the largest population of Liberian refugees and immigrants? For this reason, people often call Staten Island "Little Liberia." They call Liberia "Little America," because it was founded by freed American slaves. This professor told me there were child soldiers on Staten Island who had never told anyone about their wartime experiences. And when he said that, I felt a tingling in my spine. I knew I was meant to go to Staten Island. Whatever the next chapter of my life would bring, I would find it there.

Flying back from New York and over the North Atlantic Ocean to Europe, I couldn't believe my luck. But then, as the plane crossed over the Sahara and I looked out at the bleached sand, I started wondering what I had signed up for. Ten thousand feet above Africa, I thought about all the people who had come before me. People blame inequality on many things, but I come from a place where inequality is the way of life, and all my life I had been luckier than most Africans. Here I was getting another chance. What about the chances I'd already been given? I had started something. My boys were depending on me. Was it my duty to stay and help them, or to try and help the child soldiers on Staten Island? Could I do both? I thought I could. I wanted to do the right thing, but I wasn't sure what that was.

In life, we make the best decisions we can with the information we have on hand. In the end, I decided that going to America to get this trauma training would benefit my boys and me. Also, I wanted to meet the former fighters on Staten Island. The professor said they were living in the shadows, memory prisons. Nobody had broken through to them yet.

My boys thought I was deserting them.

"What we do?"

"How we eat?"

"What gonna *happen* to us, Mommy?"

"I am going to do something," I explained to them at our meeting. "But I will be right back."

I told them there were boys like them across the ocean. "These boys are really suffering," I said. "You remember how you boys used to suffer?" They nodded. I told them these boys had not opened up about their actions or made strides like the members of Straight from the Heart Center. The boys in America had no center. Could they understand my desire to help them? My boys thought about it, and eventually most of them agreed it was a good idea. As for our center, I promised to keep in touch. Because I would not have a salary, I would not be able to provide for them as I had been doing. But most boys understood that I could not support them forever, and that it was time for them to start seeking opportunities for themselves. If anything went wrong, I said they should tell Ebenezer. He was a good leader, and he knew how to reach me. Finally, I congratulated them. I reminded them how far they had come . . . they had confessed to their crimes, apologized to their victims, and participated in peace-building activities.

"It's a big thing that you boys have done," I said, feeling as though my heart might burst. "Keep doing it."

When I went to collect my visa at the embassy, the man at the desk congratulated me. He said the embassy had awarded me a multiple visa.

"What's a multiple visa?" I asked.

"It means you can come and go for one year."

Gazing at my new visa, I knew that my life had taken an important turn. It would take time, but I would make use of this visa: do something for the child soldiers on Staten Island and come back and do something here. Right before I left, I went to see Jerome. He said the TRC would soon be collecting statements from Liberians on Staten Island. Did I want to help? I said yes. I imagined it would be a good way to meet former child soldiers. Good, Jerome said. Go and talk to the Truth Commissioner in charge of the overseas statement-taking, Massa Washington, and get in touch once you've gotten your bearings.

Finally, I called a Liberian man named Jacob. He ran a community center on Staten Island called African Refuge. I met Jacob on my trip to America, and he had promised to pick me up at the airport and assist me when I arrived. I was so relieved. He said to call before I left. But when I called him, Jacob said plans had changed. He was too busy with work and getting his master's degree. He couldn't help me look for a place, either.

I boarded the plane and didn't sleep the whole way. I didn't know what I would do when I got to America. Feeling anxious and homesick, I hoped and prayed that Jacob would change his mind. But when the plane landed in New Jersey and I walked outside the terminal, there was no sign of him. I waited at the curbside for three hours, burning up coins at the pay phone and leaving desperately worded messages on his answering machine: "Jacob, please. I don't know what to do. I know a Liberian in Florida, but that's it!" I begged. At last, even accounting for "African time," I realized Jacob wasn't coming.

It was scary, you know? My whole life, people had been there for me: my mother and father, my stepfather, my stepsister Regina, Patrick, Kojo, my boys . . . Now I was alone in a new country with my support system across the ocean. I thought about Grace, who had looked so lost and scared at the baggage claim when nobody came for her. So, I thought to myself, this is what it feels like to be Grace.

I hailed a taxi. "Where to?" the cabdriver asked.

I said I didn't know. I was here on a scholarship. My professor had recommended I try the Liberian community, and I felt abandoned by them. He eyed me strangely. Then he noticed I was wearing African clothes and nodded like he understood. "Manhattan's good," he suggested. "Okay, Manhattan," I said, trying to conceal the panic in my voice. The bill would be forty-five dollars according to his fare card. I only had three hundred dollars with me, which I planned to live on for a month! How would I afford a hotel? Eat? All the money I had was in my hand. I told the cabdriver I needed a cheap hotel. He recommended Times Square but then remembered a cheaper place in Brooklyn.

"Okay, Brooklyn then," I said. It was clear I had no idea what I was talking about. He dropped me at a hotel, but it was full of drug dealers.

Staring out the window of my hotel room, I looked at the silver buildings that had once seemed so inspiring. Now they were a wall of discouragement. A week passed. All my money was finished. I was eating Chinese food at every meal—it was the cheapest option. Lying alone in my small room, I prayed to God that life would improve and wondered how I had managed to make the biggest mistake of my life. I had had a good job in Liberia. My family and friends were there. My boys were there. If I had known this was going to happen, I would never have left. "This was the place Liberians were running to?" I said to myself. "Why?" I was so angry with myself.

I fell asleep. Morning came. The hotel manager said I had a telephone call. It was a Liberian family who knew my stepsister, Regina, and lived on Staten Island. Regina wasn't around, but they had heard about my situation. They could put me up for a few weeks if I liked.

If I liked?

"Stay here until you sort yourself out," they said.

The overcast New York sky might as well have been a rainbow. I packed my suitcase, paid my hotel bill, and boarded the subway in seconds flat. The sign said STATEN ISLAND FERRY. Boarding it brought back my memories of the war and searching for refugees at the port in Sierra Leone with my father. It all seemed like such a long time ago. I was standing on the outer deck of the ferry when the Statue of Liberty came into view. I had seen that statue in movies, but this was the first time I was seeing it in real life. I thought about the slaves who had immigrated from America and founded Liberia. Almost two hundred years later, we were still cleaning up their mistakes.

The Liberian family lived in an apartment beneath a noisy bridge at the tip of Staten Island. When I arrived, they embraced me. When I described my unfortunate beginning in New York, they nodded and clicked their tongues like they understood. They had a six-year-old daughter named Destiny. She grabbed my hand and showed me around. I met her dolls and pet fish. She reminded me of my daughters, Diamond and Ogechi, who were still living with Jeff and his wife in Nigeria. I visited them right before I left. It had been so hard saying good-bye to them that time. Still, I told myself I was doing this to build a better Liberia for them and their children. People who come from countries like mine often make difficult choices like that.

Soon my bumpy arrival was a distant memory. In the morning, I ate breakfast with Destiny and her father, leaving for work, or her tired mother, coming back from her night shift at the nursing home. I completed my school assignments and kept in touch with my boys and family on the Internet. As for my classes, I was used to being among young people and found I had a lot to say. Many of my classmates didn't know about Liberia. They were shocked to find I had something to say on every subject. When we studied transitional justice, I told them about the TRC and my work as a citizen statement-taker. When we discussed human rights, I described my boys and how they were coming to terms with the war. They were fascinated to learn that there were Liberian child soldiers living on Staten Island. Aside from a few interested reporters and refugee agencies, no one knew they were there.

"Why don't people know about them?" they wondered.

I said I wasn't sure, but I was going to find out. I agreed it was strange. In Liberia, many people wished child soldiers would disappear. Here in America, they had actually succeeded.

25

THOSE GATES LOOK LIKE a prison. And I thought about the babies being born there...If you give a child something to play with, he'll play. If you give a child nothing, he'll grow up in a wilderness and go to crime.

—Marjorie, Park Hill community organizer

IN SEPTEMBER, right after classes started, I took a volunteer position at African Refuge. This is the Liberian community center the Liberian man Jacob runs. Eventually, when Jacob explained why he hadn't picked me up at the airport—he is a religious man and had been worried people would look at him strangely, a woman staying in his house!—it made more sense to me. "I wish you had told me this before, Jacob." I smiled sweetly but forgave him. I could tell his heart was in the right place, and I needed his help meeting child soldiers.

African Refuge is located in Park Hill, Staten Island. This is a neighborhood that non-Liberians tend to avoid or read about in the police blotter. In the late 1980s, Park Hill acquired the nickname "Crack Hill" for the addiction so many residents fell into. I commuted to African Refuge on the weekends and as my class schedule allowed. There, I tutored Liberian teenagers, helped adults with their résumés, and children with their homework. I performed my duties, and paid close attention. I knew it would be a good place to watch, listen, and do what I'd come to do. I knew child soldiers were there, so many were there. Drifting in and out of African Refuge, or hanging around the basketball court and the apartment complexes with a purpose but, seemingly, nothing to do.

How did I know they were former child soldiers? It was just an instinct. I have never seen a fighter who has given up his weapon but doesn't still look like a fighter. He might carry a pistol instead of a *panga* knife, or smoke weed instead of opium, but I am not fooled. Although he may have left Liberia to begin a new life, he still lives in a jungle somewhere. In his mind, he has been fighting all these years. As soon as I see one, I see the fight in his face.

Occasionally, they drifted into African Refuge to check their e-mail. Looking at them, I saw similarities between them and my boys. Tough attitudes, empty eyes. There were differences, of course. These boys wore nice clothes. Their tennis shoes weren't full of holes. My boys in Liberia would have sold these boys' shoes and the flashy chains they wore around their necks for a bag of rice.

When these boys came to check their e-mail, I tried asking them questions. None of them wanted to talk to me, though. Some threatened me and even wanted to fight me. They would sneer, "Miss, miss, if you touch us we will call the police!" It really surprised me. I hadn't encountered this behavior in Liberia and wondered why they were so harsh. I asked around the center, but nobody seemed to know. Or, if they did, they didn't want to tell me.

Sometimes I tried following the boys. I hung back at a distance so they wouldn't notice. Or, if I sensed that they were getting suspicious, I would disappear around the corner and do a loop. They were intelligent and knew that I was shadowing them, though. "One day," I told myself, "I'll pick out a boy and follow him home. Or, as far as my courage lets me."

"Park Hill is a dangerous neighborhood," Jacob warned me. "Ask the wrong question and you might get a hole through your head!" Jacob told me the former fighters belonged to gangs, drank alcohol, and did an industrial amount of drugs.

"You have to watch your back," Jacob said. "I know the laws of the jungle. You don't. I have informants. You don't."

I looked at Jacob. What did he mean "the laws of the jungle"? And why wouldn't the boys on Staten Island talk to me?

Then one day, Jacob got a call from the principal of a local high school. There had been a fight. A Liberian boy was involved. Jacob said that we should go there. When we arrived and heard what had happened, I told Jacob we should investigate. "Let's get to know the boy to find out why he was fighting," I said. So we made an appointment to speak to the boy's father.

When we got to the house, I sensed that something was wrong. His father was acting fishy. He wouldn't answer my questions about his son, not even simple things about the boy's age or their county. When I asked him when and why they had fled to America, Jacob stopped me. He put an end to my inquiry, shook the man's hand, and shoved me out the door.

I didn't understand.

"Yes," Jacob said. "That is the point. You *don't* understand how things work in Park Hill."

"Jacob . . ." I said calmly. "Are you worried for my safety? If so, don't trouble yourself." Getting child soldiers to open up was just a matter of time. Of course, Jacob could speed along the process by introducing me to boys he knew . . . boys with stories.

"You say you know everyone." I smiled.

He wouldn't, though. Just like Mohamed, Jacob always had an excuse as to why they weren't available, or he wasn't available. It was odd. Either Jacob didn't have time or didn't want to show me who fought. I would have to investigate on my own. Eventually, when I started making inroads, Jacob would look at me and smile and say, okay, just remember what I had signed up to do and who ran this center.

"Of course," I would reply, my confusion and curiosity mounting. "I am just a volunteer."

26

PEOPLE ARE TALKING like that, making noise. I say I ain't got time for this one man! You don't know about the war, so that's it. Some people can be lying and say they fought the war, and they don't even know. They just be talking, they just be lying. Say, "Oh we were there! The people were doing this one!" I get vexed! I get vexed. I get vexed … They say what you vexed for? I say, "Listen, you don't know nothing about the war. We all suffer in the war. Don't be coming here telling me this one was good, this one was bad." And you know man, we suffer, we suffer. We suffer in the war and *you* come and tell me?

—Edward

I HAD BEEN VOLUNTEERING at African Refuge for several weeks when he walked through the door. He was tall and thin with short dreadlocks and an army cap pulled low over his eyes. He was holding a cell phone as if it was a walkie-talkie and speaking into it in Liberian English, which was my first clue. I nodded. He ignored me. I shrugged and returned to what I was doing: teaching a Liberian grandmother to use the Internet for the first time. She had grown up without lights or a toilet. Now she was surfing the Web and reading articles about Ma Ellen's efforts to bring electricity to our country.

I smiled and watched her eyes absorb the flood of information. When I looked up, the boy had vanished.

The second time I saw him was in the park across the street. No one needed to tell me what he was doing there. It was a children's park, but I had never seen children playing there. Instead, boys loitered by the playground equipment, exchanging slow high fives with small plastic bags for wads of bills.

When I saw him the third time, I was helping Liberian schoolchildren with their homework. I was wishing I had paid more attention when I was their age and could actually be of some use. The boy was sitting at one of the computer consoles. "You guys keep working," I patted my small students' heads. "I will be right back." Then I walked over and introduced myself.

"How are things?" I said.

The boy looked at me. Then he extended his hand in the traditional Liberian way: a high five punctuated by a prolonged finger snap. His eyes were glassy. He was skinny as a shadow. I asked him what he was working on. Schoolwork, he said. But when I looked at the computer, I saw MySpace on the screen.

"Are you taking me for a ride?" I put my hand on my hip. There was a rule against using the African Refuge computers for social networking.

"Aw, miss . . ." he grumbled.

Then I smiled to let him know I was not too serious. I asked the boy his name and where he lived. He didn't answer. He said he had seen me hanging around the neighborhood and knew I was a Liberian lady. "What else do you know?" I asked. That I followed people around. Asked a lot of questions. That I worked for the government and was probably some sort of spy. I laughed and told him I was not a spy. I was interested in collecting stories from the Liberian war. Also, in people's coping mechanisms: how they dealt with the things they had experienced, or, I looked at him, done.

The boy pulled his hat brim down. He thought for a moment. What would I do with the stories? he wanted to know.

"Help Liberians recover." I smiled. "Get the car back on the road."

This seemed to make sense to him, so I figured it was my turn to ask him a question. I asked him whether he was in school or working. He nodded vaguely. "And how is America?" I asked. "Do you want to go back to Liberia someday?" And he said no, he didn't think he would go back to Liberia. I asked him why. And oh, it was a long story. And I said do you want to tell me the long story? And he thought about it for a moment and said, yes, he might do that.

"Give me your number then," I said.

He gave me his cell phone number, and we agreed that I would call him soon. I telephoned Jerome. "I think I've found someone," I said. Jerome said to keep him posted.

From that day forward, I got to know the young man, whose name was Edward. I learned who he was, what county he came from, and who he could introduce me to in Park Hill. It took time and multiple telephone conversations. But I was happy to take my time getting to know him. He seemed to know important people. When we traveled around the neighborhood, he would point out some of the boys I'd had my eye on. "You see that one?" Edward would gesture toward a rough-looking boy who had bullied me. And I would nod. "He goes to this school, he joined this gang, this is where they hang out."

I learned how tough life was in Park Hill for Liberian refugees like Edward: "They call us 'African booty-scratcher.' They think because we come from Africa, we have *nothing*! No clothes, no food. They think because we Liberians, we sleep in *trees*!" He grimaced. He described the fights that broke out between Liberian gangs and the African-American gangs who had ruled Staten Island until the Liberians showed up. Still, compared to life in Liberia, Edward said the people in Park Hill had it pretty good. He had gone to school. Joined a soccer team. He was away from the war.

Edward took me around the soccer field where he used to play. He told me he was at soccer practice one day when he saw a boy he had fought with.

"I know you!"

"I know you too . . ." the boy answered. "But you look strange."

"So do you . . . Remember how we used to suffer?" Edward asked.

"Yeah, yeah," the boy said, and waved his hand. "Let's forget that thing."

In that moment, Edward learned that you were not supposed to talk about the war.

It was a slow process, getting to know him, but I was grateful for his information and time. Edward told me what factions the boys fought for, and how they bought their expensive cell phones (with drug money). I asked Edward about the tough clothes that he wore. "Don't you think people call you 'street boy'?" I said. And Edward said, "Oh, that's the way." "Don't you want to be president of Liberia someday?" I asked. Edward said he wouldn't rule it out. "Well, you can't wear those." I pointed to the baggy pants that ballooned around his ankles. "When you come to African Refuge, I won't treat you like an American," I said, pulling up his trousers. "I will treat you as a Liberian," I said, and Edward blushed.

Edward struggled with memories of the war—battle flashbacks. When he gave me his story, his eyes would cloud over. Sometimes he could barely speak. Often, the tears in his voice took over entirely.

"You are not alone," I told Edward. "There are other boys like you." I told him about my boys in Liberia. Many of them had been through the same things. Talking with each other really helped, I said. And then I asked Edward why the fighters on Staten Island were unwilling to talk to me. And oh, it was complicated, he said. It wasn't the war, but what happened *after* the war. But I didn't understand what Edward meant.

"Edward," I said when I finally figured it out. "Is it because of how you got to America?"

Edward told me his family had applied for asylum and put his brother's name on the refugee papers. Believing Edward was already dead, they didn't include Edward's name. By the time the approval came through, Edward had escaped, but his brother had gone to fight. Edward used his brother's name to get to America. He lied and fled with his mother and sister:

> When I come to America, I ask my uncle. I say, "Is this America?" He say yeah. And it was funny, because it was the same Liberians, the same people. I start seeing old faces. Most of the guys I knew from Liberia I started seeing here. They say, "How you reach here?" I say, "How *you* reach here?" Everybody just start running away, that how most people get too much of the war, that's how they get here. Too much.

I asked Edward if people on Staten Island knew who he was, and what he had done. "Some people know," he said. But because Edward had been small when he committed atrocities, most people didn't recognize him as a child soldier. Edward said there were people who talked about the war who weren't there and didn't know, and this is what made him angry.

"Did you ever talk about your fighting with other boys in Park Hill?" I asked. Edward shook his head. "You don't want to talk about it?" And Edward said no, and his voice was hushed. And I stopped asking questions after that, because I could tell we had talked enough that day.

Then one day, Edward told me his story:

I was ten when the rebels got me. We were living in Sinoe County at that time. My father screamed, "Get under the bed!" We all ran under the bed when they started shooting. I was in my blue pants, because I had just come from school.

They called my mother and father outside. They say, "Bring all the children!" They were big guys with big guns and wearing chains around their necks. One guy had a pot of fire on his head.

They say, "Who the oldest?" My sister was the oldest, but they can't take women to the front. My dad told me to follow them, because they could have killed our whole family if I didn't. When I left, my mother was in tears. My father was not crying because he thought I would be back. But it didn't go like that. They wanted small, small rebels.

We trained in a big yard. The training was just basic physical training, push-ups every morning. After one week they say, "You are going to the battlefront." I was scared! I won't lie to you, because the things those people do was wicked.

They issued us guns for killing. I didn't even know how to shoot a gun. The guns were too heavy for me to lift, so I carried the guns on my back for the other fighters. We started looting houses in different counties. I did domestic things, too, like making food for the big fighters and washing their dishes. This is how me and the other small boys started out.

Everyone was fighting each other—tribe on tribe, ethnic group on ethnic group. Guns were given to each and every man that walked by. My commander was Nelson Taylor, Charles Taylor's brother. When our regiment ran out of ammo, he went to get more but he was killed. Another general called Rebel King took over. You didn't mess with that man. He had one ear. He lost his other ear during the war. If a boy wasn't listening, he would grab the boy and cut off his ear. He would put a pepper on top of the boy's ear and chew.

Eventually, I started shooting. I had no training. They just told me to "shoot everywhere." We would rape, loot, kill, take different-different drugs that make you high and kill more easily. They give you a drink, "Drink that!" I remember one pill they called "10/10." Tiny white tablets we took before the big battles. You take that pill, you kill your own mother.

We would see someone on the road and go and rape and kill her for no reason. No reason. One time, my sister passed by. The boys just rape her on the spot. It could have been worse. If they had known we were related, I would have had to kill her to prove that I could, and the others would laugh about it. Instead, I disguised myself and walked right past. I'm glad she did not know it was me.

Finally, I turned fifteen and I began to doubt the rebels. Me and another boy decided to escape. We plan, plan, plan. During the next attack, we took our chance. We ran on tiptoe— silent. If they catch you, they kill you! When we reach the Ivory Coast, I say, "I looking for my ma." The people say, "Your ma just left." I felt weak. Weak now.

Finally, I find her. But my ma, she did not even recognize me. I was big. My hair was long. I go and stand there and my ma not even know me.

Hell, I feel bad. I say, "Oh! I fifteen year already. Where the children? Where my brother?" She said, "Your brother not here. He in the war." I say, "What?" She say, "He heard you was there, so he go there." So I say, "I have to go back and look for him." But she said, "No, you can't go! He will come. If they find you, they will kill us." And I never go Liberia no more.

There were things Edward wouldn't tell me. His real age, for instance. When I asked him why, he said, "Oh, my age is a 'refugee age.' If I tell you my real age, my mother will get in trouble."

I grew fond of Edward. He had a sweet disposition. Still, it was clear he was really traumatized. He was a combination of my boys in Liberia—intelligent like Ebenezer, emotional like Fofee . . . and soon, like Mohamed, a disappearing act.

Without warning, Edward stopped coming to African Refuge. He didn't return my calls. I looked for him everywhere. I went to Jacob.

"Jacob," I said. "I met a young man. His name is Edward. I need you to help me find him."

Jacob placed his hands on his desk and sighed.

"This boy has stories!" I said. "He has a need to talk to me. Even if he doesn't know it."

In Liberia, it was simpler, I said. There I could just go and cook for the boys. But here in America, it was delicate. There were immigration laws, the police, and people's rights to worry about. I had learned that some boys had given false testimony to gain refugee status and enter the United States. They had doctored their stories on immigration forms using false information and kept lying when they arrived. They were terrified of being sent back to Liberia. I wanted to tell these boys that nobody was going to send them back for talking to me, but I hadn't been in America long and didn't know what would happen. I didn't want people taking me to the police. Or in Park Hill, where I didn't know who was linked to who, carrying me far away from the police. Oh, I had to be very, very careful in dealing with all these things! I started to share some of these feelings with Jacob, but he interrupted me in mid-sentence.

"Don't go spoiling my center!" he cried.

"I'm not trying to spoil anything, Jacob," I said. "I am trying to *help.*"

Then I told him about the threatening phone calls.

"Jacob," I said. "There is something else. You will not believe who called me."

"Who?" Jacob asked.

"Prince Johnson," I said.

Jacob's eyes bugged out. "Prince Johnson? Wow!"

I had been talking with some Liberian boys, hearing what they had been through. They came from Nimba and had fought for the warlord Prince Johnson, though I didn't know this at the time. I was grateful when they decided to speak to me and started asking them lots of questions. A week later, my cell phone rang.

I was home alone when it happened. I saw the familiar Liberian country code, +231, and a string of unfamiliar numbers behind it. "Hello?" I answered. I couldn't make out the voice at first. It was a man's voice, cool and low. When I recognized it, I felt as though I had been hit by lightning. It was Prince Johnson!

"Why are you calling me?" I asked. My voice was shaking.

His was calm. He told me he had heard I was conducting investigations and trying to discover things about him. He said that this was "not a good effort for me," and that I should stop my searches immediately. I was spooked. I wondered how he had gotten my cell phone number—from someone on Staten Island who was still loyal to him?

It happened a few times. The message was always the same: "Lay off your investigations! Stop asking people questions—or else!!!" It really rattled me. Each time, I would think of the video of Doe's execution, and of Prince Johnson sitting there watching the mutilation over a beer. If Prince Johnson was capable of that kind of behavior, what else was he capable of?

I told Jacob I was a little bit worried, but I assured him I could handle it. I knew Prince Johnson's weight (what he is "made of," you might say) and wouldn't let the phone calls interfere with my work. Nothing and no one would get in the way of that.

Jacob paused before speaking.

"Listen," he said at last. "Park Hill is a big place . . ." If Liberians gave me their telephone numbers and addresses, fine. I could go and visit them at home. On my own time. But he would not allow his center to become a "crime scene investigation."

"Jacob," I complained. "Don't you want to know the truth? What really happened in our country?"

Then I looked him squarely in the eyes and asked him a question I'd wanted to ask for some time: "What were you in the war, by the way?"

The room was silent. The groove on Jacob's forehead deepened into a pronounced *V*.

"You know, it is a long story," he said after a pause. "And I will be happy to tell you another time."

"But—"

Jacob left. I was frustrated. I didn't understand Jacob's reaction and I had no idea how I would find Edward again. I went home and did what I do when I need to unwind. I lay down on my bed, put on my headphones, and listened to Bob Marley. I got up the next morning, ready to try again. But when I showed up at African Refuge, the door was locked. I tried my key but it didn't turn. When I finally reached Jacob on his cell phone, he said people had been stealing things from the center. He had no choice but to change the locks.

"Okay," I said. "But I am your volunteer. If I had known African Refuge wasn't open, I would not have come all the way down here."

Jacob apologized. He was in a rush, had a lot on his mind, etc.

"Jacob," I said, "is there something else you want to tell me? Your story, I mean?"

Jacob groaned. "Agnes, if you want to know my story, it is all over the Internet. It's there in black and white!"

And it was. It was all there. Video clips, newspaper stories, and radio interviews. Jacob had been interviewed on NPR and CNN. On World Refugee Day, Jacob spoke to Soledad O'Brien and was identified as a human rights activist who had spoken out against Charles Taylor. Jacob told Soledad O'Brien that soldiers threw him in a dark room and tortured him for days. He narrowly escaped an attempt on his life before fleeing to Staten Island. Now he ran a center that helped Liberians talk about similar horrors they had endured.

It was all there, exactly as Jacob said. Still, I wondered if he knew more. I asked around. People told me Jacob's uncle was a powerful general during the war. And I thought, if Jacob's uncle was a powerful general, didn't it make sense that Jacob saw things, heard things, and experienced more than he was letting on?

But when I tried to reach Jacob again, he jumped from here to there, bringing me this way and that, zigging and zagging. I felt frustrated I couldn't reach him.

"Are you sure you don't want to talk to me? About your experience?" I would press.

Jacob didn't want to tell me. Every time I tried to talk to him, he made as if he was the busiest person in the world.

"I have told you where I was," Jacob would say. "I'm a Gio boy. When Doe started killing Gio boys, God spoke to me. I changed my name. And now I am an advocate for the Liberian people."

I sighed and acknowledged that this was true. As director of African Refuge, Jacob has helped Liberian refugees secure apartments, health care, and legal services. He has a university degree and could go anywhere, but he was here, nobly assisting his people after the war. I said I knew Jacob had made huge sacrifices, bodily and otherwise. And that whatever he had told CNN and other news outlets about his past was extremely valuable and probably very difficult to share. But I was interested in learning what else he had to share. I wanted to help him communicate his whole experience.

Jacob's cell phone rang. He picked it up and gave me the "hold one minute" sign. Apparently, the call was important. Jacob placed his hand over the mouthpiece and whispered that he was a busy man, working full-time, getting another degree, had to take the call, etc.

27

DON'T BE SCARED to give a statement. I gave my own statement. And I have to admit I was apprehensive. I was scared in the beginning. I wasn't scared because I felt I had security concerns for me, or for my family in Liberia, or here. Or that I had a precarious immigration situation, you know, and I *do* understand and respect people who have that situation. But I was scared to relive the memories. To relive the things that happened to me...That happened to my family. It's a scary thought.

...But it was very powerful. It was a healing experience. It was very liberating. I felt, wow, I just did something noble. I actually talked about my family that can't speak for themselves. I actually talked about my parents' property that was destroyed that the world needs to know about.

—*A Quest for Justice*, Minnesota Advocates
for Human Rights TRC video

YOU MIGHT THINK the people who escaped the war would be the first to leave it behind. But in America, I learned that isn't the case. Walking around Park Hill, home to scores of war-displaced Liberian refugees, I came to learn the people who flee from something often have the least distance from it.

When I started volunteering at African Refuge, I met a lot of Liberians who were coming in to check their e-mail and find out how to get jobs. As I helped them and started getting to know them, I wondered how many of them had stories to tell. How many had fought? How many had children who fought? These questions were running through my mind.

I called Jerome and Massa. There are a lot of Liberians here, I said. How many had stories? What happened to them in the war, *if* they were in the war? "That's a good question," Jerome said. "Go and find out." So I started taking statements on my own, and then when the TRC came, with other statement-takers.

The TRC began taking statements from Liberian immigrants and refugees in February 2007. TRC Commissioner Massa Washington flew over from Liberia. There was a kick-off celebration. She explained the process and thanked members of the Liberian Diaspora who had "paid their dues," and "stuck with their homeland through thick and thin." Never before had a truth commission sought to engage and give voice to a Diaspora community in its proceedings. But considering an estimated 25 percent of our population had fled the country during the fourteen years of fighting, it's obvious why Massa and the Commission felt it needed to engage them.

The TRC enlisted the Minnesota Advocates for Human Rights, a non-governmental organization based in Minneapolis, to document statements from Liberians in the United States, the United Kingdom, and Ghana, West Africa. This is where the majority of Liberians outside Liberia live.

The Minnesota Advocates were training pro bono lawyers to take statements for the TRC. They enlisted my professor at the International Trauma Studies program to help prepare the lawyers for what they might encounter. I was already an official, full-time statement-taker for the TRC but attended the Minnesota Advocates training

and gave the lawyers a few tips of my own. I listened closely as they reviewed the process: Liberians could give their names and testimonies on the record or confidentially. As statement-takers, we must emphasize the fact that no one was obligated to tell us anything they didn't want to. We should not press Liberians past the point they felt comfortable. Also we could highlight the benefits of giving statements—it could be a powerful, cathartic experience, a chance to make your voice heard, and become a part of the historical record. Finally, we should remind people that counselors and mental health professionals were on hand.

The lawyers were nice enough, but there were no Liberians among them. As a consequence, many had no real grasp of the situation in Liberia, or the poverty most Liberian immigrants and refugees found themselves living in. As I sat through the training, I worried that the Minnesota Advocates' approach was the wrong one. Their plan was this: If a Liberian had a statement to make, he should call the Minnesota Advocates to book an appointment. Then, the Minnesota Advocates would schedule statement-taking days at various centers on Staten Island. On the appointed days, the Minnesota Advocates would invite Liberians to sit down with pairs of statement-takers.

I hadn't been in America long, but I was living with a Liberian family and knew that most Liberians were just trying to get by. Many didn't own cars. Some were living on such a tight budget, or wiring such a huge portion of their paychecks back to Liberia, they couldn't afford an extra bus fare. Not only that: No one had time for the statement-taking days the Minnesota Advocates wanted to organize. "Do you expect these Liberians to skip work and miss a day of pay?" I asked a lady who worked for the Advocates. Many Liberians worked two jobs to pay the bills. They couldn't just come and go as they pleased. "If they must come to you, at least let them schedule their

appointment times," I suggested. The lady agreed this was a good idea. Still, she didn't seem to comprehend what I was saying.

When I explained my statement-collecting techniques, the Advocates shook their heads. They said I would not be allowed to do what I had done before. "No recording devices?" I said. "No recording devices," they confirmed. Also, they insisted we work in pairs, when I worked better alone. "Who do you think Liberians are going to open up to? Them or me?" I wondered, gazing at the pro bono lawyers in their pressed suits. At a certain point, I knew I had to step back and take direction. Following orders is not my strong suit, but this was not my country. And who knows, maybe the Minnesota Advocates were right?

The Advocates organized the first statement-taking day at St. John's University on Staten Island. I completed my school assignments early and went. I waited the whole day with the lawyer I had been paired with, but the Liberian who had signed up to give his statement never came. Only three people did. To say it was a "poor turnout" would be an understatement.

Eventually, the Advocates realized they would need to go and knock on doors. It would be time-consuming, but it was the only way to get through to people. Only soon, walking down the streets of Park Hill with the statement-takers, I realized this wasn't going to work, either. Home visits were more convenient, but most Liberians were still afraid. Many lived next door to their enemies. Would you tell your story if this was the case?

The Liberians who did open their doors didn't open them widely. Some were so traumatized they didn't even know what they were saying. I remember we went to collect a story from a man in Park Hill who was drunk. He kept saying he had a story to tell: "Put this down!" and "Write that there!" That man did not say anything of use. Still, I patted his hand and thanked him for his time and told him

about the TRC's counseling services. We tried another house. No one was home. When the Liberian at the third house peeked through his keyhole, he shook his head and indicated that he had changed his mind. The last Liberian we visited was a young woman who said she had been raped. It was something, but I knew she was leaving things out. She wouldn't name names or go into detail.

"It's not just about knocking on doors," I tried to tell the lawyers. "You have to mingle with these people, get to know them." *Be one of them*, I thought, but didn't say. "It takes time . . ." I said. "You must reach. You can't just ask one particular question and get the whole story. You have to make a commitment. When you find someone with a story to tell, you must go and come back at a time that's convenient for them."

In the meantime, Jacob had posted signs at African Refuge, encouraging people to come and give their stories. The signs said HELP PUT LIBERIA BACK TOGETHER! and TELL YOUR STORY TO CLEAR YOUR HEART! A Liberian woman saw the signs and approached me. She seemed strange, but I scheduled an interview. Because the Advocates required us to work in pairs, a social worker named Jane would accompany me.

Jane was thrilled. It was her first statement-taking. She was from Denmark but volunteered at African Refuge and knew more about Liberians than the average Joe. I was optimistic. But when the Liberian woman arrived, she was talking up and down, too quickly for a normal person. I told the woman to wait a minute and pulled Jane aside.

"Jane," I said and tapped the side of my head with my index finger. "We need to listen to this woman before taking her statement. I have a feeling something is not right."

Jane was too excited. "It's a story, it's a story!" she insisted.

I didn't want to disappoint Jane. So I said, fine. In keeping with the Minnesota Advocates' protocol, Jane would ask the questions and

I would transcribe the lady's answers. We sat down with the woman for five minutes before it became clear the woman was not well. At the end of the session, I thanked her for sharing her story. I made sure she knew where she was going and had someone to help her. Then I turned to Jane.

"That wasn't a statement, and we're not going to submit it," I said. Jane looked confused.

"Trust me," I said quietly. "That lady needs help of a different kind."

Jane looked crushed, but I told her not to lose heart. "Many people will tell you they have a story," I said, "but you have to *analyze* it to see if there is truth inside." I told Jane that in my experience, statement-taking was a painstaking and laborious process. Most people didn't open up right away. When they did, it felt like prying open a door or a paint can. Sometimes you succeeded. More often, you didn't. Still, even when it didn't yield anything, listening to someone and making him or her feel validated was important. I told Jane we would know a statement when we got one, because it would be hard-won.

I collected a few stories over the next several weeks, but nothing groundbreaking. Sometimes I would return to the houses I had visited with the Advocates on my own. I tried to explain the Advocates' mission, but many Liberians said they didn't want to share their stories with the statement-takers. They had all kinds of reasons—fear, mistrust, or deep-seated depression. Some said they couldn't remember their stories. Some said they remembered too much. Who would listen or care? Who would turn away from them for talking? Many Liberians had told their stories to friends, and for whatever reason, their friends hadn't believed them. Besides, what good would come of it? If they told the Advocates their stories, would they get their loved ones back? Would they suffer the pain and relive the rape and violence all over again? But the number one reason Liberian refugees and immigrants didn't want to talk to the TRC was they didn't believe anything would change.

I called Jerome and Massa.

"This isn't working for me," I said. I told them I saw myself getting through to the Liberians, but the Minnesota Advocates were cramping my style. They said yes, yes, yes, we see, we get where you are coming from. I said I believed I knew what the Liberians needed, and I thought my techniques might work. Jerome and Massa considered for a moment. Luckily, they are people who understand that sometimes the only way to get somewhere is to go your own way. Some things you learn how to do, other things you just know how to do.

"America is a different place," Massa said. Did I think I could do what I did so well in Liberia over here in America?

I said I thought so.

"Good," Massa said. "Then go ahead and do it."

28

IT HAS HURT. I can't tell anybody it didn't hurt me. It hurt me.
Okay? But I am not going to sit down and become hateful and say,
"I'm not going to talk to a Krahn man, I'm not going to talk to a Gio
man, I'm not talking to a Bassa man because he did this to my father."
No! My father's first love was his country, and if I am to believe that
I must see that this country is rebuilt.

—Counselor Yvette Chesson-Wureh

YOU REMEMBER the Park Hill boy, Edward? I did not see
him for some time. Then one day, I was driving down the
street and nearly ran him over. I slammed on the brakes. He said a
friendly "Hi" as if nothing had happened. He was dressed nicely, too,
so I suppose I won that battle.

"You promised to talk to me." I smiled, rolling down my window.

"Aw miss . . . I'm busy," he replied.

"Too busy for your country?"

I love that boy, but I can sense when somebody has reached his
limit. You must thank that person for helping you learn the truth to
the extent they can. At that point, I knew I would not have much luck
reaching out to ex-fighters on Staten Island. Despite my assurances
they could talk to me anonymously, boys like Edward got a fishbone

in their throats whenever I started asking questions. Those who had doctored their stories to gain asylum worried the immigration authorities would deport them. Even when I told them they could give their stories confidentially, they shook their heads. "Don't you want to be a part of Liberia's recovery?" I asked. But they feared Liberia and didn't feel an allegiance to it anymore.

"Don't take it too hard," a man who coached a Staten Island soccer team many ex-fighters played for said. "These boys are used to being on their own." Edward's disappearance had nothing to do with me or my methods, he said consolingly. In his experience, it was difficult for ex-fighters to maintain friendships, hold down jobs, or shoulder responsibility of any kind. "When you're in a relationship, you share ideas. When you're in school, you listen to instructions. When you're at home, you wash dishes. But they're not used to that," he said. "You get a lot of incompletes."

Take Edward, for instance. This coach had helped him enroll in an auto mechanics school, but Edward dropped out. He found Edward work as a security guard, but Edward showed up late one too many times and got fired. Over and over again, this coach found himself pleading with Edward's teachers, supervisors, and the Staten Island police to give Edward another chance. Edward left his soccer team, the clubs he joined, his girlfriend. Edward left everything he had been a part of except the war.

I decided to change tactics for the time being. I would concentrate on older Liberians living in Park Hill and try to gather their testimonies. I felt hopeful. When I greeted these people in the street, they returned my smiles. It was a good sign. I started going around the neighborhood collecting cell phone numbers and making friends.

I would stop people in the street and ask, "How is it?" in Liberian English. And, "Oh, fine," they would say, or "Fine-fine."

"I can see the Liberian face in your face," I would respond, which got them laughing. "I am a Liberian, too!" Then I asked them questions: Where were you during the war? When did you leave? Do you have relatives back home? Kids in this neighborhood? Based on their answers, I could determine whether they saw or heard things that might help the TRC. It typically took me two to five minutes to establish whether somebody knew something valuable.

The Liberian street market was my favorite place to gather stories. This is a strip of Park Hill where Liberian women wearing brightly patterned African headscarves and American sweatpants wheel shopping carts piled high with favorite foods from Liberia. Hot peppers, fried plantains, fried fish, potato leaves, and plastic bottles filled with blood-red palm oil. You'll be walking along or driving by in your car when a fistful of peppers is thrust through your passenger-side window.

The women chat and sing. They sway their hips to Liberian music bleating from small stereos. When it rains, they bring out trash bags to cover their wares and heads, and gossip. And they always talk about Liberia. It is a lively place, and a nostalgic one, too. These women are conducting the same business they did before the war.

I frequented the Liberian street market and alternated whom I bought my groceries from. I wanted to support the women and collect stories while I was at it.

"Old Ma," I would say. "I want pepper. You got pepper?"

"Yah, I got pepper," a lady would say. She fetched me peppers and mentioned, in passing, her superior potato leaves.

We negotiated a price. I handed her money.

"You remember your home?" I asked as she counted out the change. The lady would get a faraway look in her eyes. "Yeah . . ." she would say. "The pepper in my home is good."

And I would nod. "You have moved on. You need to go back and help your country. Let me help you."

Then we would set up a time to talk.

"Now don't get me wrong," I would say when the woman offered me a folding chair from a refugee agency in her small apartment. "I like America. The roads are smooth. The ferry leaves on time. The seats are comfortable. When they say two thirty, they mean two thirty. In Liberia, you wait for hours and there is no place to sit down."

The woman would clap her hands. "It's true, oh!" she would say. "In America, the taxis are yellow and quick. You hop in the backseat, and it's just for you!"

And I would nod and agree. Not like in Liberia where they smash you into a bus, if you can even *find* a bus. No electricity, the heat, the mosquitoes.

"Yeah, yeah, it is better here . . ." the Liberian lady would agree. She had clean water, her husband got paid on time, her kids went to school. After so many years in America, she still marveled at the appliances in her apartment: the electric stove, the refrigerator, the air conditioner. It was a big improvement on Grand Bassa or Bong County.

"But it's not home . . ." I would say.

And yeah, she would agree. That was so.

"I would rather earn five hundred dollars in Liberia and keep the money than make a thousand dollars and give it all to bills." I would take her hand in mine.

And, oh yeah, she would agree with that!

"Americans live alone in their apartments," I would continue. "They eat their own food. They don't share. In Africa, what we put in the pot is for everyone."

And yeah, yeah, that was true . . .

And when you got old? Ah! When my father got old, I would bring him to live with me. Not like these Americans who stashed their parents in nursing homes. "You should know," I would say. "Your kids work in those places."

And, "Oh, we know, we know." The old woman would shake her head sadly.

"Liberia is a different place now," I would say. And some of the women would nod their heads and admit that they had thought about returning. But more would shake their heads and reply that it could never be. These Liberians missed Liberia, but they feared it. They had escaped death once. Does a person get lucky twice?

Well, let's talk about it, I said. Let's discuss what is going on in Liberia. But for some people, speculating about the future was more frightening than remembering the past. No matter what I told them, Liberia was a lost place. Our bright-eyed politicians were wearing disguises. Schools today would be rebel hideouts tomorrow. They feared their old home. They feared their new home. The fear had followed them here.

This old woman Amelia, for instance. She had been a vice principal at a Liberian school and now worked as a home health assistant in New Jersey. On her feet all day and tired, but she swore she wouldn't return. Amelia had lived through two terrible regimes, Samuel Doe's and Charles Taylor's. She said she didn't imagine Liberia was capable of much better.

"We were under the slavery of the gun." Amelia described Doe's ten-year rule. "That man said all kinds of stuff to us. 'When two elephants fight, it is the grass who will suffer. And you Liberian people are the grass. You will suffer!'"

Amelia told me about a priest who led a protest march to Doe's presidential mansion. When the protestors arrived, they demanded that Doe step down and hold elections. Doe flew into a rage. How dare these Liberian people talk to their president this way? You think you put me in that chair? I put myself in that chair! My M-16 brought me to power, and only a gun will remove me! He said, "Liberian people, you do not know me, but you will know me today." Amelia shivered as she spoke. "Then he went and brought some lions. He fed the pastor to those lions in the basement of his presidential mansion."

I shook my head in disbelief.

Then there was Charles Taylor. His army entered the country while people were sleeping, Amelia said. When she woke up, the country was crawling with rebels. But the thing that amazed her? She still couldn't get over it. "You couldn't hear any birds," Amelia said. "You couldn't see any dogs. The place was quiet. I still don't understand how the animals managed to know that something was wrong."

Amelia had stories, so many stories. An old man in her village who lived in a house Charles Taylor wanted for himself. Taylor sent his militia to seize it. "They didn't use a gun," Amelia said. "They didn't use knives." Instead, they tied the man's legs together. They hung him upside down inside a well and sealed it. "When I think of it—" Amelia shook her head. "My skin creeps."

I asked Amelia whether she believed in reconciliation. She said that human beings were hard to forgive. She said people "talk with their lips and say beautiful words, but have evil hidden in their hearts." She said her tribe came from the forest and their hearts were like the forest: "We don't forgive."

Then she paused.

"I may be wrong. Let them try it and see. Let them try and see if it will work. The bloodshed was too much."

It was enough for me. That glimmer of hope. When people have that, it is something.

Before I left, I asked Amelia about the former child soldiers in Park Hill. They had never been treated as victims, I said. I said I believed they were traumatized. Was it too late to help them? What did Liberians on Staten Island think? Amelia said they were "Rude boys. Fresh." She told me there were many Liberians who didn't believe they were sorry for what they did and instead had hidden agendas in their hearts. "They say they will go back to Liberia and avenge the deaths of their relatives if it takes a hundred years," Amelia said. "They say they will go back home and repay their debts. So the thing is not finished!"

It was then that I knew the Liberian community on Staten Island had a long way to go.

A reporter from the *New York Times* accompanied me to this interview. She had heard about my work and wanted to write a story. She said she wanted to "get a sense" of my methods and techniques. I looked her up on the Internet and learned that she was an accomplished writer who had chronicled the lives of many Liberian refugees living on Park Hill. I was flattered and a bit nervous after that, but she made me feel very comfortable. The story appeared in the *New York Times* on October 31, 2007.

29

WE MUST STAND shoulder to shoulder as our brother's keeper, not as Congo or country, not as Krahn or Mandingo, not as Gio or Mano, but as Liberians. Indeed, we are the harvest of only one banana tree and that banana tree is our beloved Liberia.

—Agnes

YOU KNOW what we say about Liberians? If we fall in the water, we turn into fish. We make the best of our surroundings. In time, I grew to like America and felt I had a unique opportunity to help Liberians living on Staten Island. Emotionally or physically, I could help them go home.

I continued volunteering at African Refuge and gathering testimonies for the TRC. Each day brought something new. I met a man who lived in the apartment building Charles Taylor fled to when he broke out of prison in Massachusetts. Do you know that story? Taylor fled to America when Doe accused him of stealing government money. He didn't get far before he was arrested and thrown in jail. Bars can't thwart some ambition. Some people say Taylor escaped by sawing through the bars of his jail cell. Others claim he used a knotted sheet and slipped out the laundry room window. I suspect that the Americans facilitated Taylor's getaway. They wanted Doe out of power just as much as we did and were willing to hand Taylor over to the Liberians living in America. Escape or release (the jury is still out), Taylor's wife was waiting in a getaway car and drove him from Massachusetts all the way to Staten Island, where he disappeared . . . or so I thought, like everyone else, until I met a man named Larry.

"Charles Taylor used to live in my building," he said. "Building 160. He lived down the hall. Right on my floor!"

Larry showed me the place: a red brick building like the one where African Refuge was located. Gazing at the building, I shook my head, imagining how different things might have been had that man stayed in a cell.

I attended the Staten Island Liberian community election. There, I met an old woman who had lived on Staten Island for thirteen years and was voting for the first time in her life. It touched my heart, because she was exercising a right she had never enjoyed in her own country.

I went back to Africa from time to time to see my children and check on my boys. Sometimes, I participated in TRC events: the Lutheran Church candlelight ceremony, for instance. The Lutheran Church is the site of one of the worst massacres of the war. More than three hundred people were slaughtered there in a single night. This ceremony was held to honor them. When I went, I met a young warlord with a tortured gaze and long dreadlocks named "Peanut Butter." He fought for Charles Taylor and his real name is Adolphus Dolo. He was sitting next to Prince Johnson, so I decided to sit somewhere else. But then I noticed that Peanut Butter was crying and sweating in the air-conditioned room with his coat and tie on, so after the program I went and knelt beside his pew.

"Do you want to go outside?" I whispered to Peanut Butter.

Peanut Butter indicated that he did, so we went outside, whereupon he broke down in tears. Peanut Butter told me he had led his villagers to the Lutheran Church twenty years ago. He had led them there for safety. Instead, they were slaughtered. Something snapped inside him. The Lutheran Church massacre was the reason he *fought* the war. It was the reason he became a warlord. Nobody knew this. Not even his wife knew this! If only people knew this, they might understand where he was coming from, and that he wasn't an evil person. Eventually, I convinced Peanut Butter to give his statement to the TRC.

And then, in December 2009, the TRC of Liberia released its final fact-finding report. It is difficult to express how much that document meant to Liberians. For so long, we had endured corrupt regimes, bloodthirsty warlords, massive carnage, and unimaginable pain. Now we were being presented with our history and the TRC's recommendations for the future. The 370-page document was the culmination of a three-year effort, comprising some of the stories you have read and many more from hundreds of Liberians. It is our living history, and I was proud to have contributed to it.

While I couldn't wait to read the report, like everyone else, my eyes skipped to the recommendations at the end. Although the TRC could not prosecute anyone, it could recommend that certain individuals be sanctioned. There were fifty-two people on the list. Number one: Charles Taylor. Number two: the president of the Interim Government of National Unity, Amos Sawyer. Number three: the president of Liberia, Ellen Johnson-Sirleaf . . . The report suggested that she be barred from public office for thirty years when her term ended. The reason: She had not expressed remorse during her TRC testimony, or gone far enough to apologize to the Liberian people.

In the wake of the media outcry over Ma Ellen's inclusion on the list, people's eyes skipped over the other names. I didn't. I recognized so many of them. There were names of warlords who had kidnapped my boys and turned them into child soldiers. Other warlords who had taken girls like Rita as concubines. Warlords I had interviewed on *Straight from the Heart*. Warlords who were banned from *Straight from the Heart*. The warlord who bought our groceries at the Lebanese supermarket those many years ago, when I was a young woman with a small child and living with my father. Prince Johnson. Alhaji Kromah. Sekou Damate Conneh, Jr. Jacob's Uncle, Vanni. Peanut Butter.

There was another list containing the names of people who shouldn't be prosecuted, despite their involvement in the war. The TRC said these people had spoken truthfully and expressed anguish for their actions. Among these names—the reporters couldn't believe it—was one Joshua Milton Blahyi, alias "Butt Naked."

What can I say? The road to justice is full of challenges. No one ever said peace would be cheap, easy, or make sense.

30

WE HAVE SEEN the worst, and there have been lots of challenges. But this does not mean we don't know where we want to go. This nation *knows* where it is going to go.

—Leymah Gbowee

SOME TIME AGO, I found myself entering a tall building in Manhattan and riding up a mirrored elevator to watch a documentary film about the lives of several of my friends. The film is called *Pray the Devil Back to Hell*, and I had been invited to the premiere by Abigail Disney, who has dedicated herself to organizations that assist people living in rock bottom places. I met Abigail when she came to Liberia with a group of women philanthropists. I helped her when she returned to Liberia to shoot her film. She met with some of my boys, and since then she has become a mentor to me. I was excited and honored when she invited me to her premiere.

When the movie started playing, I couldn't believe the familiar faces I saw on screen. There was old video of Liberians who had torn our country apart. There was new video of those trying to rebuild it. The heroine of the film was a woman named Leymah Gbowee. She helped bring peace to Liberia by inspiring ordinary women to rise up and force the Liberian warlords to sit down at the negotiating table.

Leymah's women organized marches, staged sit-ins, and used other forms of nonviolent demonstration. It was a tough road, and those warlords made many demands, but Leymah didn't give up. After the war, she worked with child soldiers. The more she worked with them, the more convinced she became that they were victims, too. I had invited Leymah on my program several times to discuss the challenges these children faced. We saw eye to eye on many issues and were excited to help the American filmmakers. Leymah's was a powerful untold story, they said, and a fresh lens into the Liberian conflict.

Abigail and her team told Leymah's story powerfully. People in the audience gasped. A few of them cried. Me? I gasped for a different reason. I *came* from this country. I lived this untold story.

When the film was over, Abigail got up to speak. Another woman named Gloria Steinem joined her. Together, they asked us to help spread the word about the film. They told us they would be taking it to international movie festivals, universities, and even refugee camps. I marveled that some people would pay lots of money to watch what is essentially my country's suffering. But that is the way the world works. Somebody's life is another person's education—or even entertainment.

Afterward, we were shown into a room with fancy food and important people. Many of these people wanted to speak to me. I spoke to them for Abigail's sake, but really I just wanted to talk to Gloria Steinem. A person sitting next to me in the audience had told me she was a powerful woman who helps other women do big, powerful things. Kojo always said I should never be afraid to talk to anyone. "If the president is over there, go over there!" he used to advise the staff of UNMIL Radio. "Gloria Steinem has a mission," the person in the audience said. And so do I. So I went up and introduced myself.

Since then, I've gotten to know Gloria Steinem and her beliefs on women. She and Abigail got me thinking maybe there was something I could do for the women and girls in Liberia and on Staten Island.

And so, I'm working on two new projects now: a Liberian women's radio station and a farm outside Liberia where girls who fought the war and sex workers can come to sort themselves out. And I started speaking to young women in Park Hill about what they can do to help their country. There are some girls who remember the war and others who escaped before it touched them. They are about the age I was when I fled Liberia with my father, and I want to make sure they learn all they can about our country.

Just the other day, I spoke to a group of young Liberian women who call themselves the "Ladies of Prestige." They have big plans for Park Hill. I told them not to forget about Liberia. We discussed events we could do together to help Liberians on both sides of the ocean. "Someday you may go to Liberia and become a minister or president," I said. "But you girls have to *really*, really push it."

I am enjoying it, you know? Helping these girls realize their potential, being a "feminist?" And you know, I have Leymah to guide me. She is in America, too. She lives just up the street from my apartment. Leymah says she came here to get her head clear and to understand our people. She says Liberia is a work in progress. She says Liberians are a people the rest of the world is still trying to figure out.

31

I CAN'T LIVE such a life where I can't see my people. And I just living lonely! I got to try my efforts where I'm not used to. Where I'm not doing it before. And I'm doing these things. I don't know when I will fall into a predicament again. And maybe the people do not consider me, or they may not know me. They may not feel for me.

I will not like to be suffering, sleeping all around, on a market table, in the night, sleeping here and there, going around, doing these things that will not benefit me. I think it will not be necessary. And I pray for the Republic of Liberia, and we extend our greetings and thanks, send praises to our government of Liberia today, and even the UN. They are in the country, this is what they here for. To get people from the street, people who are traumatized, you know. Me, I'm traumatized.

Some days, even when I sit down, I think and think. I can't get rest! Because twenty-four hours, I walk all around, and I can't even know what make me to move from here to there, I can't really know. I dislike it, but there is no way. No one can come to our call. I'm only saying this: Those that have the opportunity, the UN in the country, to hear us and come to our need, come to the youth of our country.

—John

RECONCILIATION IS a long process with ups and downs. I know in my own life there is still work to be done, to reconcile with people. To grasp the full, personal effects of the war. Sometimes you ask yourself: Is reconciliation necessary? Is it possible? What will I lose? What will I gain? Can I survive the process? Are *we* really going to survive this process? It's strange how life keeps taking you back to the beginning.

Do you remember Mariam? The girl I lived with when my father and stepmother threw me out of the house? We were sleeping in Mariam's room the night Taylor's troops reached the Coca-Cola factory and changed our lives forever. While I fled to Sierra Leone, Mariam stayed behind with her family in Liberia. We lost touch. According to friends, Mariam never told anyone what had happened to her. When I came to America, I discovered that Mariam lived in New Jersey, right across the water from Staten Island. I found out she worked in a nursing home. I looked up Mariam's number and held my breath as I dialed, wondering what I would say when she picked up. I got her answering machine:

"I Ii, you just missed me, the African princess. Leave your number and God bless!"

For the first time in years, I heard my old friend's voice. "Mariam," I said. "It's Agnes . . . your old friend. Call me."

All that day and the next, I jumped whenever the phone rang, hoping it was she. I tried two more times. Nothing. Just Mariam's recorded voice, which sounded normal enough, but I knew better. Even after a long time passes, you know your friends.

Recently, I went back to Liberia. I asked around and learned that Mariam's family still lived out by the airfield, so I went to visit them. It had been a long time since I had been there, and as I wound through the narrow streets, the memories came flooding back to me. Mariam's father, J.P. The bedroom Mariam and I shared. The conversations we used to have. The last words I had spoken before the war: *I will write!* And Mariam's tears, she who always seemed to know better.

When I came upon the house, I almost didn't recognize it. The house was the same shape and color, but the porch was full of children. They were laughing and playing loudly, as we'd never been allowed to do. Had my informant been wrong? Had somebody else moved in? In the center of the porch, sitting on a banged-up chair and resting his chin on a cane, was an old man. He looked familiar. Could it be? I waded through the circus of playing children.

"J.P., sir?" I said.

He didn't reply. Too bad, I thought. This was not Mariam's family. I had gotten the wrong house.

Then a young man approached.

"It is J.P.," he said. "He doesn't speak anymore. Our father lost his mind during the war."

Mariam's brother.

I met more of Mariam's siblings that day. Many had been young children when I lived with them. They told me what had happened after I left. There was no food. Boys were being kidnapped. Mariam's brothers were afraid to leave the house, so Mariam and her sisters ran to the frontline. They got caught behind enemy lines. They returned a few weeks later. Mariam's brother didn't know what had happened, but she was never the same.

"I am in America now and trying to reach Mariam," I told her brothers and sisters.

"Tell her to call us, sister?" Mariam's brother asked.

I promised him I would. Before I left, I sat with J.P. for a few minutes and tried not to cry. It was sad to see a man so changed, especially a strict man like J.P. I wondered why he had lost his mind, what he might still remember, and if, for some Liberians, losing one's mind weren't a blessing.

Back in America, I tried Mariam again. Now I knew I needed to talk to her. I had a message from her family. And I wanted to apologize.

Mariam is my childhood friend. We grew up together. We were living like sisters the night war came and ripped our lives apart. Everybody's luck is not the same, but I had been lucky and Mariam had not. Just like when a storm comes and tosses up a garden, war tears through and separates people. Branches fall. Blossoms are separated from their stems. Leaves that once hung side by side on a tree are blown apart. Some land on the soft grass; others cluster around the drain. When the storm passes, there is chaos. It's the same elements from before, but the bad weather has rearranged them.

It is the same way for Mariam and me. We grew up in a country in a part of the world known for its storms. We might have continued walking the same path had fate or luck not blown us apart. I wanted Mariam to call me. I needed to hear her voice. I was friends with a memory and wanted to know Mariam as she was now. Could friendship survive these things? I didn't know. I knew I wanted things to be the same.

Then one day I was checking my messages:

"Agnes, it's Mariam . . . your old friend. It's been a long time. Call me."

EPILOGUE

—◆—

W AR IS not something you understand. It is not something you grasp. It is something you endure, survive, and work to prevent from recurring. And that process, the process of prevention, involves hard work, day after day, a total commitment. Recently, I ordered a dual time zone watch to help me keep track of my work in Liberia and America.

Monrovia, Liberia, 11:02 a.m.
Straight from the Heart Center is no longer in its former location. The land was taken over by Liberians who wanted to rebuild their homes. Now we work out of my house. It's not too far from the old center and relatively convenient for my boys and girls. Our mission has changed. We work on peacebuilding projects now, instead of running a feeding and jobs center. This is as it should be. My boys and girls need to move on.

Ebenezer recently found work as a prison guard. Now he's earning money and has the dignity of putting on a uniform every day. It isn't easy for him. The last time I visited Liberia, there was a jailbreak. The prisoners learned the guards weren't carrying weapons and escaped. Ebenezer is optimistic. "It's the job I have taken," he says. "I just have to stay until I find something better." Not long ago, something better materialized. Ebenezer won the lottery and the chance to apply for a visa to come to America.

Rita is another child soldier who beat the odds. Unlike many girls who were taken as fighters and concubines and turned to prostitution, she is going to school and wants to open a business someday. She has stopped drinking, too, and smiles proudly when I suggest that maybe one of her sons will become president of Liberia. Benatta, who did become a sex worker, is now living and working at my project in Bong County, learning to farm and live a clean life. A step forward, a step back, a step forward again.

Do you remember Fofee, the boy from Tubmanburg Junction? Fofee joined the Liberian police force after all. I recently saw him when I went back to Liberia. He stood proudly in his uniform and showed me pictures of his kids. He is so much happier now, more so because his people have accepted him. As for my other boys, some are doing well and some are not. Some have returned to their villages and gotten jobs. Others want jobs and are working hard to find them. Many need education and counseling. I say, why not take boys like them and get them to repair what they destroyed? But people can't comprehend how a boy who committed murder can make an honest living. And you know, I understand. But I encourage Liberians to accept that perpetrators are Liberians too, and have a stake in our country. They are dangerous to work with, but they belong.

Some people realize this and are opening their hearts and doors. Humanitarian organizations continue to provide former child soldiers with mentoring and professional skills training.

I see Mohamed from time to time, when he wants to be found. He still pressures me for money. I press him to move on with his life. He says he doesn't want a job and continues to rely on juju with God as his "backup," whatever that means. I worry about him and the people he hangs around with. Mohamed brags that he knows warlords who can send our country back into war "like that!" Liberia can't afford that. We can't risk having Mohamed's information fall into the wrong hands. After all, we have the next generation to think about.

Staten Island, New York, 7:02 a.m.
Edward and I are back in touch. I am organizing a discussion group with him and other ex-fighters. My plan is to create a safe space where they can talk about their pasts. I will bring in child soldiers from other countries, who are living in New York, to help facilitate it. Soon I will go to see my old friend Mariam. I will ask her so many questions. Everyone needs to open up to someone, and I hope Mariam opens up to me. She is my sister until the time that God calls me from this earth.

As for my actual stepsister, Regina, she has two daughters, Libby and Lucy. Lucy is named for our mother. Lucy is also best friends with Destiny, the little girl I lived with on Staten Island when I first arrived and everything was a mess. Playing with Lucy, Libby, and Destiny takes me right back to Sierra Leone and all the tricks Regina and I played.

"Don't you mean the tricks you played on me?" I can hear Regina saying now.

I missed critical years of my son Reginald's life. Thanks to my mother, he had a far better upbringing than I would have been able to provide. Going around Park Hill, or working with the boys at Straight from the Heart, the same thought enters my head each time: I am so lucky Reginald did not fight the war. Now he is helping me run the Straight from the Heart Center. I am very proud of Reginald and know he will be a role model to the boys, as he has been to me. Reginald unknowingly allowed me to be a mother to boys who needed me. In spite of how little I gave him as a mother, he's always understood I had given it somewhere else.

My father visited me recently. I showed him around New York, took him to African Refuge, and introduced him to many of the people you've read about in these pages. We talked about new projects and old times. "You created a better world for yourself," my father said. "It is a dangerous but outstanding achievement!" Those words meant everything coming from the man who devoted his entire life to helping other people, and who never gave up on me, no matter how many times I disappointed him.

He still worries about me, of course. When I told him I was visiting the Democratic Republic of Congo to speak to former child soldiers, he nearly fell off his chair.

"You remember that song you played, Agnes?" he asked.

I knew the one he meant.

"'It's my life, it's my life, it's my prerogative . . .'" my father recited. "You would often 'rehearse' it to me. I think, in retrospect, it was a clue of things to come. It meant, 'I will take care of myself and in the end I will make it.'"

❖

EVERYONE HAS DIFFERENT STARS. My destiny introduced itself to me over time and after a series of wrong turns. It paid visits at my doorstep, knocking and then scampering away. Finally, it decided to enter and nearly knocked me over.

The story I have told you is based on memories of the war and stories I have collected from other people. I've done my best to chronicle the details and set them down accurately. I'm sure I've made mistakes. Liberia is a complicated place, and these are complicated stories.

You have a saying in the West: "A man is known by the company he keeps." We have this saying in Liberia, too. And if you judged me by the company I keep, you might not want to know me. But I hope that in sharing these stories with you, I've helped you understand the former child soldiers of Liberia a little better. To grasp that they are good boys and girls. Or rather, they are good at heart and were forced to do terrible things.

Let me be clear: I am not saying these boys and girls did no wrong. They are responsible for horrendous actions. Murder, torture, rape—a fourteen-year nightmare. But many who fought the Liberian war were very small or confused when they were taken. Traumatized the day a powerful warlord stormed into their villages, massacred their families, and gave them a decision: kill or be killed. Many were too little, or too drugged, to realize there was a choice. Many don't remember or understand it even now.

Everyone has a choice, that is what I believe, but most of us make poor ones along the way to making better ones. For boys like Edward or Fofee or Varlee or Mohamed, the path was so dark, a commander so powerful, or the consequences of disobeying his orders so frightening, that they ended up making the wrong decision for a very long time. Who's the good person? Who's the bad person? It's difficult to say, and perhaps useless to ask at this point.

What I want to say is this: For too long, my country, my Liberia, was a difficult place to love. The war came and took everything that was good and loving and peaceful. People grew older and older and still peace did not come. But it's different now. The sorrow is subsiding and individuals are making peace with the past. A woman is president. Children go to school wearing pressed uniforms, satchels on their heads. "Did you finish your homework?" their mommies call after them, steadying their own buckets of water and bundles of wood. After school, boys shoo cows from the fields to make room for soccer matches. Girls skip rope under trees that look like elephant legs. They are not oblivious to what came before. The vestiges of war and the humanitarian organizations are everywhere. Still, most of the time they are doing what children should be doing, and that is progress.

We need to include former child soldiers in this process. They want to learn. They want to work. There is a lot of work to be done and we need their help. They need our help, too. It is a new time. Now the real work begins. We Liberians are getting the car back on the road. But this is not like that afternoon driving back from Tub-manburg Junction when we left the suffering on the road behind us. We need to stop the car this time. We need to get out and help these people. We must bring them along with us. Together, we must keep driving.